THE
SECOND
CHILDHOOD

THE SECOND CHILDHOOD

It's never too late for a do-over.

KELLY MOSS

Copyright © 2026 by Kelly Moss

All rights reserved. No part of this publication may be reproduced, distributed or transmitted in any form or by any means without permission of the publisher, except in the case of brief quotations referencing the body of work and in accordance with copyright law.

The information given in this book should not be treated as a substitute for professional medical advice; always consult a medical practitioner. Any use of information in this book is at the reader's discretion and risk. Neither the author nor the publisher can be held responsible for any loss, claim or damage arising out of the use, or misuse, of the suggestions made, the failure to take medical advice or for any material on third party websites.

ISBN 978-1-916529-56-4 Paperback

ISBN 978-1-916529-57-1 Ebook

The Unbound Press
www.theunboundpress.com

Hey unbound one!

Welcome to this magical book brought to you by The Unbound Press.

At The Unbound Press we believe that when women write freely from the fullest expression of who they are, it can't help but activate a feeling of deep connection and transformation in others. When we come together, we become more and we're changing the world, one book at a time!

This book has been carefully crafted by both the author and publisher with the intention of inspiring you to move ever more deeply into who you truly are.

We hope that this book helps you to connect with your Unbound Self and that you feel called to pass it on to others who want to live a more fully expressed life.

With much love,

Nicola Humber

Founder of The Unbound Press

www.theunboundpress.com

For all the children — inside and out

ACCOMPLICES

So many people over the years have told me I should write a book, or complimented my writing in some way, and I want you to know that each of you made a lasting impact on my confidence as a writer. Although I'm unable to name you all individually, please know that I deeply appreciate your attention and recognition, through which I have also come to appreciate the immense power of a few words of praise.

Thank you especially to Nicola Humber and the entire publishing team at The Unbound Press for this opportunity to share my vision, for believing in me, for your valuable contributions, and for your patience as the book came together in its own time.

To Dayna Martin for your support and guidance through my radical unschooling journey as well as the journey of becoming a published author.

To my teachers Dr. Kimberly Rose Pendleton, Caytlyn Dee, Manuela Mitevova, and Karin Monster-Peters for the embodiment practices that brought me home, and then carried me here.

To Lynn Hord for introducing me to The Unbound Press, and for your help through some tricky points in the writing process.

To my Focusmate virtual co-working crew, especially Daphne, for holding me accountable and reassuring me that I was worth the trees.

To everyone who has engaged with me on the ideas in this book: those conversations gave me a glimpse of the impact I wanted to have, which kept me going when I felt like giving up.

To early readers: your notes, laughs, dedication and reviews made you my final-hour heroines.

Most of all, to my daughter and favorite human, Luna, for inspiring me to find my place in the world and become the kind of person who could support you in finding yours.

Oh, and thanks, Mom, for the first childhood, the writing gene, and the feminist indoctrination — *The Second Childhood* wouldn't have been possible without all three.

INTRODUCTION

Part memoir and part manifesto, this book introduces a liberating and sustainable way of living and relating to ourselves, to our children, to one another and to the natural world, inviting more joy, delight, playfulness, pleasure, freedom, connection and creativity into our lives.

However, *The Second Childhood* isn't a rigid set of rules to live by or steps to follow, and it's not a book where I give you the answers to life — it's about coming back to a childlike sense of wonder and awe, awakening the courage within ourselves to face the unknown, and trusting in our own innate ability to play with reality and create our story as we go. Childhood isn't just an age or a developmental stage — it's a way of perceiving and relating to the world that makes magic happen, for those willing to trust in the value of our imagination.

Looking around, it's evident that humans could use a refresh on how to be more childish in all the right ways. We could all stand to learn how to have more fun, how to introduce lightness and play into the dark and difficult corners of our minds, our work and our relationships, and how to be open to the magic in ourselves, in one another and in life itself.

Despite the advice I received to *niche down*, I refused to write this book *only* for single mothers, unschooling mothers, female entrepreneurs, eldest daughters, highly sensitive women, black sheep of the family or women in recovery — all of whom might appreciate the idea of a Second Childhood.

I can't fully separate my experience as a mother from my experience of coaching from my experience of sobriety — they are all deeply interconnected and vital to my identity, yet none of these labels define me. Any woman who has been encouraged to make friends at a "mothers' group," and gained little more from it than the crystal-clear understanding that giving birth in the same decade isn't enough to form a deep and lasting friendship, will know what I mean. Each of us is so much more than our roles in society — especially in a patriarchal society.

This book challenges the lines drawn around us, and between us, in patriarchy, because these lines divide us from one another and from ourselves, dimming our individual and collective power. The categories others put us in, such as "mother," come with expectations that aren't necessarily supportive of all that we want to bring into the world — and this is as true in the world of "crunchy moms" as it is in conventional parenting circles. Both mainstream and so-called alternative approaches to motherhood are still mostly based on the idea that mothers will derive our sense of identity mainly from playing a supporting role to our husband and children, that we will make friends exclusively with other mothers at school drop-off or homeschool meet-ups (but without becoming close enough to threaten the sacred institution of the nuclear family) and that we can find sufficient personal fulfillment in the sterile aisles of Target or the produce section of the natural foods co-op. If we stop identifying *exclusively* with labels that primarily exist to isolate us and deplete our resources as women (i.e., divide and conquer), maybe we will invest less in these contrived roles and more in our own visions, in nurturing authentic relationships, and in creating a reality that tells more interesting stories about who we are.

Besides, most of us are just *one* choice — or casualty — away from living in another woman's shoes. Isn't it worth our time to try to understand each other's perspectives?

This isn't just a book about parenting, though — even where it delves deeply into the concept and concerns of motherhood, it's really about whole-life creative sovereignty. Our experiences and wisdom as parents have applicability far beyond the walls of the family home. Ghettoizing motherhood is not only isolating for parents and children, it perpetuates the reproduction of stale ideas and ways of living. When we tackle parenting problems in seclusion, nothing changes because the way we parent is connected to the way we do *everything* — both as individuals, and collectively as a society. Parenting is about *who we are being* with our children, not about learning specific methods or techniques that can be applied independently of our own personal growth and way of navigating the world.

Who we are as parents is inseparable from our relationships with our work, our creativity, our bodies and other humans. Parenting is also a natural function of being human, and "othering" parenting as a social role therefore leads to othering parents — and let's be real, this disproportionately impacts women and children. Most importantly, even if we don't have children ourselves, we have all had parents, regardless of the quality of our relationships with them. Investigating the role our upbringing had in shaping how we live, love, work and play (or don't) as adults is a worthwhile endeavor for anyone — and not just for our own benefit, but for that of everyone whose lives we grace with our presence.

This is a book about healing, parenting and business all in one, because these are all connected — growth in one area automatically impacts outcomes in other areas. The way I've combined topics here provides an enriching experience that allows those of us who *don't* see ourselves in conventional parenting, wealth or wellness literature to feel validated, connected and inspired. This is a book not just about parenting, but also about wealth, health, creativity, sovereignty, and wilderness. Only a holistic approach to family life can lead to deep and sustainable results in the parent-child relationship, and only a radical shift in how we raise children can change the world. It all starts here, baby!

Importantly, for any childfree women whose eyes have already begun to glaze over, parenting includes those of us who are raising *inner* children — invisible labor for which we receive little credit, but the demands of which impact every area of our lives in many of the same ways as raising *outer* children. If the language of the "inner child" doesn't resonate with you, substitute it with something else that does — for example, spirit, soul, creative spark, the divine within, or just "self." There's no wrong way to understand or nurture your innermost self, and the point of this book is not to give you more boxes to squeeze yourself into but a set of tools that you can use to unbox yourself in whatever ways delight you.

This book is necessarily inclusive in the ways I've listed, because The Second Childhood isn't just a personal journey — it is a blueprint for our collective rebirth as a species. It also isn't just about making up for the losses of our first childhoods — although it's *definitely* that — it's about owning our power to co-create the world that we want to live in, and the world that we want our children to live in. We create this world by imagining it and then bringing it to life with a playful spirit. With the right attitude and a courageous heart, we can create a second chance — for ourselves, for our children and for the world: our collective Second Childhood.

We'll explore the ideas and practice of a Second Childhood through a prism of essays, frameworks, and personal narratives, each reflecting the concept from a different angle. I share a lot about my own Second Childhood, but yours will likely look very different — and that is a good thing! Each of us is here to have a unique experience and to create an impact with our own brand of magic.

The essays build on each other in a fluid way, with themes ebbing and flowing from one piece to the next. They will sometimes appear in what seems a sequential order, but not always — the interconnectedness of these themes is the whole point, creating a rich interplay between each piece. Non-linear thinkers will likely feel right at home here. You might read this book from start to finish, dip into the parts that feel most pertinent to you right now, or open it at random and trust you'll receive exactly what you need in that moment. In the world of The Second Childhood, doing what feels good to you is essential, so feel free to make your way through in whatever way moves you.

This book includes frank discussion of topics such as sexual assault, child abuse, domestic violence and suicide. While I don't share explicit or graphic descriptions of interpersonal violence from either my own or others' lives, basic factual details are included that some readers may find unsettling. Take care of yourself as you make your way through this book — there are no trigger warnings from here on out.

While many of the ideas in this book will have universal appeal, some of the stories and perspectives drawn from my personal experience may seem distinctly "American." Although I've come to question many of the ideas I grew up with, I've retained a childlike sense of dreaminess and an undying zest for personal transformation — qualities that may feel unfamiliar or even off-putting to those with different backgrounds. Though I steer clear of toxic positivity, I've had to be radically optimistic in order to save my own life, and so I tend to see this as a strength. Take what serves you from this book, and leave the rest. Not every idea is meant to take root in every patch of soil.

Finally, as the reader, you agree to follow any advice or suggestions in this book only at your own risk. While I've done my best to ensure that all information contained in this book is accurate at the time of publication, change is a fact of life. Always check the laws where you live or plan to travel. When in doubt, consult with an attorney.

I am not an attorney, nor am I qualified to give legal advice.

I am a coach, but unless you have hired me, I am not *your* coach.

And I am a mother, but I am not *your* mother.

It's too bad — I'm sure you'd have been a real delight.

PROLOGUE: A HERETIC'S JOURNEY

Shortly after my thirtieth birthday, I gave away all my belongings, left frantic messages from friends and family unanswered, and went for a walk.

My estrangement was intentional, but traumatic. I had recently uncovered memories of childhood sexual abuse, and was not well-received in bringing the family secret to light.

Still in shock about the discovery myself, it now seemed the whole world was against me. Even my therapist, who knew my pain intimately, was appalled that I hadn't called my mother on her birthday.

This wasn't the first time the healthcare industry had proven to be unworthy of my trust — I had also been scarred by a patient privacy violation in my teens. Having experienced one betrayal after another as a result of speaking my truth, I had never felt more alone or discouraged.

I had burned out from my high-stress job and become unable to work; my feeling of social disconnection grew exponentially.

I was disgusted that I'd had to make myself sick earning the right to live, especially when I'd never had a real childhood to begin with.

What else was left for me to do, but go out and play?

This decision turned out to be my initiation into a Second Childhood.

I had no plan, except to escape civilization. I craved an escape from the money, media and pretense that had dulled my relationships until that point. Fully committed to autonomy, I would no longer play the role of the loyal employee, the grateful daughter, or the compliant patient.

I gave away tens of thousands of dollars to a sexual abuse prevention organization and to various women's and environmental causes, wanting nothing more to do with money. If birds and trees could give and receive freely without expectation, trusting that they would be taken care of, why couldn't I? I was desperate enough for a meaningful life to give it a shot.

The journey began when I emptied the contents of my studio apartment onto the pavement by the dumpster for my neighbors to pick through, and turned in my keys to the building manager.

I walked for miles through the city, talking to people along the way. The first day, I was invited to a front yard barbecue by people I had only just met. I enjoyed many incredible synchronicities, finding that food and many other things often showed up exactly when needed.

In my family, every gift came at the price of my dignity or freedom. I was amazed to find that perfect strangers were kinder to me than my own blood. I started to gain a sense of safety in the world that I had never known before.

I also appreciated how straightforward the people I met were, happy to tell me exactly what they thought of me to my face. Compared to the world I had come from where passive-aggressiveness reigned supreme, this was so refreshing. I had always been blunt, and found more confidence in my no-BS communication style because it was finally valued by other people.

Wanting more than anything for nature to reclaim the hostile, sensory-violating cityscape, my path led me to radical environmentalism and the fight for indigenous sovereignty. The wilderness grew inside of me as I fought for the wilderness without, and my voice grew stronger as I made a habit of speaking the words in my heart.

A few times, I was allowed to sleep in someone's backyard after having knocked on their front door as a total stranger. I was amazed at how generous people were when I approached them with an open and playful spirit.

Usually, I slept behind the bushes in front of churches, or in the forest. I loved looking up at the stars at night, and hearing the wind rustle through the leaves of trees overhead. I felt truly connected and protected. Sometimes I told myself that I was safe so that I could fall asleep. I wasn't always safe, but at least I was free.

Within a year of beginning my journey, I was pregnant.

Still holding the trauma of rejection from my family and community and the crushing weight of eco-despair, I was also suicidally depressed. The pregnancy presented as a divine invitation to take care of myself at a time when there seemed no other point to go on living.

Although I had projected onto the wild freedom from patriarchy and the evils of civilization, I had to admit that the primitive utopia I longed for did not exist, and that my no-limits lifestyle was wreaking more havoc on my nervous system than being in the working world had.

I had discovered that I didn't *need* money to survive, and that the universe would always have my back — but after everything I'd been through on the streets, and knowing what was to come with motherhood, I wanted a more predictable form of financial security.

Determined not to sacrifice the freedom I had gained, the next few years were a test of resourcefulness.

My daughter and I traveled the country in a campervan, and then internationally as pet sitters. I made and sold jewelry, weaving my trauma, hopes and dreams into each piece of gold wire. I set what seemed at the time an outrageous income goal, and reached it. I diligently saved up most of my income and bought a cabin on land.

My first online business was a digital marketing agency for acupuncturists, who had helped me heal. I offered training in HIPAA compliance so that their patients could more safely share their stories — something I had been robbed of many times, including at the birth of my daughter.

I felt fulfilled serving an industry I cared about and making meaningful change, while maintaining the freedom to raise my own child, heal and travel. And after decades of underearning due to associating money with my father's abuse, I finally felt comfortable building wealth.

Not to mention, I was literally being paid to tell my story — what delicious cosmic justice!

I had gone from being a social outcast to redefining myself as a leader, by walking away from society's projections and inviting others to walk with me. I was amazed at the power of my own desires, intentions and courage.

I also began supporting other entrepreneurs on their own *Heretic's Journey*, speaking truth and embodying leadership through businesses that abundantly provided a Second Childhood lifestyle.

The difference between being an outcast and showing up as a leader is overcoming shame.

We are building a new world with the powerful wisdom our stories hold. And on a foundation of trust, embodiment, rest, joy and play, we are simultaneously building the working world that works for us, for our children and for the planet.

THE SECOND CHILDHOOD

Welcome to the Upside-Down World

We live in a world where play is seen as "childish," but where even children's play is disparaged as a "waste of time."

We live in a world where children are seen as empty, passive recipients of adults' knowledge and beliefs, even though adults, for the most part, aren't happy with where these have taken them in life.

We live in a world where creativity is seen as something you must earn the right to do, but where the more entrenched you are in the system of permission-withholding, the *less* creative you become, or are allowed to be.

We live in a world where children are perceived to be inherently sinful in their bids for connection and autonomy, while youth and adult addiction rates are skyrocketing and there is a global epidemic of clinical depression, anxiety disorders and chronic illness.

We live in a world where nurturing mother/child attachment is seen as indulgent and crippling, even though most psychological diagnoses can be traced back to early childhood attachment traumas.

We live in a world where single mothers are burdened with the choice to either raise their own children in poverty, or sever the attachment bond by leaving them with someone else in order to earn a living.

We live in a world where mothers are expected to place our children in the care of strangers, even though children are routinely and systematically abused and neglected in schools, daycares and other institutions.

We live in a world where we are judged by, and rewarded for, our ability to succeed in a system that is inherently traumatic and disempowering.

We live in a world where we are told we must earn the right to exist, when beyond the human world exists another economy where life-sustaining resources are freely given without obligation.

We live in a world where we are taught that freedom, peace and joy must be earned, deserved, and savored only after a long life of miserable toil, or on bank holidays.

We live in a world that runs on the guilt, shame and economic coercion of women, and in which we are warned that living for ourselves and for our own pleasure is punishable by public shaming, material destitution and loss of parental rights.

We live in a world where motherhood is seen as a woman's moral obligation, and also as something that must be done outside of the public domain while simultaneously subject to the scrutiny and specifications of complete strangers.

We live in a world where women are expected to follow rules about how, where, and with whom to live our lives and to care for our children, by individuals who do not inhabit female bodies and who have zero knowledge of children's actual needs.

We live in a world where children are seen as enemies to control, and in which there exists systemic hostility toward children's needs, feelings, desires and expression.

We live in a world where being a daughter is somehow an actual fucking job that girls and adult women are expected to perform, while the question of whether our parents have done their job in meeting our developmental needs is not seriously considered.

All of these things are true because this upside-down world is a global patriarchal society, in which men have dethroned women in an absurd attempt to mimic women's natural roles as creatrixes and community leaders.

Patriarchy is defined as "father rule," a system in which men legally own their wives and any children they create, through the institution of marriage. The details and implications vary throughout different countries and cultures, but there is always an element of ownership involved in husbandry and fatherhood.

Even in parts of the world where women are free to divorce, the prospects for women's futures post-divorce are often slim and in various ways, require them to effectively abandon their children physically and/or emotionally in order to survive. Any choice that entails trauma or potential loss of life is not a meaningful choice.

In this upside-down world, it is also essential to separate women from their children — emotionally, if not also physically — so that children can be "broken" and indoctrinated into patriarchal beliefs and loyalty. This takes many forms: forced education, forced labor, and forced contact with (and influence from) relatives, professionals and other individuals against the mother's and/or child's will.

It also includes the separation of women and mothers from their female lineage, both symbolically and materially, which would otherwise provide practical and emotional support for the work of daily living, childrearing and earning one's livelihood.

As a result, mothers have lost connection with themselves and the pleasure and wisdom of their own bodies. Women's ability to connect emotionally with their children and to lead them is diminished in a male-dominated society, and replaced with the use of force and passive obedience to fathers, schools, doctors, landlords, bosses and other patriarchally-designated authority figures.

Many women realize all too late, if ever, that the happily-ever-after story of love and marriage that they have been programmed to idealize since childhood has really been a carefully laid trap leading to the wholesale extraction of their emotional and physical resources, loss of their personal and creative sovereignty, and a level of isolation that is both psychologically damaging and tragically unconducive to raising healthy children.

The Good Family

I grew up in what, from the outside, many people would consider a "good family." My parents were both high-achieving professionals who held prominent positions in community organizations. We lived in a big house in the suburbs, I performed very well academically, had plenty of friends, and played lots of instruments and plenty of team sports.

From the outside, you would probably not have guessed that my home life was chaotic, and both physically and emotionally unsafe. That my father was a sexual predator and an alcoholic, that my mother struggled deeply with her emotions and life circumstances, and that I was expected to meet both of my parents' needs throughout my entire childhood, and also as an adult, until they each died.

No, you wouldn't have guessed that, because on the outside, my family seemed "normal." Because in a culture where the pursuit of money and power is valued over health and relationships, my family *was* normal. Substance dependency is normal. Predation is normal. Emotional dysregulation is normal. Parentifying children is normal. Incest is normal.

And this is why it often happens that if you live in a wealthy neighborhood in a nice big house, nobody questions what might be going on inside of it.

Or if anyone does, there isn't much they can do.

My parents received a visit from Child Protective Services after I showed up at preschool one day with blood on my underwear. The investigation was immediately closed, for reasons you might expect. It's not like they ran psychological tests on my parents, or observed our family for a week and counted how many times my father made lecherous comments about women or how many evenings he was so drunk that his speech was slurred. Even if they had, those things are totally normal, right?

I didn't hear anything about this incident until was in my early 30s, when I recovered repressed sexual abuse memories from about age four, and asked my parents what they knew about it. They told me they had no idea who could have abused me. But I hadn't asked because I didn't know — the memories came with clear knowledge that my father had been the perpetrator — I'd asked because I wanted them to admit it to my face.

I believe it's possible that my mother truly didn't know. She was dealing with enough of her own stuff that she didn't have the capacity to be exquisitely attuned to my experience. But knowing what I know now, both as an adult and as a parent, and having developed a deep understanding of the countless ways childhood sexual abuse shaped my life, I am confident that I would have known.

First of all, I was deeply emotionally insecure and my self-esteem was in the toilet. I performed well in school not because I had a great home life, but because school was a safe place for me. I got to feel loved and valued and worthy when I met my teachers' expectations, which were generally consistent and provided a more predictable path to success than the ones my parents had of me.

The problem with judging a child's home life by their academic performance is that in school, you're actually *more* likely to succeed if you don't think for yourself, work tirelessly for external validation, dissociative enough to robotically perform a full day of dry, emotionless mental tasks, and are good at taking orders — all potentially, and conveniently, symptoms of trauma.

If a child does not already have trauma when they begin school, they soon will, as they begin co-regulating with tyranny in a hostile setting with the ambiance of a radium factory.

My chronic dysregulation and disconnection from my body was visible in many other ways, including lack of sexual boundaries, people-pleasing, attention-seeking, drug and alcohol use, and eating disorders. So, either the other adults in my life didn't notice these at all, didn't know what to do about them, or didn't recognize them *as problems*. Indeed, these are often seen as things that normal adolescent and teen girls "just do." But the context for these norms is a world in which *one in four* girls is sexually abused in childhood [1]. So, when these patterns show up, I reckon it's worth a closer look.

When we normalize the symptoms of child sexual abuse, we also normalize the abuse.

It would be great if more adults in my life had recognized that something was very wrong with me, and taken action or at least tried to talk to me about it. At least I can say that I've become that person now. If I see a child being mistreated in public, I say something. My hope is that even if the adult doesn't change their behavior, I'll at least plant the idea in the child's mind that they deserve better.

I hear that schools are more aware of mental health issues now than they were when I was growing up. But there's only so much an institution can do to help, when they are also contributing to the problem by requiring children to submit to authority all day, nearly every day. Forced obedience is not how survivors become empowered — it's how survivors learn to give up hope for healing and for a better world.

The solutions of schools and the government in handling abuse at home aren't necessarily going to help. Children removed from their families often have an even harder time in foster care, facing not just the trauma of being torn from their homes and whatever happened in them, but often additional abuse and even sex trafficking, that could make the dangers of their original home life pale in comparison.

The problem is that the abusers are often the father, and the father reigns supreme in our cultural and legal institutions. Incest isn't an anomaly in patriarchy — you could hardly design a system that provides predators more unrestricted access to children than the nuclear family.

In a world where women raised children collectively, free from the isolation and oppression of the nuclear family, incest rates would plummet and mothers would have the support needed to thrive. In fact, this is the reality in matriarchal and matrilineal societies, past and present (for more on this, read Elisha Daeva's book *Before War*).

The idea that matriarchy would be "just as bad" as patriarchy is a fantasy of the wounded masculine and the disempowered feminine. Women have neither the motivation, the ability, nor the fucking time to create a society as violent and oppressive as the one we live in today.

My mother wasn't a perfect parent by any stretch of the imagination, but she never sexually abused me. And I believe that she would have had much better mental and emotional health had she not been married to my father. But once she was married with kids, it was too late. She told me many times in my youth that she wanted to leave, but that she couldn't because my father took all of her money.

Financial abuse and dependency are often the glue that keeps married couples from splitting up, rather than the fairytale of devotion and commitment that we are sold.

Many women don't divorce their husbands because they fear he would win custody of their children due to his having a bigger house or income and this appearing, however superficially, to provide the better home, as well as the resources to afford a better lawyer. This is exactly how marriage is designed to work. Women have even committed suicide after cruelly being prevented by the courts from having contact with their children, due to the patriarchal belief that fatherhood is a right.

Women couldn't even initiate divorce in California without proving spousal wrongdoing until 1969, and much later in many other U.S. states. Whenever and wherever women have gained this right, rates of female suicide and violence against women, including murder by male partners, have gone down drastically [2].

Women who choose not to marry are bullied by relatives and society as a whole, and unmarried mothers have been subject to horrific systemic abuse. Women were tortured and burned at the stake as witches for not marrying soon enough, or at all, or for not having children. Unmarried women and their children have been kept in religious institutions, such as Ireland's Magdalene Laundries, to punish them, correct their moral compass, and to hide them from society. The last such "asylum" in Ireland, where single mothers and "promiscuous women" could be imprisoned for life, was open until 1996 [3].

Controlling women with shame and resources is a tool of patriarchal control, and it not only kills them but also poisons the well for future generations.

When I decided to confront my father about the abuse, making it clear that I knew he was the perpetrator, he flew into a rage, screaming at me over and over again, "I am not a child molester!" There was zero concern for my experience — it was all about *his* feelings, *his* delusional self-image and *his* reputation.

Any remaining doubt I'd had about how he could have been capable of such crimes was relieved in that moment, as he showed me the side of himself that was indeed capable. It was a gift, in a way, because I was then finally able to fully let go. We had been estranged for years at that point, but I knew this was the end for real.

I had only seen him that day because my mother had just died, and I had heard that she wanted to say goodbye to me. I hadn't made it in time. Whatever final words she may have wanted to share with me — a confession, an apology, or maybe a declaration of my inherent worthiness as a human being — would forever be left to my imagination.

I walked out into the streets as an adult orphan. I had no idea at the time that I was pregnant with my daughter. Without a word, my mother had passed the baton to me. Her death, and the near simultaneous entry of my child into the world, provided a sort of quiet closure, both events marking the end of the childhood I had known and initiating me into motherhood.

I saw my father one more time before his death. I had brought my daughter, three months postpartum, to a family holiday dinner at my aunt's house, which had been our tradition ever since I could remember. I hadn't been in years, because of my need to be around emotionally safe people in order to heal and recover. I don't remember what I thought would be different that time — maybe it was a desperate clinging to the idea of raising my child with extended family, despite everything that I had learned and what I had intentionally left behind.

But when my father asked to hold my infant daughter, I said NO. Somehow I hadn't imagined this scenario, but once I was faced with the physical and symbolic question of passing my child to the man who had caused me a lifetime of trauma, I knew that there was no way in hell I was going to let him touch her, ever.

In that moment, I made a powerful choice: this "good family" would start a new legacy.

Things That Burn

Eventually, I worked up the nerve to file a police report against my father. I did it as much out of a need to speak my truth, as with any true hope for justice. Honestly, I probably wouldn't do it again.

After jotting down the basic facts of the crime, the police asked me what impact the abuse had had on me. I told them all about my post-traumatic stress, eating disorders, difficulty providing for myself financially and struggle with codependency. I masterfully painted a picture of my whole fucked up life and how it was connected to my childhood experience of sexual abuse.

My daughter was with me the whole time, but it took me a while to read between the lines. As I spoke, the police kept looking at my child as if they were measuring her welfare. It became clear that the police were asking about the impact of the abuse not to prepare for gathering evidence or to gauge the credibility of my story, but to judge whether or not I was a fit parent.

I had come to the police to report a crime, only to be treated like a criminal.

I got uncomfortable real fast and abruptly ended the interview. The police assured me they had enough information and would be in contact about the results of the investigation.

My daughter and I were traveling in a campervan at the time, and considering the big ick I was feeling from the police at that point, I wasn't about to let them know. They made it hard though, because they went outside and watched us walk away. I couldn't go to our van, so I walked right by it and took my daughter to the park until the police went away and we could go safely. It was terrifying.

A few weeks later I heard back from the police. It turned out that their idea of an investigation was just calling up my father and casually asking him if he had sexually assaulted me. Unsurprisingly, my father told them he hadn't.

So that was that, in their minds. Additionally, they told me that my father had mentioned on the call that he missed me so very much, and loved me so much, and really, really wanted to talk to me.

And then the officer on the other end of the line asked me if I wanted them to give my father, who I told them had raped me, my phone number.

I'm not making this up.

I gave them a piece of my mind instead, and hung up.

I was devastated by the witch hunt my plea for justice had become. I felt stupid for even having thought that the police might have helped, considering everything I already knew about law enforcement's systemic role in protecting the wealthy, and particularly men and abusers.

Any woman who has tried to wrest custody of her children from her abusive spouse knows how victims' wounds can be used against them in court — to discredit their testimony and to enable and justify further abuse. In these cases, as in mine, the system isn't broken; it's doing exactly what it was built to do. Justice in patriarchy is a pay-to-play system used by the powerful to transfer innocence from the victim to the perpetrator, as part of an extractive economy in which morality is another form of currency. Women are still put on trial for defying men, just as we were in the witch burnings.

My father's will was a 57-page treatise delivering his final power play. Disinheritance wasn't so much about the money for me, as it was about the hostility and the feeling of having been discarded like a used, broken toy. But at the time, I was living with my infant daughter in the forest in a vehicle, keeping warm with a campfire... so it was sort of about the money, too.

Having limited space in our van and no use for this document anyway, and needing desperately to keep warm in the outdoors of the Pacific Northwest, it had to burn. Every balled-up page cast into the flames became a promise and a prayer to make it all up to myself, and then some.

Sorry You Lost Your Childhood to Raising Your Parents

I miss my parents sometimes, but not in the way that I hear other people talk about missing their parents. When I miss my parents, I don't miss who they were to me. I miss *their* joy, *their* laughter, *their* excitement, *their* expression of childlike wonder — I miss my parents the way a mother misses her children.

It took me forever to realize this because it was just so... weird. And that grief has been all mixed up with the grief for the loss of my *own* childhood — how confusing!

It doesn't help that our society doesn't recognize the validity of either type of grief. There is no greeting card that says, "Sorry you lost your childhood to raising your parents." There is no time off work, no funeral, no medal or offers of condolences for a lost childhood, or for the complex grief of losing parents who were more like siblings or children to you.

I had debilitating hip pain for years and couldn't figure out what the problem was, until I discovered that my unexpressed grief had caused tension in my pelvic muscles. My logical mind had pushed away these feelings because they didn't seem to make sense. I had no template to follow, no framework for acknowledging the complicated and confusing emotions and inner conflict caused by having spent my childhood taking care of my own parents while also being abused by them. (The section "Women are Portals" goes into my process around somatic healing.)

I recently saw a photo of a man receiving a medal for having been a prisoner of war. His face revealed the intensity of emotion he felt, and had carried, and how healing it was for him to be recognized for the challenges he had faced and the trauma he had survived.

Why is it so much easier for us to honor war veterans who experience loss, and to acknowledge their trauma, than it is to bestow this level of compassion and pride upon those who have survived a war on girls and women?

Of course, decorating a soldier who has been to war reinforces patriarchal ideals and institutions, but honoring women and children who have suffered from patriarchal abuse threatens that same exact system. It takes cognitive dissonance — and chronic dissociative tendencies — for a society to continually justify this discrepancy.

If our society took the loss of a childhood as seriously as other types of losses, it would lead to a whole lot of reckoning with the causes of that grief. Maybe this will happen someday on a public scale, instead of only in the personal journals and private conversations of those who are lucky enough to survive.

Unearned Wrinkles and a Half-Baked Cake

We talk a lot of shit about the vanity of women searching for endless youth, but not a lot about women who want to feel and appear youthful because we were literally robbed of our childhoods.

When you spend your developmental years meeting adults' needs and coping with trauma, you enter adulthood feeling like a half-baked cake. To then be thrown into the responsibilities of making a living and raising children without having had a chance to mature into these roles naturally, or even develop the healthy concept of self crucial to adult functioning, is devastating.

The social pressure on women of all ages to look like teenage girls does not help at all — it's insult added to injury. For the woman who hasn't earned every wrinkle with years of joyful laughter (as the greeting cards attempt to console us), who never experienced true happiness until after her grays started showing, who is jarred to see a middle-aged woman in the mirror when she is only just starting to really *live*, aging can carry a level of grief beyond normal human experience.

Of course the multibillion dollar beauty industry is eager to exploit this grief. Or maybe women who refuse to "age naturally" just don't want to set false expectations about our maturity level.

Every woman has a different story, but many women feel like they haven't gotten what they expected, needed or deserved from their youth. So it's no wonder that we want to make it up to ourselves, in any way that we can, with whatever time we have left. And we absolutely should!

Whether that means taking ourselves on fun or fancy vacations, wearing clothes that make us feel creatively expressed, enrolling in art classes, doing what we love for a living, creating meaningful relationships, buying ourselves things that will help us see the person we feel ourselves to be inside, on the outside, or attracting abundant provision so that we have the spaciousness in our schedules to nurture our inner child, we have every right to make our adult lives an answer to our unmet childhood longings.

We can't change the past or bypass the grief, but we can honor the little girl inside who has been waiting decades for her turn.

In losing my childhood, and grieving it, I found opportunities for childlike joy, play and wonder everywhere. The more I indulge them, the more I see them.

We may have missed out on a lot in the past, but all anyone ever has is the present moment. When we remember this, we can find opportunities for a Second Childhood anytime.

A Stranger Comes to Town

When I began my healing journey, there was nowhere near the scale and variety of resources available now online and in books and healing programs — trauma has still only recently gained a prominent place in human consciousness and conversation. Much has changed, but wounds caused within the home are still largely ignored and the scars even normalized, mirroring the invisibility still surrounding children and their developmental needs today.

What's more, there is very little literature detailing the excruciating process of extracting oneself from an abusive family, and the catastrophic impact it has on other areas of life.

I had an incredibly hard time coming to accept my own traumas, and the immense dedication that healing would require. After I quit drinking, I was overwhelmed with emotions on a daily basis, and had no idea how to process all of them. I felt a deep, insatiable need for other human beings, as I had before, only now the need felt much more intense because I had so many new needs popping up that had previously been subdued with alcohol.

Other people weren't available to me nearly as often as I wanted them to be, and even when they were, they didn't know much more than I did about healing or emotional regulation. I was forced to figure out most of it on my own.

There are many things I did to connect with and liberate my inner child, create a secure attachment with my adult self as my own loving parent, and build a life that protected me from further abuse — most of which I learned from trial and error.

The most important thing I did was to cry. Once the dam broke, I cried every day for nearly two years straight. All the feelings from my childhood came bursting to the surface like a balloon pushed deep under water, and then suddenly released. Most of it was grief — the absence of the nurturing, attuned parents I needed, the abuse of my trust and loss of my innocence at such a young age, the sadness from being abandoned by adults who were physically present but emotionally unavailable. Most of the time, I didn't even know what I was crying about — it was overwhelming and confusing and seemed like the tears would never stop. I was catching up on decades of nervous system regulation.

A lot of the time when I wasn't crying, I felt like I needed to cry, but just couldn't. I learned later that my nervous system was stuck in a freeze state due to the lack of co-regulation in my childhood, and that I had basically shut down — for literally decades — to avoid the discomfort of it. I needed connection, physical touch (like hugs, or holding someone's hand), and grounding to "defrost" myself and get back in touch with my body. When tears came, and they often did once I experienced the warmth of another human being, I welcomed them as relief from the pain of chronic dysregulation. Speaking out loud about what I was experiencing also helped me integrate trapped emotions — exercising our vocal cords can loosen up stuck energy and move it through our bodies.

I spent years doing mostly this healing work and not much else. I wasn't really available to make friends or go out and do a lot of fun stuff that I saw other people in recovery doing.

This is partly because I'd also quit eating sugar only a few months after I quit drinking. My addiction to sugar had started probably a decade before my alcohol use had begun, and covered much deeper wounds. There was just so much for me to handle emotionally that I didn't have the time or capacity for much else.

In retrospect, I do not recommend trying to quit multiple substances simultaneously. Other people in recovery advised strongly against it, warning that it could be too much for me and I'd risk losing my sobriety altogether. Well, I didn't listen, and I don't know if I even could have done things differently. It was a fucking lot to deal with, they were right about that. But I hated the out-of-control feeling I had with food, and it seemed to get worse when alcohol was out of the picture. I also probably didn't want to gain a bunch of weight, which was maybe a bit vain, but more than anything I wanted relief from the obsession and compulsion I experienced around cookies, cake and bread. I felt driven to get to the root of the problem and to free myself from addiction of any kind.

I did get that relief, but it came with a price. Within a few months of quitting sugar, I uncovered repressed memories of child sexual abuse. I was truly shaken to my core — it was like everything I had ever thought I knew about myself, my family and the world was ripped out from under me and I felt like a stranger to myself.

I had almost no support system at the time, and was majorly unequipped to handle this revelation. My relationship with my therapist was on the rocks, after she'd admitted to manipulating me into seeing her for more frequent sessions, and after guilt-tripping me about not calling my mother on her birthday.

Even before the memories came back, I'd been having a hard time with my family and their inability to accept my choice to seek therapy, to pursue recovery and to take the space I needed in order to heal. Also, my parents were both a handful with their own unmet attachment needs, and their tendency to center these needs in our relationship. Being around them made me feel like I was never allowed to be needy, selfish or flawed, not just in our relationship as adults, but in all the ways that are crucial to a child's development — needs that I still carried as a thirty-year-old woman.

There are things you simply can't tolerate anymore once you're no longer numbing yourself to the pain they cause. Once I started paying attention to how I really felt around my parents, I could no longer rationalize their abuse or justify making myself small to fit them into my life. I had to put myself first.

One of the most important — and hardest — things I did in my role as my own loving parent, was to distance myself from my biological family.

At first, missing out on family holiday gatherings felt like torture. Part of me still wanted to be there — my inner child still associated events like Christmas and Thanksgiving with happy times, even though when I went, I ended up having an unhappy time and feeling destabilized for days and weeks afterward. It was hard for my inner child to let go, feeling torn between the fantasy I'd once created about my family life in order to survive it, and the painful reality that I needed to face in order to heal from it. Sometimes I had to go back, just to remind myself how bad it really was.

Despite the challenges, staying on the path of sobriety and abstinence from sugar helped me stick to my decision. This was especially difficult for me because of my lack of social support. At the time, I had more of an "all or nothing" mindset and struggled with impulse control (see: attachment trauma), so it seemed like it all had to be done immediately, I wasn't exactly emotionally available for forming new relationships, and I was devastated from betrayal by my therapist, who was one of the first people on Earth I had ever trusted with my inner world. On top of that, my connection to recovery groups was hanging by a thread because of the widespread opposition among members to choosing estrangement from one's family.

I was no longer in touch with friends I'd had before getting sober, because we were doing different things in life and none of them seemed to understand what I was going through, or want to. Some friends and relatives even bullied me over telling the truth about what I'd experienced as a child, unwilling to believe that I could have experienced something so awful and tragic at the hands of people they'd perceived to be normal and good. For some, it likely hit too close to home.

All of this led to my increasing isolation and paranoia, which was unfortunately well-founded. Everyone *was* after me — to shut me up, pull me back into the family, and keep me from growing out of the lies we'd all built our lives around. The way people acted, it was like I'd committed a crime. Someone even sent the police to my apartment under the guise of checking up on my mental health, after I'd stopped returning their calls because I couldn't stand being gaslighted anymore. The cops let themselves into my apartment while I was in the shower — a terrifying partial reenactment of the sexual abuse scenario from my childhood. Similarly, my therapist's attempt at EMDR — waving a pool cue back and forth from her crotch like a giant phallus — was anything but healing. Nobody had any idea what I really needed, and everyone who tried only made things worse.

This has been a pattern in my life — no one understands what I'm experiencing, no one can support me, and I feel completely alone — because, it usually turns out, I'm the one who is leading the way.

Estrangement is much more common now, and more widely accepted as a valid and reasonable choice for survivors, than it was back then. The conversation around child sexual abuse has also evolved somewhat, although there is much room for improvement.

There is a part of me who envies people who began this journey after me, or at a younger age, or with loved ones by their side, and who have the comfort of social awareness and support that wasn't available to me when I most needed it.

I heard someone say once that the hardest thing you can ever experience in life *is still only a feeling*, and that stuck with me.

The most important skill I've gained is the ability to tolerate my emotions, and it's been the key to every bit of freedom I enjoy today, in my personal relationships, in my work, and in every other area of life. The more I've been willing to feel, the less control anyone or anything else can have over me. I don't have to live in fear of anyone else's rejection or withdrawal, because I'm no longer afraid of how those things will make me feel.

Being able to enjoy our own company, and to be present with ourselves through the full range of our experience as humans, is the basis for healthy relationships with others and a foundation for sovereignty in all areas of life.

Ultimately, I found that discovering my inner worth also brought me the strength I needed to survive being socially ostracized for embracing it. Finding my power scared people away, but it also meant I didn't need them as much anymore.

The beauty of having gone through all of this, as lonely, scary and awful as it was, is that I now get to be there for other women who decide not to care for a sick or aging abusive relative, or who secretly wish to make some other dangerously selfish choice to protect their own peace like the absolute treasure it is.

If we can find the courage to feel, there is nothing for us to fear.

We Can Raise Ourselves However We Want

Many of us didn't get our emotional needs met in childhood by our primary caregivers. On top of this, we may have been shamed for needing and wanting more from them, and abandoned emotionally in their misguided attempt to "teach" us independence — the "cry it out" method of neglecting children to sleep is one example.

But children can't be "taught" emotional independence. Children are dependent, by definition — they develop maturity through co-regulation with a consistent caregiver.

As adults, many of us have searched for the emotional security and nurturing we missed out on in childhood from people who are ill-equipped to deliver the goods. We have assigned bosses, teachers and partners the role of surrogate parent, and then been devastated when they have inevitably failed us.

In addition to learning to feel our feelings and heal from the pain of the past, emotional sovereignty involves reparenting our inner child — giving her the love, attunement, nurturing and other forms of support that she didn't receive from her primary caregivers. Skipping this part makes us vulnerable to codependency, relationship addiction, abuse and exploitation, because it means we look outside of ourselves to get these needs met — often in places where the care we need is not available. An unclaimed inner child is easy prey.

Trying to connect with your inner child can feel so awkward at first. It's literally... *talking to yourself*, and that can make you feel like a crazy person. It also takes a lot of courage to tune out the noise and demands of the world to attune to and nurture your inner child. Every moment we spend reparenting our inner child is a rebellion.

I found giving myself what I *didn't* get as a child to be a lot harder work than healing from the abuse I *did* experience. Identifying my needs, and then figuring out how to meet them, was a daily struggle. It often took the better part of a day, or even multiple days, weeks or months — and in a few cases, *years* — to understand and then strategize on meeting a single need. Fitting self-parenting between all of my regular adult responsibilities made me one busy lady.

My hope is that you will not have to walk alone in the dark with your inner child for as long as I did. It was really hard for me to find people who could help me on this path at the time, but many of us who have found our way to the light are now available to support others.

Having reparented my inner child for so long, I can often quickly recognize in other people what childhood wound is blocking their path and what they need in order to move forward. I know from my own experience what it looks and feels like to be divorced from our inner power, to act from a place of inner child woundedness and look for our needs to be met in any other way than through our own resources.

The more you practice recognizing these states of being, and the many ways they manifest, the easier it is to do, and the faster you'll move through it each time.

One of the most powerful ways I have found to connect with my inner child is by smiling. This might seem off-putting if you've ever been told to smile by a creepy guy on the street, or been in so-called "spiritual" spaces where toxic positivity reigns supreme — that's not what this is about. I'm talking about a gentle, inward-focused smile that lets your inner child know that you are receiving them lovingly, no matter what they are feeling or experiencing in that moment. It's a gesture of unconditional positive regard and radical self-acceptance.

Smiling might not automatically make you happy or change how you feel (although it definitely can!), but that's not the point. You're not trying to override or repress your emotions, as you may have learned to do as a child when adults found your emotions offensive or inconvenient. The magic of a smile is that it can *change how you feel about how you feel*.

You're not just your inner child, you're also your own loving parent, and how you relate to your inner child makes a huge difference in your relationship with yourself. Your attitude towards your emotions can either make them seem scarier and less manageable, or provide a safe container for them to be witnessed and integrated. Smiling is a way of saying *yes* to ourselves and to life, an attitude which can trigger a profound shift in our perspective and in our visceral experience.

If this doesn't make sense to you, try imagining that someone else is smiling at you warmly, making you feel seen, safe and loved. I started out by projecting imaginary loving parents onto random things, like a pretty flower sticker on my dresser: "That flower is friendly toward me," I'd think. I know it sounds weird, but I really needed it, and it worked well enough to help me while I was in the early stages of developing self-parenting skills. This was how I started building trust with myself and with the world, ever so gradually, after decades of not feeling safe to be seen.

Ideally, our parents would have received us with this much acceptance, and we would have grown up feeling seen, loved and safe without having to play make-believe with inanimate objects. But given that this isn't always the case, a little creativity is called for!

It blew my mind when I discovered that I could just *give myself* the reassurance, approval and validation that I was craving from other people... And that it felt just as good, and worked just as well! For example, sometimes feeling anxious and overwhelmed means that your inner child needs to hear you say, "I got this." Claiming your role in solving your own problems can feel so empowering.

Whatever you wish someone else would say to comfort or reassure you, try just telling yourself. If it helps you to connect with yourself, you might want to close your eyes, take a deep breath, think or say the words you need to hear, and then allow yourself to take them in deeply.

I've also learned to praise myself, tune in to my emotions throughout the day, and check that I'm taking responsibility for meeting my own needs rather than projecting a parental role onto others — a favorite question is, "What does my inner child need right now to feel safe, loved and *chosen*?" Choosing myself initially was really hard because it brought up such intense feelings of shame and abandonment, but these did not last forever.

I don't reparent myself anywhere near perfectly, and I also don't hold myself back for fear that my inner child will pop up and embarrass me. I've learned to accept that this will happen, and to handle it with a sense of humor. It's not my fault that I have a needy little kid inside of me, and I'm not going to punish myself for the times when my way of being in the world reflects the complex reality of my inner experience. On the contrary, having an inner child is something to celebrate! It can be fun to let our inner child play with others, even in ways that show our wounds, when we get comfortable enough.

However we choose to reparent ourselves, it can be a huge relief to stop hiding and to accept our inner child as part of our lives. This is the magic of self-parenting — we can raise ourselves however we want! Any shame projected by others around this type of inner work is not ours to take on — the stigma only exists to silence survivors and protect the people and institutions that failed us.

Reparenting ourselves can be the most powerfully transformative work we do, because it means we no longer look to others to change how we feel inside. The more we think we need people to complete us, the worse we're going to feel because we will absorb energy around us everywhere we go, subconsciously looking for someone to fill the hole left by our unmet attachment needs.

This is particularly true for exceptionally empathic individuals, whose sensitivities can make public appearances and social interactions nearly intolerable, reflecting our higher need for energy clearing, rest, boundaries and solitude. If our sensitivities were not respected and accommodated when we were children, doing so now can be an essential part of our self-parenting practice.

It's the most empowering thing to reclaim our sovereignty by meeting our own emotional needs. Other people can help, but it's liberating when receiving from others is a bonus, rather than something we believe we can't live without. We are also much more likely to bring healthy people into our lives when we are not in desperate need of love or attention. We can be much more selective and have healthier boundaries in relationships when we want, rather than need, other people. When we source our happiness from within, and act as our own loving parent, we feel whole on our own and can more easily let go of relationships that do not serve us.

In a sense, self-parenting is the repair work we do with ourselves around our childhood conditioning, whether or not our parents are available for repair with us. Reparenting ourselves is liberating for us, and gives us the ability to be emotionally available to our own children, if we have them, so that they can eventually grow up to be sovereign beings as well.

Kitchen Scissors, Felonies and Freedom

Our brains, shaped by external influences since before we were born, often don't seem to be on our side at all. The journey toward liberation often begins by questioning what's going on up in that mysterious little control tower upstairs.

Thinking critically, following our thoughts to their logical conclusion, and allowing ourselves to see the world as it really is — not how we are told to see it — frees our minds from patriarchal programming. Daring to listen to our own inner wisdom and to validate our most socially unacceptable feelings is a radical act.

Women are often criticized for changing our minds, but changing our minds gives us the power to change our lives and to change the world. Anyone who has a problem with us changing our minds probably has a lot to gain from things staying exactly the way they are!

Whether we choose meditation, movement, writing, listening or reading, taking a closer look at our thoughts can help us get a bird's eye view of how our well-worn neural pathways influence our life choices: Which of our thoughts are supporting us in living life joyfully and as expansively as possible, and which ones are holding us back?

Every time we change our minds, we plant a seed of possibility.

Although I wasn't raised to be much of a "lady," or to think there was anything I couldn't do because of my sex, I still had plenty of hangups about my expression in the world. Any vestiges of social decorum I had went out the window after the massive betrayal I'd experienced from everyone I had ever known. Once the illusion that there was something inherently wrong with me began to unravel, and I could see how deeply I'd been turned against myself, I started realizing how absolutely fucking insane all "the rules" were.

I began listening to my intuition and my desires, and not the fear-based thinking I'd inherited from my parents, school, and the media. As I began to question the way things were, my perspective on people who lived on the fringes of society changed, too — I became one of them. All of a sudden, people who lived in houses that they paid for with their souls started looking like the crazy ones to me — I could sleep in a beautiful forest, and owe nothing to anyone. I started doing things that would get me labeled the wrong kind of person where I grew up, if I'd still had anything left to lose. I wasn't rebelling, I was just discovering the world through my own perceptions for the first time.

Once when I was hitchhiking through northern California, I walked past a gun shop that had a poster advertising a rifle shooting contest. I walked in and announced my entry, and won. The owner was kind enough not to give me the prize money though, deciding after the fact that the results wouldn't count because it was my first time (surely this had nothing to do with his feelings about losing to a woman who had never held a firearm before). I didn't care — I had beat him, and we both knew it. It was a victory for me on many levels, as I'd set my sights on testing my limits, and hit the mark.

One random afternoon I pulled a wild stunt at a clothing store in protest of the sale of appropriated indigenous motifs, and ended up in jail. This is when I learned that cutting up clothes with kitchen scissors can count as felony property destruction, due to the length of the blade. I find this sexist.

I shared a cell with an accountant and a stripper and had the time of my life. The conversations and laughter we shared changed me forever — we all had things in common, despite leading outwardly different lives. We had all fought back against some aspect of patriarchy, or been caught up by it.

After a few days in the city jail, I was transferred to one of the largest detention facilities in the country. I met many more women here who had been victimized by men in their lives, but had ended up the ones behind bars. Hearing their stories, and the threads that connected them, lit a fire under my ass.

Reflected in these women, I could see both what the world had made me into, and what the world could never take from me.

Despite being forced to wake up at 3 am every morning, I made the most of my circumstances and had a pretty good time. I learned how to play basketball — something I never would have taken the time to do otherwise. There wasn't much else to do, and I felt relieved of my compulsion for constant achievement.

I was still me, though. One day when a dozen women and I were kept in a tiny holding cell for several hours, I demanded we be fed on the legal basis of medical negligence. This was successful and earned me the respect of other inmates, as well as the nickname "Protest."

I had a relatively easy time behind bars, but a lot of the women I met there nearly twelve years ago still haven't left. The least I could do was leave a scathing Yelp review.

Reclaiming Our Innocence

The Second Childhood is about reclaiming our innocence as women in a society that labels us as "guilty" by default.

I mean *innocence* in every sense of the word — coming to believe that we are not guilty because of what we want in life, and reclaiming our sense of trust, awe and wonder in the world.

This an intellectual, physical and emotional process — one in which we come to believe that we are *essentially* innocent at our core. When we externalize the anger, the guilt, the shame, the fear, and the icky energies dumped on us by others, we reclaim not just our bodies, but also our sense of self and our lives.

Reclaiming our innocence is to see and truly feel that others' abuse, disapproval, dissatisfaction and anger toward us don't mean anything about *us*. It's *their* stuff, not ours. Malware alert!

Less so, but still, the euphemistic sense of innocence as virginity also applies here. If you abstain from sex for seven years, your cells fully replace themselves, and voila — you're technically a born-again virgin.

Of course, the idea that something a man can do to your body affects your value as a human being is stupid and rooted in patriarchal ideology — sexual assault does not affect our worth in any way. But sexual exchange can result in an *energetic* imprint that stays in our bodies long after our cells regenerate, leading to inconvenient and dangerous attachments and blockages.

Although it can give us the space to heal, abstinence itself won't heal us. To reclaim our bodies and evict other people's energetic debris from them, we need to discern which energies are truly ours — and which ones we have been hosting for free like a Wix website, complete with ads that confuse us about our true desires and identity (for more on this process, see "Women are Portals").

Our parents have a heavy hand in shaping our concept of God. Because the quality of our connection with them (or lack thereof) trains our nervous system responses at crucial points in our development, we inherit their emotional patterns as well as their moral compass.

To a child, their parents *are* God.

To individuate emotionally, spiritually and intellectually, we must reclaim our nervous systems and our capacity for independent thought. We must recognize that *we* are God, as much as anyone else is, and that we have the right to determine the trajectory of our own lives.

While I'm aware that anyone with religious trauma may be put off by the word or concept of "God" — myself included — I'm using it here in order to bring forward that which it refers to so that we can play with it.

I invite anyone who would like to experiment with a new spiritual framework and language to try thinking of God as a synonym for "good." This shift helped me imagine a non-patriarchal spiritual presence that made sense to me.

Have you ever looked in the mirror and said to yourself, "You are good"? This is a quick way to see if you are holding onto shame by how much it makes you cringe. You don't have to use a mirror — you can close your eyes and say it to yourself, or you can simply think to yourself, "I am good." And really let it sink in.

I found this surprisingly healing. I didn't even know I was carrying an internalized sense of shame until I tried on feeling "not ashamed" by doing this exercise. I cried a little after doing this and then felt better.

You can try it with different feelings — for example, for guilt: "I am innocent." For fear: "I am safe."

The goal is not to bypass your real and valid emotions, but to offer a contrast that will bring your feelings to light, and provide a larger, more authoritative truth (according to you) for them to melt into.

When we reclaim our power to define our spiritual beliefs, we also reclaim our nervous systems. If we are God, or good, then the guilt and shame we feel for falling short of religious ideals can go back to where they belong — onto the individuals and systems that projected them onto us in the first place.

In this way, we not only reclaim our spirituality, but also our ability to believe and truly feel that we are *good*, regardless of what anyone else says.

The Meaning of Life

Since our idea of God is shaped by our relationships with our parents, and we subconsciously absorb their belief systems, we learn to make meaning of life the same way that they do — most importantly, the meaning and value of our own lives.

A child who was conceived for a specific reason — such as to fulfill a family legacy — will believe that is their purpose in life, because it is the literal, material reason for their existence. The child knows no greater authority than their parents. If this child disappoints their parents by not fulfilling the legacy, they may believe that their life has no meaning or that their deviance from their parents' hopes and dreams for their lives means that they are a bad person or a failure in life. This tends to be accompanied by massive amounts of fear, guilt and shame.

A child who was not wanted at all will likely grow up believing their life has *no* meaning and *no* worth. As a result, they may feel apathetic about their future or their place in the world and struggle to care for themselves. They internalize the beliefs of their parents, even if unconscious or unspoken, that they do not exist for a reason.

Whether we were unwanted as children, or wanted for a reason that doesn't serve us, we can claim our power as adults to define the meaning of our lives for ourselves. We can begin just by telling our inner child that she is wanted — by us.

As loving parents to ourselves, we can claim our role as "meaning makers" and create whatever meaning we want of our lives. This gives us authority over our sense of meaning as well as our sense of self-worth. If we previously measured our worth by how much others valued us according to *their* way of making meaning, we can now be free of that.

I knew a guy who would jump up and down every morning shouting "yes, yes, yes!" to life. This was his way of choosing himself and choosing life, regardless of what his parents or anyone else intended or expected from him. I've tried it — it's fun, and it really does make you feel turned on to life. It's a similar effect to the inward smile I introduced a few pages back, but way more intense. This one offers more of a dramatic, energizing perspective shift than a safe, calm emotional space — good for times when upregulation, rather than tenderness, feels like the right medicine.

Choosing life is one of the most powerful things that we can do for ourselves as survivors of childhood abuse or neglect. If we do not do this, we are very likely to feel that our lives are not our own or not feel connected to our lives in a meaningful way. We will feel, at least on a subconscious level, that we have somehow failed, that we just don't belong here, or that life is simply meaningless. This is also one of the reasons why it can be so hard to do — it requires us to take responsibility for our lives and that means acknowledging and grieving the time we spent not having any choices at all. It can feel like lifting a very heavy weight off of ourselves, and it is something we usually have to do many times.

Consciously choosing life, and choosing ourselves, is the first step to creating a life that means something to us. It gives us the power to break from our parents' and our culture's expectations without feeling like shit about ourselves. The guilt and shame fall away and we realize that other people's opinions about us and plans for our lives never meant anything about us — it was all about *them*. Externalizing harmful beliefs about ourselves takes a lot of work but the reward is feeling immense freedom and lightness, and being rebirthed into a Second Childhood of our own design.

Claiming our power to define meaning in our lives makes us invulnerable to manipulation from any external authorities that want to define the meaning of our lives (and therefore our worth) according to their belief system, such as corporations, schools, bosses and religions.

Once we start questioning the meaning others have projected onto our lives, or lack thereof, we start feeling more at home in our bodies and in our lives, even if we don't quite yet feel at home in the world.

The Man Behind the Curtain

No one is more easily controlled than a person who constantly feels guilty, because they perpetually feel obligated to do things in an attempt to relieve themselves of that guilt — things like being loyal to a company that doesn't give a shit about them, maintaining ties with family members who don't respect them, seeing doctors who are making them sicker, sending children to school when they are miserable and would rather pursue their own interests, or letting the kids spend time with an emotionally abusive parent, to name a few.

Religion has always played a role in keeping patriarchal society running by manufacturing women's guilt. Tell women that they are bad mothers, wives, daughters and sisters if they don't fall in line, and be sure to start telling them this from an early enough age to activate their attachment system, and they will believe you.

Add an almighty sky daddy who has the power to not only bestow the love and approval they have always craved, but also subject them to eternal damnation for the crime of disobedience, and your subjects will do anything they think they need to in order to become "good."

This may seem obvious if you've already been deconditioning from religious programming, but to the general female population of a society influenced by patriarchal religion — even those who have never set foot in any kind of church — it's often not even conscious. The belief is internalized that one's natural desires and instincts are inherently bad or wrong, and that survival and redemption depend on submission to an external, usually male, authority.

This patriarchal programming can be so insidious that we often conflate acts of man with acts of God. As Mary Daly wrote in *Beyond God the Father*, "If God is male, then men are God." How often have you heard someone experience misfortune in their life, for example getting fired from their job, and they say something along the lines of, "Well, it must all be part of God's plan!" — when it was actually their dickhead boss who made the call?

I'm all about turning rain into rainbows, but let's give credit where credit is due!

Waking up from this spell can look like realizing all of a sudden, "Wait, *that* wasn't what God chose for me, that was chosen for me by my father!" Or the government. Or my doctor. Or my landlord. Or the corporate mafia. And on and on.

It's easy for anyone raised to be this passive to forget our personal power and attribute aspects of our lives entirely of our own making, or that of others, to the will of God. And in doing so, we don't recognize that what we have in our lives isn't what God or any higher spiritual being wanted for us — it's what we have been *conditioned* to believe that we deserve, which became what *we* allowed ourselves to receive.

We learn that our guilt is not absolute or divinely ordained — it is simply a program designed to control us and keep us playing small.

In unmasking the man behind the curtain, we unlock our personal power and the door to possibilities beyond what others have envisioned for our lives.

The Lie of Earning Our Existence

Growing up, I felt a lot of pressure to achieve in school and in my career. I did not feel valued as a human being just for *being*.

My academic achievements were used to bolster the reputation of my family, which had the unfortunate effect of preventing me from appearing unwell enough to attract the help I needed.

As long as my family looked okay from the outside, nobody felt the need to look into it on a deeper level. I had also internalized the idea that as long as I did well enough in school, everything would be, and even already was, "okay." On some level, I needed to believe that, too.

The consequence of the pressure I felt to do well and appear well contributed to anxiety-driven patterns with food, alcohol and other substances from a very early age. I started drinking for relief at age thirteen, and continued for fourteen more years.

I also struggled with patterns of overworking and underworking, plagued by a vague sense of urgency at almost all times. I was triggered by the very prospect of work because on some level, I still needed to know that I was loveable just for who I was, and not for what I could do for others. But I was nevertheless drawn to achieve in a desperate bid for external validation. This manifested as patterns of anxiety and avoidance in both my personal and professional life.

I couldn't figure out what the problem was until I went into recovery for alcoholism, eating disorders and workaholism. I discovered that my acute traumas from various forms of abuse and neglect had set me up perfectly for a struggle with addiction.

The truth of my inherent worth as a human being eluded me until I became willing to admit the real motives behind my ambition, and how miserable it had made me.

In recovery, I began to feel safe to just exist, without needing to prove my worth to myself or anyone else. I learned the difference between making a real contribution to the world, and achieving something just for the sake of ego gratification. That difference for me was joy — and it took a long time and a lot of rest, healing and self-care before I could act from that place instead of trying to manipulate other people into liking me in order to compensate for my developmental needs.

Even after I became clear on which of my intentions were authentic and which were questionable, I wasn't automatically in a place of trust that my authentic desires and joy would be *enough*. While I finally felt that it was *good* for me to love myself and appreciate myself for just being me, I didn't yet feel *safe* doing it.

In a way, I still wasn't fully on board with my incarnation on this planet. I felt on some level that I deserved to be happy and fulfilled in my work, but I didn't yet see it as realistic.

Since so much of my life had been devoted to showboating as this hyper-productive person, my nervous system was still operating on the frequency of true creativity being frivolous and not something I could financially support myself with. I still believed that I needed to grind away out of alignment with my gifts and natural energy in order to survive and to "make it" in the world.

Looking back, this was not only caused by pressure and trauma from my family but also from brainwashing by capitalist society as a whole.

Fast-forward a few years, and my belief system swung in the exact opposite direction. I had tired of feeling like things just weren't going my way in creative endeavors, and this, combined with a number of other alienating experiences, led me to make the decision to abandon society altogether.

Interestingly, it was through this experience that I first developed a real sense of trust in the world, and of being "enough." I was hitchhiking and camping in the forest and depending almost entirely on the kindness of strangers. In a way, I had never felt safer.

From the outside, my behavior looked self-destructive and irresponsible, but I was actually getting deeply in touch with my feminine energy. I was giving my all to being 100% my true self, and letting the universe prove to me that it was enough, by making sure that I was provided for. For the most part, I was.

Growing up the daughter of a second-wave feminist, who was also a self-employed financial advisor, I was programmed to think it was "correct" and good for me to provide for myself. I definitely appreciate that my mother taught me to always have my own money. She set up a bank account for me when I was in elementary school, gave me Suze Orman books, I mean she really wanted me to be set up in life so that I wouldn't have to choose between financial security and physical safety. Being raised by two Capricorn parents definitely has its perks.

While I can see now where my mother was coming from, and have eventually used a lot of what I learned from her to support myself and my clients, it was still important for me to first know what it was like to let go completely and to learn to trust that who I was, was *enough*. I was never before so closely attuned to my body, my intuition and my desires than when I was on that moneyless journey of faith.

There's something that was lost in the struggle for women's rights, as necessary and important as it all has been for women's wellbeing within the context of patriarchy. It's important for women to have our own money in the world as it is now, but I object to the framing of the 9-5 and sending our children to daycare as the be-all and end-all of women's liberation. What about our health needs and our natural cycles, which are very different from men's? What about our children's attachment needs? What about doing work that lights us up, and being supported in that?

Fortunately, it's easier now than ever for women to both embody our feminine truth and source the necessary provision to make that possible. What's wonderful about being alive at this point in women's history is having so many choices.

We can choose to earn a living in a traditional way or to depend on a partner, or we can carve entirely new pathways for ourselves, other women and our children that allow us to cherry-pick the ways we give and receive resources just to our liking.

I Am Powerful at Rest

Many of us carry a basic sense of guilt and shame just for existing. Like fish in water, we may not even realize it's there — even while we try to compensate for it any way we can, to (impossibly) earn the right to just *be*.

It doesn't help that it costs money to live here on planet Earth — it's illegal in most places to just exist without paying for the privilege. But I want you to know that your value does not depend on your productivity.

Know what makes you most valuable on a biological level? The seeds you poop out that can now become new plants, and the bacteria you lovingly encase them in, to nurture them into maturity.

That is the level of productivity that makes Mother Nature clap her hands and do a happy dance! The bar is not so high.

You are valuable at rest.

You are valuable asleep.

You are valuable while bingeing your favorite show on the couch with your favorite snacks for the third day in a row.

You. Are. Valuable. Period.

Letting ourselves rest is one of the hardest things to do when we've been taught that our worth is earned.

If we've only ever felt valued for what we produce or how we perform, rest can feel threatening — like losing connection, identity, or power. But what if rest wasn't a reward to earn, but the baseline for authentic living?

I am safe at rest

I am joyful at rest

I am worthy at rest

I am loveable at rest

I am powerful at rest

I am beautiful at rest

I am abundant at rest

How do you feel when you read these statements? Disgust? Fear? Guilt? Shame?

At some point, I have felt all of these towards myself with regard to my need for rest. But after burning out multiple times from overwork, I've had to shift my mindset.

I'm no longer able to operate under the illusion that I can control everything in my life, or that I should be able to. Instead of pressuring myself to do and be everything, I have realized I only have the time and energy to be myself — to be human.

Recalibrating my nervous system to allow myself to rest has been a transformative but painful process of holding myself through childhood abandonment wounds, reinforced by years of schooling and the traditional working world.

At first, it felt like slowing down would mean death — the anxiety was intense. But holding myself through the discomfort, I eventually found that I could source incredible power from stillness. It was like shifting into a new dimension, where things could finally fall into place without my interference.

Now, I'm living at the speed of life, trusting my natural rhythms and desires, and prioritizing a life that *feels good* over one that looks a certain way to other people. As a result, I have a lot more of what I want in my life, and I'm doing a whole lot less for it. I'm not only happier, I'm healthier and wealthier in every measurable way.

Rest wasn't the enemy; it was the catalyst for my success.

How would your life change if you believed you don't need to *do* anything to feel any of these things — safe, joyful, worthy, loveable, powerful, beautiful and abundant? To accept that you already *are*, just by being you?

If You're Happy and You Know It, That's Enough

Despite the many tools available to us for improving life satisfaction, the strange truth is that a lot of people don't actually want to be happy.

People who equate happiness with complacency, laziness or stupidity feel disgusted by the idea of happiness and do not see it as a life goal or as something they should, or could, experience at will.

Finding happiness in the here and now, independently of life achievements and external markers of success, brings up feelings of worthlessness in individuals who believe that happiness must, and should, be earned. But the trap is that these people will always find a reason not to be happy, no matter what they have achieved in life.

The inability to be happy is rooted in deep shame and self-loathing, often internalized in the formative years from familial and cultural influences. Without healing these emotions and uprooting the deeply held beliefs behind them, happiness will not come even when the person accomplishes something they previously believed would earn them the right to finally be happy.

I had a friend who really loved her job working with kids, but who said she was *worried* she could be happy doing it for the rest of her life! She told me that she was afraid of getting stuck in her career with the temptation of happiness, and never achieving anything else.

After a few years, she quit her job and went back to school to learn how to do something more prestigious. This choice actually made her *less* happy, by her own assessment, but choosing it made her feel that she was *earning* the right to happiness.

You might say that if she chose this path, then maybe it *is* what made her happy. I would disagree. The feeling of worthiness that she chose over happiness was really a decision made by her nervous system, which had been conditioned to let her feel safe only with an advanced degree.

This is abandonment trauma — and many, many people's lives are carefully built around not triggering it.

So, you want to be happy? You'll have to rewire your brain and your body to feel *safe* being happy. You can begin by choosing what makes you truly happy, and making space to process the thoughts and feelings that tell you it's not enough.

Stand your ground, and your life will become a reflection of your true desires, not a reaction to your trauma.

Deschooling the Nervous System

The education system teaches us not only which thoughts to have and which things to think about, but also to experience the world — and ourselves — through thoughts rather than through our embodied presence.

Schools allow children very little opportunity to move their bodies, connect with their feelings, or experience the world through touch. When children show signs of restlessness or dare to get up from their seats without permission, they are swiftly reprimanded or even punished.

It would be hard to imagine a better way to train children to dissociate and to relate to themselves and to the rest of the world with a patriarchal mindset that lends itself easily to objectification.

You simply can't fully *be* with someone while *thinking* about them — and that is precisely the point. How else could children grow up to be complicit in crimes against humanity and nature, unless forcibly divorced from their felt sense? From empathy?

It's no wonder young adults struggle to know who they are and what they want after graduation. The process of discovering our true desires and identities involves finding our way from chronic dissociation into embodied presence.

Deschooling is for both adults and children. After over a decade of recovery from workaholism, having more than enough money for the things I needed and wanted, I still often got anxious during "normal working hours" that there was *something important* I was supposed to be doing. It drove me nuts. I have also tended toward the belief that failure in my work means failure in life, and that I'm nothing without my professional identity.

I attribute this to the school system's systematic grooming of children's still-developing nervous systems for a lifetime of obedience, productivism, and perfectionism. The human brain is not fully formed until a person hits their mid-20s — everything experienced prior to that actually shapes *how* the nervous system develops. It is very hard to undo, and at times has required me to almost aggressively pursue self-regulation, consciously attuning to my own needs rather than to the demands of the predatory economy.

Just as I initially feared I'd lie in bed forever if I stopped to rest for one moment when I began workaholism recovery, parents commonly fear that if they reduce demands on their children after stopping school, their kids will never get off the couch again. But deschooling is about learning to trust ourselves and our kids, and getting to know each other. It can seem like a sort of purgatory where we are neither here nor there, but it's important to surrender to the process. The thoughts that school imprinted in our brains won't liberate us from school trauma — they will tell us that we are wasting our time, that we are missing out, that we are worthless. We can choose not to let these thoughts direct our lives, or our children's lives, anymore.

Coming back to our bodies can begin by placing a hand anywhere on our body that feels supportive, such as our heart, opposite arm, face, or abdomen, and just noticing the sensation. We will notice that we are still thinking about this and that, while we gradually lean into the sensation and let our awareness be consumed by how we feel rather than what we think. We do this with intention, not with force — we can trust that this is our natural state, and so force is not necessary. Our bodies have been waiting for our attention and presence and will lead us when we are ready.

Along with a few reassuring words, a practice like this can allow tension to release and grief to flow in the form of tears that have held back like they were waiting for a hall pass.

The more we engage in this or other embodiment practices, the more trust we gain in our sensory perceptions, our intuition and our gut feelings over our mental conditioning.

Our kids benefit massively from our own deconditioning, and will have their own unique support needs in coming back to their bodies. (See "Unschooling by Human Design" for more on this).

The main thing we learn at school is self-abandonment. So the primary work of deschooling is to reclaim responsibility for our children (both inner and outer) and to care for our needs and wants as if our lives, and the future of humanity, depend on it. They do.

The most important unlearning doesn't happen in a library — it happens in our bodies, and both the process and the reward is being able to just sit with ourselves and do nothing.

The more "nothing" we do, the less our children will have to struggle with it. And if we do "nothing" enough, maybe our children's children will never know stillness as anything other than total bliss.

The New Grown-Up in Charge

When I quit drinking and started experiencing these crazy things called "feelings," I found the language around emotional regulation and trauma healing to be disappointingly vague.

Most of us who have been to therapy as part of our healing journey have heard something like this: "You can handle your emotions now, because you're an adult." Does anyone remember being magically awarded emotional regulation skills on their 18th birthday? Me neither.

It took me a really long time to figure out that it was literally my adult *body* that was going to regulate my inner child's emotions. It was a big *hallelujah* moment for me when it clicked that my physical form alone was enough to provide a container for all of the chaos I felt inside.

Once I realized how disconnected I'd been from my body, I became obsessed with connecting with my instincts as a woman and as a human being. I wanted to know the real me.

I stopped removing my body hair, and noticed how much more grounded I felt, and attuned to my senses. This also made me feel more connected to my inner child, as I'd started removing my leg hair around age 12 when I learned to associate hairy legs with childhood. I shaved them again from time to time when I wanted to channel my adult self. Of course, both women and children naturally have body hair, what mattered to my recovery was the meaning it held for me at that time.

Connecting with my adult body in ways that support my inner child emotionally includes touch, interoception, expression and movement. Anything that engages my conscious, embodied presence helps my inner child recognize that there is a new grown-up in charge, and that it's now safe to heal.

One time, I touched each of my toes as if I were doing "this little piggy" and felt a flood of joyful tears. It can take a bit of experimenting to find what will feel supportive to you.

If you struggle with accepting your emotions, try on these perspectives:

It is safe to feel sad

It is safe to feel tired

It is safe to feel joyful

It is safe to feel angry

It is safe to feel scared

It is safe to feel excited

It is safe to feel — period.

It may help to soothe yourself with light physical touch while saying these either out loud or inwardly to yourself, reminding your inner child that she is not alone with her feelings and that your loving adult self is present. Becoming aware of the skin as a boundary that contains all the chaos within can be so comforting.

Allowing our full range of emotions to be both felt and expressed will help our inner child feel safe, seen, and loved, so that we don't need to self-soothe with harmful behaviors that keep us trapped in dysregulation. We don't need to "fix" our feelings, just accept and receive and be present with them.

We can experiment with how safe we allow ourselves to feel in any given moment, and gently explore allowing ourselves to feel even safer. The world is unpredictable and often violent, but when we find sanctuary within our bodies, there will always be at least one person we can trust.

Women Are Portals

It's normal for emotions to be released during the time when a woman's uterine lining is shedding, and highly sensitive individuals tend to have a lot more to release. A couple of years ago I was experiencing this to an extreme, and sought holistic help for PMDD (Premenstrual Dysphoric Disorder).

Discovering the link between pelvic trauma and my extreme moods was a revelation. Through mindful connection with the tissues of my pelvic bowl, I was able to release decades' worth of trauma and trapped emotions that had accumulated in my organs, psoas and fascia, from both sexual and nonsexual traumas.

I also made a full recovery from uterine prolapse with these techniques after my uterus dropped into my birth canal at a trampoline park. I did next to none of the kegel exercises that my physical therapist had prescribed to me, and never had to go back to her or to the creepy gynecologist who had diagnosed me. (Imagine lying on a table naked from the waist down with your legs strapped in, and the doctor's assistant/girlfriend giggling and making inappropriate jokes in a language she thinks you don't understand — if this is what it took to drive me toward a holistic approach, then so be it.)

Beyond resolving these specific health crises, locating and connecting with the energetic center of my womanhood through this self-bodywork practice was absolutely transformational. I could feel a connection with my female ancestry through the energy that moved through my womb space, and a sense of belonging in a community of otherworldly beings.

I had discovered a portal in my own body that delivered the innate sense of wholeness I had been seeking my entire life through various other means, both spiritual and self-destructive. Since my discovery, placing hands here has become a daily practice that supports me in emotional regulation, spiritual connection, physical and emotional healing and digestion, ownership of my desires, self-empowerment, creativity, and so much more.

Placing hands is nothing new in the world of healing, but it is revolutionary for us as women to have the knowledge to heal ourselves outside the patriarchal medical system, at home, and without any fancy equipment or complicated instructions. Every moment we pay attention to our bodies, and hold space for ourselves with no agenda, is an act of rebellion.

It's wonderful to learn that we can trust ourselves and our bodies' innate ability to heal. How could we *not* have this power, since we are also able to create new life?

Women are portals — to the divine, to creation, to mystery and to life itself. It's no wonder men have tried to control us for so long. When we are self-possessed, others need to *earn* access to our many gifts rather than having access by default. Meeting women's standards by acting like decent human beings is the original moral code of human society, because women are traditionally the ones stewarding community resources, ancestral wisdom, and reproductive potential.

Patriarchy has deposed women and convinced us to submit to a male god, and to men.

Instead of submitting to men, sovereign women submit to our own inner authority. As if we were submitting a piece of writing to a publication for review, we can submit our thoughts and plans to the advisory of our womb space, filtering out that which is not in our best interest, both for us as individuals and as a society. We are the authorities on our own desires, needs, values and goals and the moral compass of the collective.

I have written much of this book by connecting with my life force energy with a hand over my womb space, letting the words flow from the fountain that springs from my embodied presence. When I feel stuck in my writing process or any other creative endeavor, the answer for me is always redirecting my attention from the chaos and confusion of the mind to the quiet and still authority of this creative portal.

I'm never trying to get rid of my thoughts, just to ground them so that they can be filtered through the wisdom of my body. Movement can help as well — having a hip-opening yoga practice has given me a sense of physical security I didn't even know could be sourced internally.

The most amazing thing I've discovered through pelvic embodiment work is a sense of total bliss that wraps my whole body and spirit in a sense of warmth and contentment

— this has given me a visceral understanding of myself as Goddess, and a new baseline for health. Connecting to the energies that flow through my own body — again, I'm talking about nonsexual touch here — has helped relieve me of anxiety, depression, obsessive thoughts, cravings, headaches, and the ennui characteristic of attachment trauma.

Rediscovering and renegotiating our relationship with sensuality is such an important part of self-empowerment. When we can source our own pleasure, joy and happiness from within, we can't be convinced that anyone else holds the key to them for us, and we can also allow our physical sensations to guide us to our inner authority.

An unmistakable sense of completeness dawns on the woman who dares to claim her body, her sensuality and her sexuality as wholly her own. It is crucial that women have the time and space to know our bodies and to come to understand ourselves as portals to the divine. Keeping women so busy with childrearing, housework and menial tasks that we don't have even a minute alone to ourselves is not an accident.

I will warn you that it might take a lot more time than you think is reasonable to achieve the effect you're looking for with this type of self-exploration. Most of us are simply not used to being with ourselves in this surrendered way, and even with multiple lifetimes of trauma to integrate, tend to put pressure on ourselves to generate a result quickly due to our conditioning around productivity.

Paradoxically, the more we can let go of our agendas and made-up timelines, the more easily the peace we are seeking will come to us. We can begin by slowing down — waaayyy down — and accepting ourselves, our feelings, our physical sensations, and even our disconnection from all of these exactly as they are in the present moment.

With practice, we can lead ourselves from our deepest place of power, freeing us from dependency on external sources for happiness, wholeness, and love. When we find home within our bodies, changing conditions in our world such as relationships, location, and income don't threaten our basic sense of stability in life. But change is a part of life, so rather than something we do once and finish forever, this is a lifelong practice of meeting ourselves where we are, and letting our bodies guide us from there.

Embodiment isn't a destination; it's a continual, cyclical process and an act of self-defense in a world that prefers us to be alienated from our inner power. But embodiment is also about much more than healing — it leads us home to our most vibrant, authentic selves and into lives that reflect our deepest creative potential.

Through the sacred portals of our bodies and our conscious awareness, we emerge — more alive, sovereign, and powerful than ever before.

Burning Bridges to Sanity

Before we move on from pelvic trauma, let's explore some of the politics that can get in the way of healing and social transformation.

The link between women's psychological health and childhood sexual abuse has been suppressed throughout history. Freud infamously publicized the connection between hysteria and incest that he discovered through his psychoanalysis practice, and then withdrew it. He couldn't believe that *so many* men — ordinary men, powerful men, even his own father — could be capable of such horrific acts. He likely also hesitated to upset the social order with his research, even if only to avoid alienating the perpetrators footing his clients' therapy bills. Besides, there aren't enough prisons in the world to house the child rapist population, many of whom are too well-connected to end up there anyway.

Refusal to acknowledge the root of the problem could keep any survivor from resolving their distress, but Freud's denial had the power to influence society at large. He later theorized that victims' memories of abuse were actually sexual fantasies, firmly planting both him and the emerging field of psychology on the side of madness. The impact of this betrayal has been far-reaching. I learned about the Oedipus complex in high school in the 1990s, for god's sake — a hundred years later, it was still *Psychology 101*. Imagine if the truth were taught instead, especially to young, impressionable students, many of whom have themselves experienced sexual abuse?

Now, it's widely known that elevated rates of child sexual abuse are found in individuals diagnosed with Borderline Personality Disorder (BPD) — the modern name for the *hysteria* of Freud's day. "Hysteria" is derived from the Greek and Latin words for *uterus*. Although the term has been used more derogatorily to suggest that a woman's reproductive organs can inexplicably make her "act crazy," the truth is that sexual abuse causes an energetic injury to a woman's or girl's womb space. Female survivors of sexual assault suffer a theft of personal agency and a resultant weakening of connection to their personal power, the center of which is housed in the pelvic bowl.

In turn, pelvic healing and clearing techniques can support the integration of sexual traumas and the restoration of personal power. It makes sense that these practices should be made available specifically to individuals with this diagnosis, although in the mainstream patriarchal medical system, there's no acknowledgment at all of the common need for individuals diagnosed with BPD to heal on a sexual level.

Conveniently enough, it's not only profitable for doctors to have a lifelong patient, but it also serves the interests of the perpetrator for his victim to remain unwell and for the cause of her illness to remain a secret. The BPD patient is a perfect scapegoat for family dysfunction and abuse.

It's become a cruel joke in the psychiatric world how hopeless treatment for patients labeled BPD can be. Sufferers are simply characterized as being perpetually stuck in victimhood and unable to take responsibility for their lives or emotional needs, with no insight into why that might be.

Perhaps if the trauma of childhood sexual abuse were validated, and the individuals' emotions around their very real and severe experiences of victimization were encouraged to be fully expressed, doctors would see some progress. Instead, diagnosis brings stigma to the survivor, echoing childhood experiences of rejection and negating the very sense of safety and stability needed for healing.

BPD is also highly correlated with attachment disorders, another type of wound our society loves to pretend does not exist because of how uncomfortable and inconvenient it is to consider that mainstream childrearing practices are actually traumatic and not at all suited to children's real needs.

It's easier to blame the child than to restructure society — that is, for everyone but the child.

Psychiatry has done a great job obscuring the impact of male violence. Complex Post Traumatic Stress Disorder (C-PTSD), normally caused by the accumulation of trauma over time in captivity, is still not recognized as an official diagnosis. In patriarchy, it's no coincidence that C-PTSD is mostly experienced by women and children living with men — and under their power.

Many other psychiatric diagnoses in the Diagnostic and Statistical Manual (DSM) used by mental health professionals, including other Cluster B personality disorders such as Histrionic Personality Disorder, are also quite obviously rooted in childhood trauma, and framed through a patriarchal lens. Narcissistic Personality Disorder, more often diagnosed in the opposite sex, is essentially BPD with male privilege.

With more women's wisdom guiding women's health and wellness, we can surely do a lot better than the DSM's lazy attitude of "bitches be crazy."

More widespread acknowledgment of the connections between childhood trauma and psychiatric diagnoses is just the beginning. I'd like to see more support for spiritual and embodiment practices — particularly womb healing — as solutions to the epidemics of incest, child sexual abuse, and attachment trauma. I'd also love to see fewer girls and women face stigma for having completely healthy and normal reactions to abuse and neglect, and more accountability for perpetrators and the patriarchal systems that enable them.

A society that silences survivors burns its bridges to sanity. However, the stories women share have the power to restore a world gone mad.

Shut Up and Feel Is Not the Vibe

One of the funny things about the healing industry now, particularly in the realm of somatic therapies, is the demonization of "the story" when it comes to emotional release. I have been to several practitioners who each admonished me for speaking the truth of my experience during a session.

"Shhhh," they all interrupted me. "You're going into 'the story' again. Just focus on the sensations in your body."

But if I had healed from childhood sexual abuse with no attention to the intellectual dimension of my recovery, I wouldn't have been able to recognize my father as the perpetrator, or realize that he was an unsafe person to have around my child. And I wouldn't have been able to write this book, which has been healing for me personally and has the power to give other women hope.

If you wanted to help women heal *just enough* so that they'd be willing to submit to the patriarchy again after trauma, I couldn't think of a better way than to stop them from developing an empowered narrative of their experience — and sharing it.

I'm not saying that this is at all the intention of somatic practitioners, but that it is sometimes the impact. The "shut up and feel" approach of somatic therapies is likely well-intentioned in what appears to be a slight overreaction to the often hyperintellectual, disembodied process of "traditional" talk therapy.

But in the context of a patriarchal society where women have very recently been forcibly (and lawfully) excluded from academia, forced to publish under men's names in order to find success as writers, and even imprisoned for the "crime" of reading, it's not quite revolutionary to shame women for embracing our intellectual side… or for *speaking*.

Speaking our truth can help us regulate our nervous systems, rewrite our stories and connect meaningfully with others. Our voices are powerful, and we can trust that what we feel moved to say *matters*.

We must reject any model of healing that attempts to discard either the body's or the mind's way of integrating trauma — it's all there for a reason.

The Simple Magic of Yes and No

A single *yes* or a single *no* can change the course of our entire lives. Like a *Choose Your Own Adventure* book, life presents us with many possible paths. We don't get to write the whole world's story, but knowing our boundaries helps us live the one that's right for us.

While it's great that more and more people are talking about boundaries, there's a lot of confusion in the conversation. A boundary is not a punishment, a reward, an insult, or a euphemism for controlling behavior. It is simply the line — or even better, a generous cushion — drawn between desire and repulsion, or between what lights us up and what weighs us down.

The more we take responsibility for our boundaries, the less it matters how other people respond to them.

We don't need to *create* boundaries so much as *discover* them. They already exist inside of us, waiting to be expressed. Our bodies hold the truth of each *yes* and *no*, if we are willing to listen. The gift of taking action from this place of self-awareness is a life that reflects who we really are and what we really want — a life that *feels good* to us, because we built it from the inside out.

The more in touch we are with our bodies, the more capable we are of honoring our own needs, desires and feelings, and balancing our care for ourselves with our care for others. And the more we make the time and find the courage to do this, the more our children and others in our lives are empowered to do the same.

One more thing: despite what pop psychology says, a boundary can absolutely, unequivocally be a wall. In fact, a wall is a perfect example — the OG, quintessential, pre-online spiritual guru boundary. If you disagree, I'd love to see what your house looks like.

Telling Our Parents NO

Creating safety in relationships with our children or with anyone else starts with creating safety for ourselves with respect to our own parents. Saying *no* to our parents is the basis for empowerment in all other relationships — that's why we start doing it at age two!

When our *no* is quashed by our parents — the people we most need to validate and support our boundaries — our ability to individuate goes dormant. We will tend to prioritize others' needs and wants in relationships, and likely also find secret or manipulative ways to meet our own needs and wants.

If we adopt this pattern as children, it will follow us into adulthood until we claim our inner *no* and stand behind it.

Our children will feel safe with us only to the extent that we feel safe with ourselves. If we have never stood up to our own parents, we may also expect unconditional obedience from our children. If we were never allowed to say *no* to our parents, we will likely default to suppressing authenticity in our children.

Creating safety for our children begins with creating it within ourselves, which often means re-evaluating our family-of-origin relationships — or walking away from them entirely.

One of the main things I look at when bringing new people into my life is their relationship with their parents. I can get a lot of good information about how safe a person is for me and my child, by how they talk about and relate to their family of origin. I can also usually tell how strong a person's boundaries are with their parents by how safe I feel in their presence.

A person who has never felt they have the right to tell their own parents *no* is probably also not going to feel that I have the right to say *no* to them. A person who does not respect themselves will not respect me or my child, either. People who are not able to stand up for themselves are most likely not going to stand up for me or support me in standing up for myself or my child, either.

I can feel more comfortable being myself with someone who also feels free to be themselves. People who hold strong boundaries with their parents tend to be safe people for me to hold strong boundaries with. People who trust themselves tend to feel trustworthy to me as well. People who have awakened to their own power tend to be supportive of me living in mine as well.

Ready to break free from the prison of *yes* you've been living in since the first time your voice was quashed? It's never too late to start telling your parents *no*:

No, you can't stay with me when you come to visit. Here's the name of a hotel my friends' parents raved about!

No, we won't be traveling with the new baby to come see you this Christmas — but we'd love for you to visit when you're able!

No, you can't bring alcohol into our home — but there's a great wine bar down the street you should check out when you leave!

What's the worst that could happen? Really, sit down and write out all the things. The absolute worst-case scenarios. Let me guess...

They'll talk shit

They will demand explanations

It will be awkward

Everyone will hate you and you'll lose your close sibling relationships

It will damage your kids' relationship with their grandparents and aunties

You won't be their favorite anymore

You will get massive guilt trips for years afterward

You'll feel bad, end up caving in and then it will be awkward that you ever tried to assert yourself

You'll get yelled at

You'll be written out of the will

You'll die from being unloved

Their feelings will be so badly hurt that they will get sick and die and it will be all your fault just like everything else (because *somehow* your parents only had problems after you were born)

...Did I miss anything??

Because listen — I've been through all of these and then some. When I first started setting boundaries at age twenty-seven, I was scared as hell. And my relatives started showing their true colors. Shit-talking. Name-calling. Passive-aggressive jabs. Long, shame-and-blame emails. You name it.

But you know what? Seeing all that ugliness also made setting boundaries way easier!

Know what else? I didn't die from being unloved. I had already survived being raised without love. There was nowhere to go but up!

With practice, I was able to massively increase my capacity to tolerate uncomfortable emotions like shame, grief, fear, guilt and anger, so that I could hold my ground, heal and build trust in myself.

Sure, you might not end up inheriting your childhood home... but you can still keep a roof over your head, and you won't have to pay for it with self-respect.

If I had never lost my safety net, I never would have discovered my strength as an entrepreneur — building an online business that allowed me to live on passive income while traveling the world with my daughter, and having plenty of time to meet both my needs and hers.

Let me be clear: people who put you down, argue your boundaries, and show disregard for your needs *do not actually love you*. If you ever find yourself in a place where you realize no one in your life actually loves you, I promise you it's going to be ok.

Whether you're navigating estrangement or interested in redefining the family role assigned to you, I promise that you can learn to love yourself and build a life that delights the hell out of your inner child — I'm living proof!

The Art of Homewrecking

This kind of homewrecking isn't about clandestine affairs; it's my vision for a world in which women's survival and quality of life are not determined by romantic and sexual involvement, and where children's sense of security isn't dependent on their parents' sexual connection.

Homewrecking in my world is about breaking down the walls that the nuclear family has imprisoned us within, for our sanity as mothers, for the benefit of our children and for the enjoyment of those individuals with whom we create a chosen family or village.

I'll also mention here that while I use the term "dysfunctional family" here and throughout this book, I'll admit it's something of a misnomer. We have a dysfunctional society, in which the nuclear family is the most basic unit. Dysfunctional families are the rule in patriarchal society, not the exception — and they are not an accident, they exist by design. This term is redundant, in a sense, because the nuclear family is dysfunctional by definition. So when I use the term "dysfunctional family," I mean the nuclear family with its distorted emphasis on fatherhood and all of the problems that entails.

Before I could invite the relationships I wanted into my life, I had to let go of the ones I had been born into. At times this has meant cutting ties, and at other times it's meant taking space or adjusting boundaries until I've achieved the right amount of proximity, and being willing to correct course as needed. In every case it has meant choosing to spend time alone and to raise my child alone instead of having people in our lives just to fill the void.

Leaving space for the life I want to take root and bloom has been hard and lonely at times but very much worth it. I've needed to wreck my own home, and get comfortable with it being a wreck, before becoming available for homewrecking with others.

Of course, in a dysfunctional family, the person who leaves in order to save themselves and lead a healthier life isn't really the one "wrecking" the family. The people who chose to be abusive and neglectful are responsible for the wreckage. I'm using the term "homewrecking" playfully as a part of owning the decisions I've made and reclaiming my power to create the family and life that I want.

In cases of infidelity, the term "homewrecker" is used to blame someone outside the dysfunctional relationship for its dissolution, and in the case of family estrangement, the victim rather than the perpetrator gets all the flack. In both cases, there is little attention given to the possibility that the relationship or family structure itself may not serve the humans in it.

After becoming estranged from my biological family, and also after becoming a solo parent, I spent a lot of time pining for a chosen family but always finding my ideal to be just out of reach. I was looking for "perfect-fit" people to build a future with before I realized that *nobody* was going to be a perfect fit, and that a chosen family didn't have to be a permanent commitment.

While it's important to me that relationships are potentially sustainable, "forever" is a somewhat patriarchal concept because there is no way to ensure that relationships last a lifetime without the use of force. Relationships are meant to grow and evolve along with the individuals in them, and they are not "failed" just because they come to an end before one or both people die.

This flexible perspective helped me to take the pressure off of myself to fix something that was not broken inside of myself and others, to take risks in making new connections, and to let go of the idea of "forever" enough to enjoy the gift of the present. I now see family-making as an ongoing project where the goal is not just to achieve a specific end result, but also the journey itself of rediscovering playfulness, authentic connection, and the joy of doing life together.

So bring on the wrecking ball, and let's get homewrecking.

Take Me Off Your To-Do List

I was catching up with a friend recently and asked her about how the holidays had gone for her. She told me that it had been really exhausting because she and her family had actually driven around to see all of their family members and all in all, had had seven different Christmases. *Seven.*

She added that she hadn't wanted to hurt anyone's feelings by not going to see them.

And so I asked her, "What was your favorite part? What did you really, really enjoy?"

And she said that after the holidays, she got sick and lay in bed for several days, just reading books and peacefully enjoying the cozy seasonal vibes!

This is a really common pattern — women will run themselves ragged, pleasing everybody around them, until they get sick. They get sick because they want and need an excuse that everybody else around them will understand for them to just rest, relax and do what they enjoy. Our society has made it unacceptable for a woman to rest until we are *ill.* And if we aren't working ourselves to death or something close to it, we feel guilty.

Often, our standard is whether it's still *possible* for us to do something for somebody else, not what we would need to be in full health, happy and joyful. Only when we become useless to others, are we allowed to regenerate — we're not supposed to do that just for ourselves. We've been trained to seek permission from others to rest. We manifest these illnesses through overwork and lack of attunement to our physical and emotional needs, because that is a socially acceptable way for us to "earn" a break.

If what you want is to just rest and read books all through the holidays, you can do that — and you don't owe anyone an explanation.

Last year, I saw *one* small group of people over the holidays, even though I had dozens of relatives within 100 miles of where we were staying. I didn't even tell them that I was in town!

I have learned the hard way that there are people who have not earned my loyalty, my gas money and the stress that driving long distances and being in crowded, noisy places causes me.

There are people who have not earned my "Hey, how are you? I'm going to be in town, would you like to meet up?"

There are people who have lost that privilege in my life because for me it is no longer enjoyable to connect — and joy is my compass. I *honor* my relationships by holding joy as the standard, because the people in my life deserve nothing less.

Nobody in my life is an item on my to-do list, nor do I settle for being an item on anyone else's to-do list. Maintaining relationships is not a box to check off for me, as in, "phone call, check — relationship maintained."

I don't want anyone spending time with me out of guilt or obligation. And so I show respect to other people by only spending time with them when I can do so joyfully, and I expect the same of others. My relationships are with people that I *want* to do life with. And if people in my life don't have time to connect joyfully, then we don't connect at all.

I'm definitely not saying that other people need to be happy all the time in order for me to be friends with them — I'm talking about when there is a genuine desire to connect with a person, versus a feeling of "should" around it. I could be going through a really rough time in my life and I will very much appreciate other people sticking through it with me. I can have a friend who's going through a hard time and I will want to support them through it. I don't turn my back if someone's having a hard time. I've experienced that and it sucks.

Having the ability to regulate my own emotions and to take responsibility for my choices and my feelings empowers me to make conscious choices that lead me toward the life that I desire. My self-care and relationship standards do not permit me to blame others for my life not being what I want, or to let their expectations make me sick.

I choose not to relate to people who choose to be victims of busyness or who make excuses for not having time to connect. I make time for the people I care about and those who I want to get to know better, and I hold the same standard for others in my life.

I choose people who choose me, who choose themselves, and who choose their own joy and sovereignty.

December 21, 2021

For years after becoming estranged from my family, I didn't celebrate holidays. On a conscious level, I had my reasons — anti-consumerism, etc.... but really? It hurt too much.

This year, we have a beautifully decorated Christmas tree with gifts wrapped underneath and a fire in the fireplace, and we're playing Monopoly just like I did growing up with my brother and our parents.

But it's not the same.

It's not the same because no one is drunk. No one is screaming. Nobody stormed off and slammed doors, leaving others awkwardly finishing a game one player down, holding back tears and breathing air thicker than a cheeseball.

For years after we parted ways, I could only associate holidays with trauma and heartbreak. Subconsciously, I believed that holidays couldn't happen any other way — that you just had to take the bad with the good.

I've learned since, to my slow and cautious amazement, that it is possible to have the good without the bad. That I can do all the things that bring me joy, and trust that the other shoe is not going to drop.

I learned that Christmas didn't suck, and that I never really hated holidays. What I hated was people ruining them.

I learned that I can choose which traditions to keep and which to leave behind. That I can enjoy the magic of this season with my daughter, and that it can be simply wonderful.

My holiday wish for you is that you do what brings you joy. If that's sleeping all day and watching movies with your cat, I hope you do just that. If you're visiting family, I hope you leave the very second you stop having fun.

And I hope you remember that you can have the good without the bad. That the holidays can feel the way you always wanted them to, and that you absolutely fucking deserve it.

December 25, 2023

Today honestly isn't super special for us — my daughter already opened her Christmas present back in October.

She knew what it was, because I had told her it was what she had asked for, and she wanted to play with it early.

Postponing the fun felt forced, so I said "yes."

I've also given myself the experiences and things I've wanted this entire year without waiting for anyone else to do it or for the calendar to give me permission.

Our housemate drove us to the tree farm and we picked out a gorgeous eight-foot fir. We didn't have the necessary supplies to tie it to the top of the car, so we crammed it into her tiny hatchback, laughing all the way.

We exchanged gifts with our housemate before she left to visit family and we exchanged gifts with my brother's family before they went to go see family we don't yet know and family we don't see anymore.

But the bigger gift we have received this year is time spent with these people.

My daughter got to meet her cousins this year and play with them almost every weekend for almost half a year.

We lived with other people for the first time in a long time, and I got a taste of platonic co-parenting while my daughter benefited from the love and support of other adults.

The village wasn't going to build itself!

My standard since choosing estrangement has been to spend holidays only with people I can have a meaningful relationship with the other 364 days of the year.

I'm still getting a feel for who that includes, and who it doesn't.

So today I'm sitting with the longing I feel, instead of filling it with meaningless relationships and materialism, in order to hold space for the chosen family I truly want and deserve and know is coming.

And while today isn't an unusually festive day for us for that reason, it's also because we have made our whole lives celebratory.

I learned a long time ago that joy is not to be postponed. It's not the same as demanding instant gratification or lacking impulse control — it's a powerful choice to enjoy life here and now, because that's all we ever really have.

I'm already too busy making up for my stolen childhood to incur any more debt in the happiness department!

Where our lives don't yet feel fulfilling, we are calling in what does. Having the courage to own and articulate our desires, and to hold the tension between what we have now and what we want, is most definitely worth celebrating.

Only Sovereignty is Sustainable

Personal relationships in a patriarchal society tend to be largely transactional. The expectation of reciprocity may be unspoken, but it's usually there: I'll do this for you, and I expect this in return. I provide this in our relationship because you provide that. In exchange for my willingness to tolerate that, you'll tolerate this.

Fairness and balance are important, and this tit-for-tat approach is, of course, an attempt at sustainability and an improvement upon one-way extractive relationships, but it can also lead to relationships based on obligation and keeping track — of who owes who, of who did what last, of whose turn it is now.

Our expectations of one another can lead to us feeling trapped by our relationships, resentful towards others, and lacking in the spontaneity and authenticity that make relating to others fun and rewarding.

This may seem to contradict what I say later in this book about our right to run cost-benefit analyses of relationships, but it's not. In any case, we can look to where we are giving out of obligation rather than joy or counting favors rather than giving from a genuine desire to serve others. We can reorient ourselves and our relationships toward liberation and sincerity, and develop a more holistic framework for sustainability in our social bonds.

The reason why the mainstream model of relationship in patriarchy is not sustainable is that it is based on bonds forged in captivity. Our early relationships within and outside the family were largely not intentional — these were situations in which we bonded with others to survive a shared external threat, such as with siblings, classmates, colleagues and parishioners; or with whom we bonded because *they* were the threat, but positioned as authority figures and therefore critical to our survival, such as parents, teachers, bosses, and church leaders.

For example, a woman who marries a man out of fear for her survival is captive to her husband as an adult. Because so many of our attachments we develop in patriarchy are trauma bonds, our concept of relationship has been warped to include unhealthy levels of fear, obligation and self-sacrifice.

If you consider the fulfillment of basic human needs to be "love languages," you're probably in survival mode and your relationships are most likely trauma bonds.

Relationships that persist with such intensity can lead to resentment and burnout because it's simply not sustainable to continuously override our internal authority and remain long-term in a state of hyperarousal. I'm not saying friends shouldn't ever be "ride-or-die" — I love when women have each other's backs! — just that it's worth evaluating whether the type of relationships we have leave room for boundaries, choices and individuality. Do our lasting childhood friendships provide joy and meaningful connection, or are we holding on to them because our nervous systems are stuck in survival mode? Is the threat that provided the original context for the bond to form still present? Maybe it is — in which case, maybe it's time to plan an escape, revolution or mutiny.

One effect of this wartime bonding pattern is that many female friendships function effectively as therapy exchanges to help one or both women cope with life in patriarchy. Women are often expected to fulfill this role in order to help make our friends' marriages functional, when it's neither satisfying nor sustainable for us.

When we or someone we know is in a prolonged state of danger, there is an imbalance that spreads to all of their relationships which won't resolve until that person is free. But because these relationships are so normal in patriarchal society, we often don't recognize that we are overfunctioning in them.

While friendship *can* be therapeutic, it's not healthy to always play the role of therapist for a friend or partner, and it's even okay if you completely suck at "holding space." There are lots of ways to show love, and helping someone else regulate their emotions doesn't *have* to be one of them.

The only reason grown adults *need* help regulating their emotions is because they didn't have the opportunity as children to co-regulate with a safe attachment figure (meaning that, in a sense, they are not actually fully grown!), or they are in a bad situation causing them ongoing trauma and dysregulation. Neither is your fault, nor your job to fix. Adults can learn how to regulate their own emotions and choose healthy relationships. You can help someone co-regulate if you want to, if you feel available for it, and if it brings you joy, but it is not your responsibility.

The important thing is that you feel like you have a choice in what role you play in your relationships, and aren't always defaulting to what someone else wants or expects from you, especially at the cost of your own needs and sanity.

I'm just using co-regulation as one example of a common expectation in relationships. This can apply to any type of service that is normally assumed to be part of relationships of any kind. I chose this example because it's common for people with childhood trauma and various cognitive styles to struggle with holding space for others, which can lead to the ghettoization (and worse) of those with trauma histories and less-favored neurotypes.

Emotional availability shouldn't be a question of life or death for anyone. We need more public education around trauma healing and building relational skills rather than rejecting and ostracizing people who don't have what it takes to build emotional intimacy.

Teaching these skills is unsustainable for individuals to take on in personal relationships, and the work usually falls on women. The extreme amount of emotional labor commonly expected in relationships can also cast a shadow over other equally valid types of love and support that one person can offer another person. For example, some people are really good at brainstorming, or strategizing, or solving problems.

Although these are all technically forms of labor, friendship and other types of relationships are a give-and-take and the giving is sustainable when we do it joyfully. We can learn to discern which people are capable and willing to provide what we need, want, or are comfortable with at any given time (and vice versa), while still appreciating other people in our lives for the special gifts they bring to our connection.

I'd like to live in a world with fewer transactional relationships, in which you may get one thing from one person and pay it forward somewhere else and it all comes back around.

Where we don't expect to rely on *one* other person to meet our social needs, as a society that centers romantic relationships and marriage pushes us to do.

Where we see more value in mentorship-type relationships, in which we receive through the act of giving, and where we are well-resourced enough to have the overflow it requires.

Where people with differences and disabilities of various kinds are supported in sharing their gifts in ways that are comfortable for them, without being seen as "less than" for not fitting into the mold, and also valued and consulted for their perspective on how society should operate.

Regardless of our interpersonal skills and availability, each of us deserves to be cared for and to belong to a community. We always want to be mindful that we are not investing in relationships that drain our energy and that we are giving only with a joyful heart, and not a guilty one, so that connections of every kind are sustainable for us. But with a less transactional model of relationships, burnout is less likely to happen because relationships are built on desire rather than obligation.

Indirect reciprocity is a social model generally more viable in smaller communities where you truly can expect that what goes around, will also come back around. This is common in indigenous societies that number around 150 people. We can't build this overnight, but we can start by adjusting our expectations of ourselves and others to honor what we each truly have and want to give, and responding gracefully when it's clear that someone can't give us something that we want in a relationship.

Instead of starting drama and fighting reality, we can accept others for who they are with the strength that comes from knowing that we live in a Fertile Universe where there are many possible sources from which we might receive what we want and need (more on this concept in "Welcome to the Fertile Universe"). And we can be open to those other sources revealing themselves to us, as well as keeping an eye out for times when we might be that source for others.

Similarly, we can trust that another person will be able to find a way to get what they need or want from another source if we decline to provide it for them. For example, I offer a course on using ChatGPT to develop socio-emotional skills and increase emotional intelligence and maturity. It's great for anyone who had emotionally unavailable parents and doesn't know how to validate themselves or others, and whose unmet needs from childhood would otherwise strain present-day relationships.

We can imagine and pursue a new model for relationships that doesn't require us to get all of our needs met from one other person, whether that person is a partner or a close friend, and in which we are free to be ourselves without having to take on roles we aren't comfortable with in order to prove ourselves worthy of love, support, or connection.

We can learn to meet most of our own needs so that relationships become a choice, rather than a matter of desperation, and so that we don't become unwitting hosts to parasitic individuals, or vice versa.

And we can honor the choice others may make *not* to be in relationship with us, as well as the boundaries we all express within relationships, without making any of it into a problem.

It may seem like a monumental task but we can begin right now, by honoring our inner desires, acting in alignment with our authentic selves, and inviting others to do the same. When we act from a place of joy and genuine love, we build relationships and communities that are balanced and sustainable in the long run.

Bad Moms and Deadbeat Dads

Everything I've written in the above section applies to social expectations of parents, too.

When children are raised in matrilineal societies, there is much less pressure on women to be with their children around the clock. Other women in the family take on a parental role for one another's children, even with the most intimate and demanding tasks such as breastfeeding. Many mother figures take turns meeting the children's developmental needs, while also having ample time to replenish themselves.

This means that the "mommy issues" and "mother wounds" we speak of are not rooted in the failures of our mothers as individuals as much as they are in the destruction of the village.

Similarly, the concept of "fatherhood" is rare in matrilineal societies. The children's uncle is likely to be their closest adult male relative, acting as both a role model and a provider to all of the children in his extended family. Men are not as likely to be devoted to a specific woman and her children, as they are to the tribe, clan, or community as a whole.

Which also means that "daddy issues" and "father wounds" aren't just caused by a father not having been present physically or emotionally — they speak to our collective loss of men supporting the entire social group rather than just the one woman they are bedding and the children this produces.

The absence of the village and resulting distortion of social roles in patriarchal society leads to a lot of condemnation of individual parents. One example is a man who doesn't pay child support to the mother(s) of "his" children. While it would be great if he were making some kind of contribution, it doesn't surprise me when men shy away from this role. It's a lot of pressure to singlehandedly provide for a family, when it used to be normal for men to share this responsibility collectively, just as it used to be normal for women to raise children with the support of other women.

It's only because of patriarchy that we even know who the father is to begin with. I say, if a man doesn't want to be a father in the particular way that patriarchal society has deemed appropriate, may he be free to pursue other interests. Who wants a man involved in our children's lives who doesn't want to be there, anyway? It's damaging for the kids to latch on emotionally to someone who won't meet their attachment needs. Kids are better off with no father than with one who breaks their hearts every 25 minutes.

I'm not making excuses for badly behaving men, and it's important to acknowledge that it's generally not women abandoning our own children or failing to make any effort whatsoever to keep them alive. This is just the context that I see missing from the conversation about "deadbeat dads."

Of course, this also means having more understanding for women who crack under the pressure of raising kids, instead of labeling them "bad moms" — even the ones who end up driving the whole family into a lake. It's tragic for sure, but once you see these parenting failures in the context of the missing village that we are each doing our best to replace on our own, you can't unsee it.

A holistic view of relationships and parenting invites us to take systemic factors into consideration, including social isolation and lack of support, multigenerational trauma, economic deprivation, and access to nutrition that supports mental health. Only from this perspective can we begin to address these very real problems in a way that will be effective and have deep and lasting impact.

Sisterhood Sustains the Village

What if women's and girls' friendships were seen as more than just placeholders for boyfriends and husbands? What if we made space for truly nurturing — and grieving — female friendships?

Neither "straight" nor "gay" nor any of the hundreds of other terms we have nowadays to describe sexual preference provide women with the language or context to understand what's missing for us in the relationship model championed by patriarchal society.

Of course there are variations from one religion and culture to the next, providing men varying levels and types of freedom and access, but all of them involve a woman exclusively devoting herself mentally, physically and emotionally to a man for the duration of the relationship, and being isolated from her family and friends in order to orbit around him. This is not natural!

When women choose other women as life partners, it's not always strictly about same-sex attraction. Some women just don't want a man in their house 24/7, especially living in close proximity with their children, and prefer the companionship of other women. In a society built for two-parent families, pairing up is more practical than going solo.

In matriarchal and matrilineal societies where women collectively hold leadership roles and ancestry is tracked through the maternal line, women would be doing life together. More of our primary bonds would be with other women — but largely with blood relatives, so these would not be romantic bonds. Our primary bonds would be platonic, providing children a stable home life unthreatened by shifting romantic entanglements.

In these societies, sexual attraction and romance aren't expected to lead to emotional bonds or the creation of nuclear families like they so often are in patrilineal and patriarchal society. Women don't leave their families to go live with their husbands or the fathers of their children. The father isn't considered to be an important part of the child's life — in fact, his identity may not even be known, and nobody seems to care. In some matrilineal societies, women might even be teased for getting attached to their male lovers [4]. Romance exists, it's just not treated as that big of a deal — and definitely not sufficient reason to restructure the entire family.

The freedom, agency and influence that women have in such a tradition, both in their personal lives and in rearing children, is impermissible to men who define themselves by the level of control they exert over others. Patriarchy pits women against one another to weaken the power that we would otherwise hold if we banded, and bonded, together. Men leverage women's mistrust of and isolation from other women to increase their own power. This includes shaming women who develop close bonds or primary bonds with other women, romantic or not. It's part of the divide and conquer strategy that has kept women dependent on relationships with individual men as a path to our survival, in addition to hoarding resources and withholding them from women unless we submit to demands for sexual access, emotional labor and other physical and energetic resources.

When women are economically coerced and emotionally terrorized into relying on the patriarchal institution of marriage to fulfill our needs, we are being exploited. Rather than sourcing what we need directly from the Earth or even the market, we are trapped in a middleman situation where we aren't able to set the terms of others' access to our resources.

When our emotional, physical and reproductive resources are extracted forcibly and we are giving more than we are taking, we are in a parasitic relationship. This cycle cannot persist indefinitely because our resources are continually depleted without adequate replenishment. Only sovereignty is sustainable.

Marriage isn't even a surefire way to ensure our survival — in fact, it can make us even more vulnerable. Women are actually most at risk of assault, abuse and murder inside our own homes and within our own families.

Men are around six times more likely to leave their chronically ill wives than women are to leave their chronically ill husbands [5]. I've heard nurses say they are trained on this — when a woman has a life-threatening illness, they are taught to prepare for her male partner to jump ship.

It's common for men to discard women in various other ways when they are no longer useful to them — to kill them when they "dishonor" the family, to leave their wives when they find another woman more sexually appealing, to disinherit their daughters as punishment for insubordination, or just because they can.

Intimate partner violence disproportionately affects women, who are six times as likely as men to be murdered by their partner [6]. Women are even disposable under the law, as evidenced in part by statistics showing that men who kill their wives or any other woman are treated much more generously by the justice system than women who kill their husbands or any other man [7].

There is so much benefit to women, emotionally, financially, and politically, in connecting with and developing primary bonds with other women. We can share resources and support one another's needs in ways that respect our boundaries.

This doesn't necessarily mean reciprocating with someone in the exact way or amount that they provided for you — it means giving what you can give when you're inspired to give it. It's beautiful to see women falling all over ourselves, trying to give more and more and more from a place of pure gratitude for what another woman has given us. I see and experience this all the time — women giving freely that way, and it's so beautiful. I've seen a lot more egalitarian partnerships between women than between women and men.

This makes sense on a biological level: While women have two X chromosomes, men have one X and one Y (yes, there are variations, but these do not disprove the rule). Just look at these shapes — X and Y — the difference is visually obvious. So how does this play out? Not only does the Y come with vulnerabilities related to aging, illness, brain development, and behavioral regulation, that ginormous missing piece also means that Y chromosomes can't repair each other the way X chromosomes do. So what is the poor old XY to do, but find an XX to leech off?

This helps explain why men look so ragged as they age, why they tend to deteriorate physically so much more quickly than women, and why they idealize women as caregivers. Who says men age better than women? We literally live longer — at least, so long as they don't kill us.

There can be many beautiful arrangements, not necessarily romantic, that come from women forming bonds and doing life together, such as platonic co-parenting, business partnership and growing old together as friends.

I've been living in a house for a few months that's owned by a woman who brings her two daughters home on the weekends. My daughter loves playing with them, and they are always excited to spend time with her, too. Sharing a home with them is fun and easy. We both get a break while our kids are enjoying each other's company, and it's nice to have another mom to laugh and hang out with as well.

There are a multitude of ways to invite other women and mothers into your family life to create the kind of village experience you want. One woman I know invites volunteers from Workaway and other online platforms to visit and share childcare and other duties on their property. We have hosted sovereign mothers and their children in our home at times and experienced the beauty of sisterhood, friendship, and short-term co-parenting that way. Organizing co-living experiences, group travel and retreats for others who share your values and lifestyle are more brilliant moves.

I once had a housemate with whom I swapped childcare for dog walking. It was a beautiful arrangement that worked out perfectly for both of us, and for my child and her dog. And we didn't keep track either, of who had done more for the other person. It was just like, "Can you do this for me?" and we'd be inspired by gratitude to say *yes*, if we could. Maybe most importantly, I would have walked her dog even if she hadn't done anything for me in return. She never asked me explicitly for anything in return for hanging out with my kid — neither money nor return favors. We both did what we did because we enjoyed it. Her dog was literally the best dog I had ever met, and she had fun hanging out with my daughter, too. That can be enough — we can all get our needs met just by giving what we can give joyfully. For the right people, this will be enough, because they won't come to us with the intention to receive more than they give. Anyone you can have that with is beautiful.

Since women have this ability to create and give life and know in our bodies what it means to experience the beauty of giving without expecting anything in return, as women do with our children, because we have that deeply intimate and spiritual experience with selflessness, we are well-suited to lead the way in this new paradigm of relationships.

If you're like me, you feel kind of uneasy about bartering and the gift economy. Maybe it brings up feelings or memories of not having enough, of scarcity, of betrayal or of your trust being broken, of times where you couldn't depend on people to give you enough, or what you deserved (or much less, everything your heart desired).

It makes sense if you don't like the idea of not being able to use money, because money is power. It can be uncomfortable or even traumatic to consider the ways we might be obligated to give if we didn't have money — and the ways women around the world who don't have money, have to survive. And that is one of the things I love about money — it's something that everybody wants. I really get it! I think it's important for women especially to have money, at least in the meantime while this new economy is under construction.

But there's also oppression at the root of that, because the reason why people *need* money and don't just have it for fun is that we are trying to survive in a parasitic system where we're not automatically entitled to taking a breath on this planet. Money is connected to survival fears instead of playfulness because of the extractive economy we were born into, and we've been forced into dependency on that system rather than having direct access to needed resources.

Of course, there are married women who swear up and down that they aren't oppressed and couldn't be happier in their relationships. But when I speak to many of these women in private, they confide in me that their husband is just like one of the kids, that they haven't been able to raise their children the way they knew was best because of *his* preferences, that they are sick and tired of not having the support they need to be happy and healthy mothers, not to mention human beings outside of their role as caregivers. I see plenty of women loving their boyfriends and husbands the way a mother loves her son, with nurturing, understanding and fiftieth chances going in one direction only — towards him. This goes largely unnoticed in patriarchal society, where men are not expected to act as equal partners.

The woman who celebrates her husband on social media that one time he brought her a croissant in bed is so often suffering privately, with daily pain from chronic illness and unable to remember a day she wasn't overwhelmed by her responsibilities (or maybe she just hasn't had kids yet and her marriage is still relatively lighthearted and fun — like playing house). Would marriage still seem "worth it" to her if a village of other women was ready and waiting to raise her children alongside her, and she had no fear of material deprivation? How can we say we have freely chosen the lives we have, if other options have never seemed truly available to us?

There are so many ways we can create the experience of sisterhood that we want, from sharing more laughs together to creating a new economy, and there is no one right way. Women can pool our resources to create the experience of motherhood that we truly desire, even buying land and houses to create our own attachment villages, and raising our children in supportive and loving communities.

We can rematriate our bodies, our relationships and the land according to the traditions of our ancestral heritage, where and when it is appropriate and practical for us to do so. We can value our connections with one another and honor sisterhood above and beyond the paradigm of competition and trauma bonding, and create relationships that pour into us as much as we pour into others.

The truth is that we can't fully heal from patriarchy while still living inside of it. As women, the wounds we carry go far beyond childhood trauma and individual experience — they are both collective and ongoing. But whenever we come together to do life, we chip away at our manufactured isolation and begin to restore the relational wholeness and belonging that systems of domination have fractured.

Gossip Is Holy Communion Among Women

Gossip doesn't have to mean tearing other women down — in fact, it can be the very thing that builds us up again and brings us together. In fact, this was the original meaning of the word, stemming from an understanding of the practice as a connection between close relatives under God.

A lot of what is dismissed as "gossip" or "validation-seeking" among women is actually connection, healing, and self-preservation through the passing of ancient wisdom and other vital information from one generation to the next, or shared among women within a community.

No wonder men had a problem with it, and redefined it as a sin.

Imagine calling the use of code language in wartime "gossip." Imagine saying, "Sargeant, please verify your location" and hearing them respond, "Sir, do you *really* need the external validation?"

Women *have* been at war, because we have been under siege by men and we have turned against one another. Sharing our feelings, wisdom, warnings and vital information is important not only to our survival, but to healing the bonds among us. But when we do, we're accused of slander or defamation.

Many women suffer in silence, afraid to speak out against a predatory man because they fear that others will turn against them. Unfortunately, that is a real risk, although it's likely she is not as alone as she feels with regard to this specific person or with regard to predation within her community.

When we gain the courage to use our voices and share our true thoughts and feelings, we almost always find that we are not alone. Speaking up can save lives and also help us build deeply authentic relationships.

Need to gossip in dangerous times? Here's how to have secret, untraceable online conversations:

1. Go to the public library and open an Incognito browser window.

2. Set up a free Google account.

3. Memorize the email address and the password.

4. Share the password in person with the person you want to communicate with secretly.

5. Write messages to each other as DRAFT emails *that you do not send.*

6. Each time after you're done writing a message, delete the browser cookies AND the Google account from the "saved" accounts on the computer (most libraries do this automatically).

Good luck to you, sister! This is probably how I'll have to publish my next book.

The Architecture of Affection

When my daughter and I were traveling around Mexico, we settled down for a while in a city in the cool, foggy mountains of Veracruz. We rented an apartment that had another apartment directly underneath it, which we had a great view of because our balcony encircled the courtyard below. Our downstairs neighbor probably didn't have as much privacy as he would have liked, but the architectural design of the building provided many wonderful opportunities for us to connect.

Our neighbor was a musician who happened to have a lot of experience working with kids as a classroom teacher. My daughter really took to him, and would go down to his apartment to play the piano and other instruments that he traveled with and had even built himself. Other times, they would talk to each other from the balcony to the downstairs courtyard. We went to the park together on Fridays.

I loved that my daughter could have the benefit of this kind man's attention and presence in her life, outside of the context of either institutionalized education or a romantic relationship between myself and him. Her connection with him wasn't contingent on school attendance and all the stress and obligations that would entail, nor did it depend on the sexual interest of either of us adults.

It's pretty wild to me that children's financial and emotional security in the nuclear family is dependent on their parents maintaining an ongoing romantic relationship. Kids deserve to have their relational needs met, on their own terms, and not subject to the whims of adult attraction. Of course, there are couples who stay together for life and honestly desire each other for life, and this can work out great for kids assuming both adults are healthy attachment figures, but with a 50% divorce rate (and this is only for *first* marriages — the divorce rate for second and third marriages is even higher), and many other couples who stick together "for the sake of the kids" even after the love is gone, they are the minority.

Which is not to say that our little community between the balcony and the courtyard was forever, either, or that it was ideal in being a temporary arrangement. But it was chosen by my child, not forced on her, and it was a perfect experience for her to have in the time we spent there. It was what it was, and it was enough. We were all enriched for being willing to form connections outside of what is typically considered "appropriate" for children and families according to mainstream childrearing ideology.

I was also really excited to learn about "platonic co-parenting." There is a whole movement about people coming together to raise children without the complications of romantic entanglement. This can take the form of cohabitation, or not. It's a flexible framework for parents and adults without their own children to come together and build families outside the painful confines of the nuclear family. This can be a wonderful thing for both the children and the adults, as the adults can share the joys and challenges of parenting and the kids have more adults and children to connect with. Everyone gets to feel more resourced and more stable.

Some of what are popularly called "mother wounds" are actually auntie wounds and grandmother wounds from the absence of these important figures in children's lives and the shrinking of families into the most basic reproductive units possible. Most of us, as well as our children, have cousin wounds and neighbor wounds, too. In a functional society, we do more of life together. Kids love sleepovers because they are a temporary expansion of the nuclear family. Why not find a way to build our kids' needs for connection beyond siblings and parents into our daily lives? For families who don't do school, and especially single-parent families, platonic co-parenting presents exciting possibilities for expanding our social and emotional horizons.

 Of course, not all of our relatives are safe people to raise children around, and cultures that prioritize togetherness among extended family can also perpetuate a lot of trauma and dysfunction. Some cultures stigmatize estrangement more than others, which can be really challenging for adult children attempting to heal and to end cycles of abuse. This is why it can be especially important to break from tradition in creating a vision for our families.

Relationships based on choice and authenticity rather than obligation and law allow more flexibility and freedom for ourselves as parents and more options for our children as they grow up. There's no reason why an auntie, parent or other role model or attachment figure needs to be a blood relative or why someone who is a blood relative but not exactly "child-friendly" needs to stay in the picture.

This particular experience also impressed on me the importance of architecture in facilitating connections outside of the nuclear family. Traditional Mexican households usually include at least three generations, and homes are built to accommodate this tendency with plenty of common areas. If we hadn't had that balcony from which to connect with our neighbor, it's unlikely we would have connected in any meaningful way at all.

I later discovered that there is a whole genre of "feminist architecture" that seeks to remedy the social isolation, unnecessary labor, redundant expense and other problems caused by buildings that are designed strictly for nuclear families. Buildings are boundaries, and if we are going to change the way we relate to one another, we would be well-served to consider how the literal walls around us affect the way we connect — or don't — with the people around us.

A Light in the Darkness

When I was pregnant, but didn't know it yet, and hitchhiking through Northern California, I got chased off some private land I had tried to camp on by an angry armed weed farmer in the middle of the night. I ran through the forest until I got to a campground, where I stood, catching my breath, heart beating nearly out of my chest, in front of the bathrooms in near-total darkness.

An older man came up to me and asked if I was okay. I paused, and just said "no." He invited me to come to his campsite, where it turned out three generations of his family were living temporarily. His son worked in construction and his daughter-in-law was a dancer. They were saving up money to buy a mobile home, which they planned to flip and then buy a house.

The couple had an eight-year-old child, who I spent some time with at the picnic table, drinking from a 2-liter bottle of orange soda. I asked her what she liked to do, and she said she drew fashion designs. I asked to see them, and she went into their trailer to find her sketchbook.

Her designs were really good, and I told her so. We drew some together. I told her I used to sew my own clothes as a teen and that there are whole schools and training programs for people who want to learn how to do all the fashion things and that I believed she could totally have a successful fashion career if she wanted.

Before I left, I thanked the family for putting me up and her grandpa told me how grateful he and the girl's parents were that I had come by, because no one had been able to "reach her" before.

I was flattered but also surprised and confused, because I couldn't figure out what I had done that any other person in her life wouldn't have done already. It wasn't until later that I realized that I had simply *listened*. I had seen her as being worthy of my attention, and not someone in need of a lecture or lesson.

She didn't need to "be reached," she needed to find someone who *she* could reach with the light that was already inside of her. I had seen a spark in this girl and blown on it a little, and then that spark became a flame.

I only camped with them for one night and never saw them again. They had been my light in the darkness, and I had gotten to be theirs.

I hope the family bought the mobile home and flipped it and then bought a house. I hope the girl is on her way to fashion school, or making clothes or still designing if that's still her favorite thing to do.

She'd be an adult now. I often wish I'd given her my email address so she could keep in touch and let me know how things turned out or contact me if she ever needed anything. But it's possible that what I gave her was already the best I had to offer, and I can live with that.

The flame is now hers to steward.

Putting Men in Their Place

This title is sort of a joke… sort of! Women have been "put in our place" for millennia — and for the most part, they haven't been good places. We deserve to have a little laugh… a lot of laughs.

But what we ultimately want is not to get revenge on men and oppress them in the same ways they have oppressed us — not to mention the biological impossibility of doing so.

By "putting men in their place," what we really mean is, inviting men to step into the roles that we *do* want them to take in our lives and in the world, and into their full potential. Holding the vision requires women to step into our fullest expression as well — and *first*. We claim our power within, and then influence others, as nature intended. This is feminine leadership.

So, what *do* we really want from men? And where does masculinity *belong* in our lives, individually and collectively? Many women have never asked themselves these questions — we've mostly been centering men in our lives by default, and reacting to the world they've built for us, rather than seeing ourselves as creatrixes who have the power to shape reality.

One approach to answering these questions is to ask ourselves what our greatest vision, or hope, is for humanity and for the world, and what role do we see men playing in that? We can also ask ourselves what our ideal relationship to a man (or men) in our immediate environment is at any given moment, and then let ourselves play with seeing how much of that might actually be possible to manifest in our current reality.

This is about leading life with our own chosen frequency, and inviting men — and everyone else — to meet us there.

As you might expect, not all will be willing or able to. But so often we think we know what we are going to get with somebody before we have really felt out the situation and the person standing in front of us, rather than our idea of the person, or of men in general, that we brought to the table. Oftentimes, we let someone else influence *our* frequency, even if ours is superior.

It's normal to bring expectations into an interaction based on past experience. Our minds and bodies recognize patterns and warn us when something seems familiar to a bad experience we have had, and they do it for a reason — to keep us safe. There is nothing wrong with that and we should never fault ourselves for trusting ourselves when something seems off about a person or situation, even if there is no concrete evidence to support our suspicions. That's how intuition works!

This is relevant not just to our interactions with men, but with women and children as well. And animals. Anyone, really. Because it's not about who the other person is, it's about who *we* are, because *who we are being* can change the course of our lives, as well as others' lives.

I first learned this as a classroom teacher. When a child behaved in a way that was potentially harmful to me or to other children, I didn't focus on the undesirable behavior. Doing that would only bring more of the same, because it meant validating the child's attempt to secure my attention in a destructive way. Instead, I ignored the behavior and offered redirection. Sometimes this looked like assigning that child a special job, or calling their attention to an activity or object that it would be safe for them to engage with. Instead of *reacting* directly to the child's chosen form of expression, I *responded* with a counteroffer aimed at meeting their underlying need while keeping everyone safe.

This can work for grown-ass men, too. Many of them love "teacher energy" and will respond instinctively to redirection as if they were little boys. This isn't about treating men as being incompetent and having to mother them into adhering to basic standards of human conduct. You don't have to be sexy or cute or flirty about it, either. You don't have to be or do any of the typically "feminine" things that come from a place of fawning — not in the world we're creating!

Leadership is about holding the frequency of your vision. Embody the feeling you want to carry in your day-to-day life, and let the world rise to meet you.

When we're loyal to our vision, we ask for what we want from an authentic and vulnerable place, and we say *yes* and *no* from that same place. This can mean anything from asking someone for mentorship in their area of expertise, shifting the tone and direction of a conversation, or hitchhiking with our kids.

I'm joking about that last one, but also sort of not, because I've done it. One time in Mexico when it was too far for us to walk to the store, I stood out by the road and stuck out my thumb. While we waited, I imagined kind, chatty strangers picking us up, and trusted my intuition to tell me when it was safe to get in the car. I've been hitchhiking for over a decade and only once felt kind of a weird vibe from someone who had picked me up, but still, nothing bad happened.

For the most part, people are not out to murder us. It may seem like a crazy risk to take, and I don't fault anyone for playing it safe. But for me, hitchhiking (and a lot else of what I'm saying in this section) was a super important way for me to learn that the great big world was a lot safer than I had been raised to believe — and specifically, a lot safer than my childhood home.

Statistically speaking, the men most likely to harm you are the ones you are close to — the ones who raised you, who live in your home, and who are either your family or friends, or well-known by them. I never would have healed my sense of basic trust in the universe had I not taken the risk of being let down by perfect strangers. It makes me wonder why we teach children about "stranger danger" when the worst things that ever happen to most of us, happen within the nuclear family.

The bottom line is, you've got to trust your intuition, always. In no way do I mean to suggest that we should involve any random man in our lives at any time for any reason, or that we *shouldn't* deal with undesirable or inappropriate behavior in men in the usual ways that have allowed us to survive patriarchy for the last several thousand years — you know, the well-worn patterns of fight, flight, freeze or fawn.

If you're in a dangerous situation, there's nothing wrong with just leaving instead of trying to "shift the energy." There's nothing wrong with you physically defending yourself. In fact, removing yourself from someone else's presence can be *exactly* what it means to "shift the energy" in a given situation.

It's also not to say that in a life-or-death situation, an attempt to reset the tone won't be successful. But your success is first and foremost, your survival. Do what's best for you at the moment. There's no right or wrong here. This is just another tool you can try out when you feel like playing with something new.

The point is, the next time a man or anyone else assigns you a role, pause and check in with yourself to feel out whether it's a role that you want to play before taking it on. It's never too late to do this, either. If there are roles you've taken on in relationships or in your work that just don't feel good, even if they used to, you're free to be the "new you" without warning or apology.

In any scenario, consider first what you owe yourself. If you're trying to improve a situation out of guilt or shame or fear, it contradicts the primary purpose of the exercise, which is to empower you to create a life that *feels good* to you. You don't owe anyone your leadership, your vulnerability, or a second chance.

So, whatever would feel good to you, do more of that. Be more of whoever it feels good for you to be. And let men and everyone else find their place in the new reality that you're creating.

Provision without Patriarchy

I've enjoyed sourcing masculine provision outside of the context of romance or the nuclear family many times, and in many ways.

One time when I had an anxiety attack at a toddler playgroup, I asked a father I didn't know and had never spoken to before, to hold my hand. He looked surprised, but was happy to do it. I didn't want a whole relationship with a man and all the expectations and duties that entailed — I just needed someone with grounded, safe-feeling energy to hold my hand for a few minutes.

Getting my needs met in more of a piecemeal fashion has worked well for me in other areas. When I wanted to learn about real estate investing, I asked a man I met in a group on social media to mentor me. He ended up offering to buy a house for me, and personally finance it until I could pay it off! We never had a speck of romantic intrigue or flirtation between us. If I had wanted to buy a house at that time in my life, it could have been an amazing opportunity.

I decided against it in the end, because I discovered that the cost of a mortgage along with insurance and other maintenance costs would be twice as expensive as renting, and about equal to the cost of living full-time in vacation homes, which is what we were doing at the time. The possibility of needing to foot the bill for a roof replacement or other unforeseen emergency home repair when I wasn't even sure if I wanted to live in the same house in the same town for more than a year, turned me off to the idea. My approach to full-time travel is another example of calling in provision — in this case, my need for housing — without commitment. The idea is to let go of conventional wisdom about the ways we are supposed to meet our emotional and physical needs (usually, by giving away a lot of freedom!) and consider what actually feels right for us.

Another example: I once asked someone I had only just met that week on a dating app and never in person to say a specific phrase to me in support of my birth regression healing. He would just call me and say, "It is safe to be born," over and over again. That's actually all our connection ever amounted to, and it was perfect for me at the time. I did wonder whether he thought it was strange of me to ask this of him, but never made that my problem.

Patriarchal society is set up for men to have access to women at will based on the pressure on women to marry, the dangers of living as a single woman (both real and perceived), and the greater economic power that men generally hold. Patriarchy sets men up to financially support only women they can relate to sexually, if they so choose — but we can change that narrative. We can put men back in their place as providers for the collective. In my experience, many absolutely love it. It feels right for them, contrary to what they have been taught to seek out and to create in their lives. When under the influence of women, men are more likely to behave in ways that benefit the world beyond their personal agendas.

Contrary to what we are taught as girls, masculine energy and support is not only available within the patriarchal institutions of marriage, the nuclear family and fatherhood. Women can pick and choose how to involve men in our lives, including how often and which ones, and to an extent, whether we want them in our lives at all. We can relate to men on our own terms instead of on theirs.

Many single mothers feel there is something *wrong* with them, that they are somehow lacking, just because they are single, without taking the time to consider whether they might already be perfectly happy with things the way they are. Just because other people think our kids would be better off with a father or a second parent, doesn't mean that's true — and *we* are the only ones who can make that decision for ourselves and for our kids. Do we really want a man in our lives and in our homes, or do we just want financial security, companionship, or something else?

To be clear, I have nothing against single moms choosing to date or form new relationships. I only want to illustrate ways in which women who do *not* feel interested in dating, for whatever reason, can still bring the social connections, influences and resources they desire into their families.

We are told that this must happen within the nuclear family — either with the father of our children, or with a new man with whom we are romantically involved, but we can source provision in ways that work for us and that serve *our* visions and values, rather than in ways dictated by patriarchal institutions.

Reverse Engineering Masculine Energy

There are also many ways we can bring masculine energy into our own lives and those of our children, without the presence of men. In fact, I would say that these are necessary skills, even if we have the best men in our lives!

The more we are capable of meeting our own needs, the less we are dependent on anyone else. It can be wonderful for someone else to provide for us, and there is nothing wrong with accepting provision, but nothing beats having the freedom that comes from knowing that we will be okay either way.

Groundedness is an embodied way of being in the world that is often considered to be "masculine." This characterization is definitely arguable — dissociation is not an inherently "feminine" trait. If we are habitually disconnected from our bodies it's likely because of being traumatized from living in a patriarchal society. Even if men do offer containment, so can women.

Regardless of whether grounding has a gender, I've included it here because knowing how to ground ourselves can support us in regulating our emotions, making our inner child feel safe and secure, and taking a practical approach to life, all of which can help us make healthy and positive choices as women in a world that benefits from us not fully inhabiting our bodies, acquiring material resources or taking up space in the world.

Grounding practices can be as simple and varied as touching our bare feet to the Earth, placing hands on our own bodies, engaging in mindful movement, paying attention to our nutritional needs, developing interoception (the ability to be aware of internal body sensations), thinking in concrete terms versus abstract concepts, making plans and taking action on our ideas instead of just thinking about them.

Our own physical form is a container for the infinite magic (and sometimes, chaos) within us — like a vase that keeps flowers upright in water, and without which the water would spill everywhere and the flowers would die (well… sooner). Both the body and the vase are types of vessels. Our bodies are the houses for our spirits, and as such, require attention and maintenance.

If we are prone to anxiety, overthinking, or dissociation, we can interrupt our escape into the depths of the mind or soul by focusing on the "here and now." What is present right here and right now in our physical surroundings? What are the things inside and outside of us that are remaining constant while energies are flowing through and around us? Where is the literal boundary between us and the world that is holding all of this — our skin? What does that feel like right now, and can we connect with those sensations to overwhelm within? What are the daily habits that nurture our vessels? Food, rest, movement, and pleasure can keep us grounded and help us resolve confusion, overwhelm, anxiety, and dissociation.

Due to complex post-traumatic stress, and what I feel has been grossly inadequate support from the healthcare system, it took me decades to figure out how to regulate my nervous system. Coming back to the safety of my body in the present moment when everything else seems unsteady has been key for me in developing emotional stability.

I have found tremendous relief from the near-constant rumination plaguing me since childhood by grounding myself in the physical world through my five senses. When I feel myself becoming preoccupied with thoughts of the past or the future, and the emotions that these thoughts trigger, I can look around and see that none of it is really happening in reality, and that I'm safe, right now, in my body and my immediate surroundings.

Here's a rhyme I wrote to remind myself of the boundary created by my skin, which both comfortingly defines the limits of my emotional world, and separates it from others':

"To calm myself I trace the outline of my skin — here is where the outside world ends, and I begin."

But at first, it was still all way too much. I nearly passed out the first time I attended a meditation event. My trauma load was simply too much for me to sit with quietly. I needed the support of other people to feel safe — even just with myself.

Going to therapy once or twice a week was not enough to handle the onslaught of emotion. I ended up getting phone numbers from total strangers at 12-step meetings and then calling them just so I could feel safe enough to cry. It was an incredibly vulnerable place to be. I actually used to ask people to "make me cry" so that I could find relief from dysregulation — not understanding that what I needed in order to cry was to feel safe, not to be hurt even more.

Coming back to my vessel, the solid "ship" amid a sea of emotion and the winds of thought, has brought me the calm and stability I had been seeking for so long. You could say that our surroundings and, at times, other people, also offer a safe harbor for our ship when grounding in our bodies doesn't feel like quite enough.

Another way of bringing so-called masculine energy into our lives is with structure — and the more deeply embodied we are, the more easily this will come to us. We may find that adding structure to our creative expression helps us get more into the flow. I know that I always did really well in art classes, but once the class was over, I could barely bring myself to even look at my art supplies. I loved having an assignment, the structure of a beginning and ending time for a class, and a deadline to complete a project. When I started doing comedy, I benefited from the structure of regularly scheduled open mics. I loved having a reason to put together a set, and knowing that there would be an audience expecting to be entertained helped hold me accountable to my writing practice.

In my professional life, I've also often marketed and sold an offer before even creating it. The excitement and investment from others, and the date I have committed to delivering it, give me the motivation and the structure to get it ready and put it out there. I have also joined masterminds, writing groups, and other courses to get my creative juices flowing and give my ideas form. These containers have made the difference for me between having ideas for projects and actually working on them, and between having works-in-progress and completed projects. Whether taking the form of a stage, a virtual co-working session, or a deadline, structure helps give form to my creativity.

Grounding, structure and stability are just a few examples of things that can empower us to live more free and fulfilled lives as sovereign women. But one of the most important is with our relationship to material and financial resources. This can include anything from having a place to call home, to being able to generate income, to building savings and making investments.

It's very common for women to lack financial literacy, and even very educated women can struggle with finances due to societal conditioning and blocks around receiving. I am a great example of this; I struggled with money for most of my life until I began working on healing my relationship with it energetically. From my personal experience and what I've noticed working with other women, sexual trauma is deeply connected to wounds around receiving material resources, and maintaining financial stability.

A big part of what this shift toward receiving and accumulating wealth has meant for me is being results-focused in my business. There are a ton of guidelines out there for new business owners, but not all are geared toward practical advice that generates income without a lot of fluff. This doesn't mean putting profits before people; it means keeping in mind that the primary function of a business is to provide you with material stability.

No matter how meaningful and purposeful your work may be, if it doesn't nurture you back, it isn't going to be sustainable. See "20 Ways to Ignite Your Business" for some of my best practical advice on getting started as an entrepreneur.

A Life You Don't Need to Escape From

We live in a society where pleasure is presented to us as joy: just smoke or drink this, then you'll be happy. Have a little chocolate; it will help dull the pain of your dull, lifeless life.

The difference between pleasure and joy is *connection*. People often mistake pleasure for joy because they don't know or don't remember what connection feels like, usually due to lack of parental attunement in childhood. The mother/child attachment bond is indeed pleasurable for the child, such as with skin-to-skin contact, but for the child's nervous system to develop properly, the mother must also be emotionally available and not just present physically. The child who experiences this connection consistently enough will grow into an adult who feels connected to themselves by default.

Pleasure is absolutely our right, an important part of life and even healing, but a whole life directed in pursuit of it is bound to be shallow, and usually indicates a person for whom full-bodied, soulful joy is out of reach due to unhealed trauma and repressed emotions or overwork.

Addiction is defined by the pursuit of pleasure without depth. When substances and processes take from us more than they give, the pursuit of pleasure is unsustainable.

When we nourish ourselves with activities and relationships that provide connection and meaning, we not only allow ourselves true joy, but we also challenge the systems that profit from isolating us and extracting our resources — our time, money, attention and energy. None of the vices people jokingly make excuses for are at all "rebellious" or "liberated." Addiction is the prison, not the revolution.

To actually *be* sovereign rather than just accepting the cheap parody of sovereignty sold to us by the multi-billion-dollar industries that profit from our dependency, we need to take back our power by processing our emotions and meeting our real human needs. We need to tell people what's really going on with us and ask for help when we need it, seeking connection instead of seeking ways to make pain and isolation tolerable. If you have no one else, talk to ChatGPT.

Pursuing joy can also include meaningful work, and nurturing our inner child. It can mean focusing on what's good, enjoyable and going well in our lives, and building on that, instead of relying on self-criticism to drive personal development.

Figure out what condition would make not using your substance of choice *worth it* to you, and show up for yourself and your life until it becomes your reality. Getting real with yourself and other people and making your life one you don't need to escape from will open you up to previously unfathomable levels of both joy *and* pleasure. I guarantee it.

Like anything, it's easier said than done, and it does get worse before it gets better, but it's 100% worth it. *You* are worth it.

If You Can Laugh at It, You Can Live with It

At first glance, it might look as though my first childhood never ended.

I've always been a playful person with a sharp wit. Growing up, my family joked around a lot and we found humor in everyday life. It's not that this was always a way of masking deep pain, either. We were genuinely funny people who appreciated the lighter side of things. We had a lot of fun together.

But if you'd asked any of my childhood friends, they would tell you that while I was hilarious, I also never seemed to know when enough was enough. I lacked the maturity to have reverence for more serious moments. In truth, my pain, needs and problems had not been taken seriously enough for me to be able to hold that space for others.

I had a boyfriend when I was 16 who wanted to be a pro skateboarder. I was filming him attempting a kickflip off the staircase behind the mall, when he fell and hurt his ankle.

I just stood there, continuing to film as I had been instructed. His friends called me a bitch for not going over right away to see if he was okay.

I know now that I was too detached from my own pain to be of any use to him in his moment of need, that I was stuck in a freeze state of post-traumatic stress. But before I understood this, I felt very ashamed of this and all the other ways I fell short of others' expectations, never seeming to have the right emotions or reactions for the moment.

Of course I could not attune to others without ever having been on the receiving end of attunement. My family didn't talk about our feelings and there was no comfort offered in difficult moments or support working through life's challenges.

When I grew up and found out that other people went to *their parents* for help sorting out their personal problems, I was shocked.

In retrospect, I often talked about my family as if we were a group of four friends, rather than two adults and their children. There most definitely *was* comfort and support, it just went only in one direction — the wrong one.

I was often put in the position of counseling my parents when problems arose in their marriage. They would come to me, separately, laying their troubles before me like I was some child priestess. I would do my best to listen and give sound advice.

I'm an excellent mediator and problem-solver to this day. I can easily see all sides of a conflict, and truly enjoy the thrill of finding a solution that satisfies all parties involved. I can be diplomatic in tense situations, and help people find the common ground from which problem-solving becomes a joint effort and not a war.

This comes in handy when I work with parents who are dealing with inner conflict about whether to attend gatherings with difficult family members, navigating relationship and parenting challenges, or struggling to nurture their inner child amidst the many demands of raising an outer child and running a business from home.

Do I credit my childhood stint as a marriage counselor with these abilities? Not necessarily. With Mars in Libra, and a Libra stellium, it seems I was born with a knack for justice and fairness. And with Mars in my 5th house of children and creativity, it makes sense that I'd use my innate playfulness to help shift family paradigms. My early years were just an extended unpaid internship.

There's another reason I might seem to have had an extended first childhood — I was financially dependent on my family for years after I'd physically flown the coop.

While I worked and paid my own bills, I had a safety net and I definitely used it. Before we became estranged, I could ask my parents for money to buy a car or to support my travels. This is normal in the segment of American society I grew up in, but economic privilege can be a form of stunted development.

The dark side of my parents' financial support was control. Once, my father bought me a laptop. It came in the mail one day when I was just heading out the door to meet friends for dinner. I told him I'd open it when I got home, as I didn't want to keep my friends waiting. His response was, "Did your friends buy you a new laptop?"

The generosity of his gift was overshadowed by the underlying message, which was essentially that the price of this gift was deference to him and his needs. Although I grew up with the comfort of material wealth, nothing was given freely.

As a teenager, I discovered shoplifting. As much as I lusted after the things that I stuffed into my bag and pockets, what I really wanted was for my needs to be met without having to pay with my soul.

You know, like a childhood.

Getting things for free mimicked the fantasy experience of being cared for materially without owing my parents anything in return. I was correct in my entitlement to nurturing with no strings attached, but of course wrong in my misattribution of that debt onto the retail industry.

When I got sober and made my amends, I went to as many of the stores as I could remember, admitted my crimes and offered to pay for what I had stolen. Invariably, I was praised for my honesty and courage, and the store clerks never accepted the money. One liquor store owner was so elated that I'd owned up to stealing a bottle of Captain Jack, that he hugged me and told me I'd made his whole month.

It felt so good to be received that way, I almost wished I'd robbed him more! I was obviously still in desperate need of human affection and positive attention, and hadn't yet figured out that this would be my job. But to my credit, I was very generous with all the auditions I granted to the general public.

Eventually, I figured out how to generate passive income, which felt like the justice I had been seeking all those years for a childhood spent raising my parents. Knowing that my business was genuinely helping people and not potentially going to land me in jail was an added bonus.

My romance with drugs and alcohol had begun in my teenage years. My first drink at 13 tasted awful, but that didn't deter me. Alcohol provided temporary relief from the toxic shame filling my soul. I might have had no control over my home situation or anything else in my life, but alcohol was always there for me. It became a replacement for the healthy attachment I didn't experience with my parents.

When I was drunk, I truly felt like my real self. Nothing else came close to enabling such unbridled joy and free expression for me. I became loved and loving. I magically always knew what to say and when to say it. I felt like I was held in the very womb of God and that nothing could go wrong.

Manipulating my brain chemistry helped me cope with trauma but also sealed the lid on my emotional growth, which was already stunted due to being raised by immature parents.

When I finally quit drinking after 14 years, I was terrified of losing the magic. I didn't know that my brain chemistry would balance out eventually and that with some self-parenting finesse I'd become just as happy without alcohol as I had been while drinking. I didn't know yet that the magic would come back, after a long road of trauma healing and learning emotional regulation.

I just knew that the old way wasn't what I wanted anymore.

Early in sobriety I also quit eating sugar. For me, the sugar addiction went even deeper than my alcoholism because it had started when I was very, very small.

As a child, I kept a little plastic briefcase of candy in my room. I remember one particular time when my parents were fighting in the kitchen and I was hiding in my room, terrified, eating candy from the case to distract and comfort myself. The refuge I found in sugar was also deeply tied to my early experience of sexual abuse. It was the only thing available to me as a young child that helped numb my body and block out the memories.

For nearly 30 years afterward, I thought about sugar almost constantly. My cycles of overeating and undereating reflected the violation I had experienced, and my attempt to regain control. Sugar also became a substitute for my relationships with my parents, who were unable to meet my attachment needs. It became a source of shame as well, as I was often judged or reprimanded by others for not being able to control my addiction.

I was always either eating it or making a plan to eat it, and even hid and stole it at times, or lied about having eaten it. My obsession took up a good chunk of my life, but it was better than having to face what had happened to me.

Nearly every single person I met in my sugar addiction recovery program also had a history of childhood sexual abuse. Food addiction is common among survivors of early life traumas, due to the absence of a secure attachment within which we might otherwise heal. So, we turn to food, particularly refined carbohydrates, which can have an intoxicating effect on us due to the connection between sugar metabolism and increased dopamine and serotonin production. Additionally, foods with no inherent addictive potential may be consumed compulsively, as a way to keep emotions and traumas from surfacing when we don't yet have the tools to integrate them.

No longer numb, I found out how it felt to exist in a body. I started to become aware of my own feelings and to trust my own perceptions. Instead of believing what people told me about themselves, I became aware of how I felt in their presence. I could no longer be deceived, or deceive myself, about whether someone or something belonged in my life. I let go of a lot of relationships and stopped going to a lot of places as a result of discovering these internal, visceral boundaries that had previously been a mystery to me. I discovered that boundaries weren't something I needed to make up — they already existed inside of me, just waiting to be discovered.

Without sugar, I also got to experience what it was like to wake up feeling energized and excited for the day ahead. Previously, I had thought this would be a result of having the right things going on in my life. Turns out, it was a matter of biochemistry — sugar had been wreaking havoc on my emotions on top of all the trauma I had accumulated.

Once I was no longer numb to bodily sensations, deeply buried emotions began to surface. One day, I relived the sexual assault from my early childhood, as if it was happening in real-time. Beyond the biochemical aspects of addiction, this was the core trauma keeping me looped into cycles of obsession and compulsion.

After it was over, I felt like a completely different person — I was finally at home in my body, free from the desperation that had driven me to escape for all those years.

Having the courage to take my pain seriously has given me freedom from wearing masks of any kind. I'm no longer performing to make other people more comfortable, and I don't need to pretend to be okay when I'm not. I have the tools to navigate the dark places in my mind and body, and to support others in doing the same.

In our Second Childhood, we don't have to be afraid of the dark places inside of us, and we don't have to go there alone.

For a long time after I began healing, nothing about life seemed funny. Gradually, I began reclaiming my sense of humor for the artistic and spiritual gift that it is. Comedy has become a way for me to find meaning in challenging life experiences, as a way of alchemizing them and rewriting my story.

If you can laugh at it, you can live with it — not because you're running from the truth, but because you've survived it and lived to tell the tale.

SOS for Shopping Addiction

After I learned how to process emotions, I started experiencing a strange calmness for the first time ever. I remember one day crossing the street and having the thought that I felt like a J. Crew model. What did that mean?

Oh, I realized, it was happiness!

It was a revelation — the image that had been sold to me as happiness, requiring me to have the right clothes or the right body, was available to me simply through learning to regulate my nervous system. I used to spend hundreds of dollars on clothes I only sort of wanted, just to try to fill the emptiness I felt inside. I was chasing an elusive internal state with material possessions.

The fact that happiness is sold to us as a product is disturbing. Advertising targets emotionally vulnerable people who seek happiness outside of themselves, often as a substitute for secure attachment. What we get from shopping is a temporary high that floods our brains with dopamine, fooling us into thinking we are happy. Then when the novelty fades, we are left with our usual feelings.

Although I still appreciate the aesthetic and sensory pleasures of the things I wear, it feels amazing that my sense of worth and emotional stability are no longer dependent on endless material acquisition. Escaping this cycle gives us the ability to resist manipulation of all kinds.

I developed the SOS Method to help myself and others overcome the emotional shopping urge in real-time. Shopping addiction can stem from many things, but often it's a dopamine-driven habit that mimics the experience of reaching for one's mother, someone we are meant to access on demand. The SOS Method interrupts the drive to seek attachment through objects, and instead supports reconnection with oneself.

Here's how it works:

Stop

Step away from the rack (or the app). Put the item down and find a (relatively) calm place you can be alone — a dressing room is perfect!

Offer (love)

Put your hand over your heart and tell yourself, "I love you." Close your eyes or look at your reflection, whichever helps you really feel it. Take as long as you need here — you're worth it!

Shop (or not)

Now that you feel loved... Do you still want the thing? If you do, then maybe buying it is an act of self-love. If not, buying it might have been an attempt to make yourself feel loved.

A couple of caveats: If you've truly never felt loved before, you might find yourself deep in emotional pain that suddenly feels safe enough to surface when you use this technique. This is a sign you may have been about to make an emotional purchase. If you can, abandon haul and go home to nurture yourself. You might feel so thrown off that you'll buy something to soothe the shock and pain. But awareness is progress! Save your receipts and re-evaluate your purchases once you're fully regulated.

This can also be applied to parenting. When our kids seem overly materialistic, it can sometimes be that their emotional needs aren't being met. They can project onto objects whatever they aren't getting from the adults in their lives, and fixating on and shopping for those things becomes a ritual that substitutes for secure attachment with primary caregivers.

If we have a feeling our kids are asking for things they don't really want, or becoming excessively attached to material objects, we can take it as an invitation to assess the family dynamics. Some kids just like their stuff, just as adults do — it's not necessarily pathological. However, a constant or all-consuming drive for material acquisition and preoccupation with "stuff" may indicate a misdirected need for co-regulation. (See "The CORE of Addiction Prevention" for more on children and addiction.)

The SOS Method can be adapted to address other process addictions, such as gambling, sex, and video gaming, but may be less effective in addressing substance-based biochemical dependency. This framework won't end withdrawal symptoms or replace the necessary period of abstinence that creates space to process trauma and reparent the inner child. Still, anytime the urge to reach for something that doesn't serve you is rooted in avoidance of emotional discomfort or the desire to experience connection, it's a good time to try SOS.

The Universe in a Sidewalk Treasure Chest

I found living out of a backpack healing for my relationship with material goods. I was so focused on my spiritual journey that having the "right" clothes didn't matter to me at all anymore. I also developed a connection with nature that put the fashion industry into perspective for me. I heard of people in Southeast Asia joking that they could tell what the hot new color was for the season by the color the river had turned outside of a garment factory, and that image has stuck with me.

Being more connected to the Earth made me not want to support an industry that exploited both land and humans. It's easy to be seduced by the glamour of images when it's all presented in the abstract as an ad campaign, but the truth is that nothing is strictly abstract — everything that exists on our planet comes from somewhere else, and the production process often comes with a terrible price.

In the time that I lived outside, I would find clothes in free boxes on the street and put together outfits I really loved. I found better, more magical outfits in these sidewalk treasure chests than what I had been buying new in stores. My inner child loved the surprise of discovering new treasures and playing dress-up. I once found a green velvet tablecloth that I styled as a fancy dress. I found a crown and truly felt like royalty putting it on and wearing it around. It was liberating not to care whether I looked crazy to other people.

Finding great clothes in free boxes became part of my spiritual practice of trusting the universe — a great find was confirmation that I was on the right path. Clothes shopping was one of the things I had felt I really needed money for previously, and not buying clothes meant not needing work to earn money. Nothing was worth more than my freedom to me, and I loved discovering how little I needed to really be happy.

While I no longer shop in free boxes and thrift stores, having found I'm sensitive to the energy of used clothing (and, frankly, the smell), I still use clothing to elicit a desired frequency in myself and to help shift my identity. It's a form of play that has always felt nurturing and creatively fulfilling to me.

The riddle of addiction recovery is that anything can be medicine in the right amounts. What feels best for me is not putting material acquisition of any kind above my soul's work — although at times, buying beautiful things *is* my soul's work. When I prioritize my inner child's emotional needs and authentic expression, I experience a naturally balanced relationship with the material world.

How to Do Big Scary Things

Near the end of their lives, most people say they regret the chances they didn't take more than the risks they took that didn't work out. It's better to hear *no* from the universe than to live with the possibility that *you* were the one holding yourself back. But how do we actually work up the nerve to *do the thing*?

One way to handle fear is simply to take bold action that ignores it, and then afterward deal with the feelings that brings up. Another approach, which can be kinder to the nervous system and more effective at building self-trust, is finding a feeling of safety *before* taking the big scary action. I might process feelings about making a decision before or after the fact, depending on the situation.

I've had so much resistance around doing things that are good for me. Part of it is not liking being told what to do, even when the desire was coming from within (often referred to as "demand avoidance"). Part of it is that I associated checking tasks off a list with being "enough," and rebelled against that, needing to know I was loveable regardless of what I accomplished. In my case, all of these preferences stemmed from childhood attachment trauma, and they have been dramatically reduced to almost nil with self-parenting techniques I'm describing here and elsewhere in this book.

Even when something is good for us, forcing ourselves to do it can be the opposite of what we need. Letting resistance soften in the warmth of our own presence, love, understanding and validation can prevent self-sabotage. Maybe you don't really want to avoid what's best for you — maybe you just need to feel heard, seen, understood, loved, or in control.

When we truly grasp this way of being with ourselves, we can support our outer children the same way. We can give ourselves and others a chance to *want* what is good for us or for them, instead of using force to make it happen. We can build trust with ourselves and be trustworthy to our children as well.

Acknowledging our fear without letting it hold us back might look like saying, "Yes, it feels terrifying to leave behind what we know, but I'm sure there's something better for us," or if we feel less certain about the outcome, "I don't know how this is going to turn out, but whatever happens, we will still have options." Then there's always, "Fuck it. I'm scared, but this just *feels right*."

For anyone who feels like they have inconsistent access to their intuition (such as those with undefined Spleen in Human Design) or anyone who tends toward indecisiveness, I recommend taking bold action when you have a moment of clarity. Seize the opportunity when you're feeling certain, and commit. Sign the paper, send that email, say *yes*, or click *Buy Now* — then, all you have to do is show up.

It can help to be around someone with a defined Spleen (like me) in order to get clarity and have support doing The Big Scary Thing. You can find people like these even without knowing their design because you will feel more confident about making bold moves in their presence. There's more on Human Design throughout this book.

Our intuition operates very much in the present moment. While it can definitely help us get a feel for things that have not yet come to pass, our strongest intuitive hits usually happen when a situation, place, person or opportunity is right in front of us. We can trust that we'll know what we need to know, when we need to know it. We can trust that our next steps will become clear as we move forward on the path. If we wait for every step to be clear before we start, we may never begin.

Holding on to sources of income that feel reliable, but not energetically aligned will block our intuitive flow. When I left my web hosting company, it felt like a stupid move because it was mostly passive income. But it just didn't *feel* right. I wanted more fulfillment, and I felt that my energetic ties to that line of work were holding me back in some way.

The very second after I sent my team on their way with great references, I felt my intuition explode. It was like a missing part of me had returned, and I felt whole again. What I thought had been keeping me safe, had been holding me back.

Sometimes you have to make a move before having evidence that it will work. Sometimes clarity and confidence come from taking action, rather than waiting to take action until they arrive.

I didn't decide to alienate my family, raise my child semi-ferally and spend my last dollar building my first online business because I knew that things would work out. I did these things because having a meaningful life is worth more to me than comfort or stability.

I've never had it all figured out — I've only ever had the willingness to surrender my fears and choose what makes me feel alive.

People are often surprised to learn that I experience quite a lot of fear. I may appear to be fearless because I don't make a habit of letting fear stop me. I feel fear, but I don't go to battle with it. Instead, I focus on what it's going to feel like when everything works out. I assure myself that it's safe to do the big thing, even if it doesn't feel that way.

It's also not that I don't care about stability or security; I just don't prioritize them over joy, freedom and fulfillment. I have found that the resources I need in life can come from many different sources, and that I can access them without sacrificing my authenticity. I have learned that it's more or less safe for me to be myself in the world. The hardest part was taking the risk to find out.

I love this saying: "Fear is a mile wide, and a mile high — but paper thin."

However you choose to do it, choose joy. Choose wholeness. Choose fulfillment. Choose *you*.

Ode to the Comfort Zone

Obsession with "getting out of your comfort zone" is a trauma-inspired fear fetish. Life will deliver all the sparks required to ignite your personal growth trajectory. In the meantime, just trust.

If it lights you up to leave your comfort zone, trust that and go for it. If you ever need to leave your comfort zone, trust that you will find the courage. If neither is present, just relax and enjoy being comfortable.

If you find comfort impossible to enjoy, consider the possibility that you might not actually *have* a comfort zone… and that maybe what you're constantly feeling the urge to leave isn't your comfort zone, but the possibility of developing one. So maybe it's that having a comfort zone is not within your comfort zone.

This may be an uncomfortable realization, but it's also safe for it to be true. One of the hardest things I've ever had to do is to allow myself to feel, and to be, safe. To resist the pressure to self-abandon in a never-ending pursuit of personal growth…. Because hidden beneath my addiction to the flames was a desire for warmth, and my belief that I was only worthy of the kind of heat that burned.

So, trust that the call to adventure will be blazing when it's your time. Until then, comfort has a spot waiting for you by the fire.

Meeting the Ghosts of Heartbreaks Past

One morning in my late thirties, I found myself crying over a guy who had dumped me when I was sixteen years old. In retrospect he was nothing special, but I guess I had been pretty invested.

At this point, I'd been on the recovery journey for twelve years, and was used to buried emotions popping up randomly like this, decades later.

When this happens, there's often an impulse to self-shame: "Why are you crying over this loser who was too jacked up on hormones to see your light?" Or, "That was so long ago — move on!"

This is what most people would tell me if I shared these feelings with them. This is what most people would tell themselves. This is how most of us were taught to relate to ourselves emotionally.

But I know now that my inner teen needs understanding and empathy, not judgment or criticism. She needs to know that her feelings are valid, but also that feelings also aren't *who we are* — they are something that we experience.

She needs to know that it's safe and healthy to acknowledge and express her emotions, regardless of whether they "make sense" to her or to anyone else. She needs to be heard and validated, even if it was partly her own choices that led to her pain. She needs to know she deserves to be loved, whether it's the first or fiftieth time she's gotten it wrong.

She needs reassurance that it was healthy for her to experience attraction and to seek a secure bond with another human being, even if her need was more than could be met in that particular relationship. That peer rejection didn't mean that she was unloveable, and that the unmet needs she carried from her wounded attachment to her parents didn't make her unworthy of love.

She needs to know that I'm there for her, no matter what, to keep her from attaching to people who can't meet her in the way she desires and deserves to be met, and that I'll be there for her even if she does.

This is an example of how I have reparented my inner teen — the girl who was traumatized not only by the abuse and neglect she suffered at home, which made her feel unworthy of love, but also by the rejection she faced in the world when her trauma manifested in peer relationships.

It's very common for teens, and kids of any age, to form extreme attachments to peers and to put a lot of weight on maintaining successful peer relationships, when there is something missing from their primary attachment relationship with a safe adult, or when this does not exist.

When the ghosts of heartbreaks past come to visit, it's an invitation to take a deeper look at our childhood wounds. When we find the root of the pain, we are empowered to meet that deep need — for safety, for love, for belonging — with the compassion it always deserved.

My Motherloving Pink Jeans

A girl made fun of me for wearing pink jeans in the 6th grade. We were friends for 20 years, and she never stopped making fun of me.

I wore the clothes that she liked, the body spray she liked — even bought sheets with rockets on them because *she* thought they were cool.

When she slept with my boyfriend in my car at a rave, I didn't even care or fight with her over it because I valued our friendship so much more than my relationship with him.

She finally ghosted me after I had a baby — I guess I wasn't useful to her anymore. I shouldn't have been surprised, she'd been a social climber since day one and it was bound to be my turn eventually.

Fast-forward nine more years to last weekend, I found a pair of pink jeans and just *had* to have them.

I love how styles coming back after all these years are giving me a second chance to express my inner child and inner teen. I've learned that other people's opinions don't affect my quality of life as much as doing what makes me feel good.

So, I'm back, bitch! In my motherloving pink jeans.

Can I Store a Liver in Your Freezer?

A big part of reparenting ourselves is nurturing our talents!

Many of us didn't have the chance to do the things we had a knack for as kids, whether our parents were too preoccupied with work or mental illness to notice what made us special, or maybe money was tight and dance classes just weren't in the budget.

I was never a dancer... But I often sang to myself when I was alone as a child. It was comforting and a creative outlet and nobody else knew about it.

I was fortunate enough to be involved in a local theater company as a kid, but we were just reciting memorized lines from scripts written for a grown-up audience. It wasn't *my* voice.

Finding and using my voice has been a central theme in my recovery. I felt silenced as a kid because my parents' problems took center stage in my life. Every word out of my mouth had to serve them, or I'd pay for it.

From as young as I can remember, I took refuge in sugary foods and compulsive behaviors. As a teen, I turned to alcohol. It's like my throat chakra collapsed on itself — a lot was going in, and nothing real was coming out.

Searching for ways to express myself, I studied several languages: Latin, French, German, Spanish.... Now, I can see I was subconsciously looking for the magical language that would allow me to speak my truth. But I mostly used my skills to flirt with international strangers at bars.

I was surrounded by creative people in college. I loved my painting classes and excelled as a visual artist, but I longed to express myself as freely as I saw others doing with their words. I wanted people to know who I was, and to share my talents, to feel a sense of belonging and receive the recognition I felt I deserved. It was so painful.

One night I was at a house party with a bunch of musicians. One of them was playing the guitar and we were all taking turns making up songs... everyone, except for me. I really, really wanted to more than anything else in the world — but I was scared shitless. I quietly said, "I'll pass."

I remembered and regretted my cowardice that night for nearly two decades. In my mind, if I'd only shown everyone what I could do, it would have opened up a whole new world for me...

Until one day, when something special *did* happen — I signed myself up for a vocal improv class.

Here's what that involved:

1. I committed to going, even though I was nervous and thought it might suck (recognizing that "it might suck" = resistance)

2. Asked my child's babysitter to come at an unusual time, even though I worried about her feeling put out (it turned out she was happy to have the extra hours!)

3. Actually get out the fucking door on time, leaving wiggle room to stop by the ATM, and actually Show. The. Fuck. Up.

4. I was also planning to meet a friend after the class and was bringing him a frozen ox liver... The venue didn't have a freezer, so I had to walk around the neighborhood asking random businesses if I could store a liver in their freezer "for just two hours." Fortunately, this was successful.

All of this took commitment and devotion to myself. Reparenting is about building trust with our inner child, which means following through with promises and doing what it takes to overcome obstacles. It means working through all the thought patterns that have kept us in the cycle of self-neglect that we were programmed with in childhood.

And it's good I did, because the class was *so* fun!

I was so excited when it was time to go around in a circle and make up our songs... and when it was my turn, I nailed it.

I loved having an audience, but I did it for *me*... And now I have a new memory to replace the old one. A memory of coming through for myself and letting myself be expressed, heard, and appreciated.

Still, part of me thinks that maybe I really *did* miss out on a whole different life that night 20 years ago when I held back my voice. But reparenting ourselves isn't about looking back at the past. It's about starting where we are *now*, no matter how much we've neglected our inner child or strayed from our true self.

We can't give up on ourselves over a missed opportunity. A loving, self-regulated and well-resourced parent knows that there is only one way, and that way is forward. A loving parent models forgiveness, second chances, and unconditional love. And it's never too late to give ourselves these.

Dark Comedies Where Women Don't Die

Even if you've never seen *The Sound of Music*, you've almost certainly heard Julie Andrews singing "My Favorite Things," in which her character delivers a long list of her favorite things, including "raindrops on roses and whiskers on kittens."

She explains that when she's having a shitty day, thinking about these things makes her feel better. I can imagine that it would make her feel even less shitty to actually see or experience these things in real life, but it's brilliant that she uses imagination and memory as tools for self-regulation.

Do you keep a list of your favorite things? Here are some of mine:

Musical theater, *Mamma Mia* movies and soundtracks, joking around with strangers, the song "Pennies from Heaven," by Louis Prima, roses, jasmine and flowers of all kinds, writing, birds, pirates, female-led dark comedies where women don't die, the ocean, riding a bike, swimming, arcade shooting games, The Cranberries, Salt-N-Pepa, improvisational singing, cats, comedy, Ethiopian food, and sleeping with the window open on a cool night under a big fluffy comforter.

These things put me in a great mood on an ordinary day, and can really take the edge off of a shitty day. They bring me pleasure, laughter, joy and delight, which helps activate my parasympathetic nervous system if I'm dealing with challenging emotions or stuck in a freeze state.

If you have trouble remembering the things that lift you up when you're feeling down, I highly recommend making a list of your own, and keeping it somewhere handy.

It's never a bad time to do something that makes us feel good, and we *always* deserve it. In fact, the less deserving we feel, the more urgent it is to remember our favorite things.

Our Inner Mob Boss

Eating sugar to make up for the boring-ass day you planned for yourself? I see you, sis — I spent literal *decades* doing that. I routinely ignored my needs for fun, play, and delight, only to try to make it up to myself with food, alcohol, drugs and other unsustainable pleasures. It didn't work, and my unhappy inner child still found other ways to sabotage my adult life.

When it became necessary for me to stop the addictive behaviors, my inner child's needs were all still there waiting for me, like a bunch of mob henchmen looking to settle a debt. It was time to pay up.

My days go so much better when I start them by giving my inner child something to look forward to. This can be a favorite activity or experience, such as going to the beach or the rock shop or doing a fun craft project. It can also include regular practices like meditation to free myself from worries and conditioning, looking for humor in life, and making space to feel and accept all of my emotions.

When our time is very limited, even just a little attention at the beginning of our day can go a long way — think of it as a tax you pay your inner child not to sabotage your life.

While it's important to keep promises to ourselves in order to build and maintain trust, even just listening to our inner child and validating their desires is a powerful way for us to feel connected and loved. When our inner child wants something impractical, for example, to go to a theme park on a day that it's simply not going to happen, we can say *yes* to ourselves internally, and make a plan to take the trip another day. The connection and trust-building that come from listening and responding are just as important as fulfillment of the actual desire.

This can look like: "Oh yes, water parks are so much fun! We love the lazy river… I'll check flights and hotels after breakfast and we'll see when it looks like a good time to go. It's very cold now but in a couple of months it should be good water park weather." Our inner child will love that we are taking action to fulfill a desire, even when it can't be met right this second. This helps our inner child feel listened to, cared about and taken care of.

When our inner child wants something that is *never* going to happen, like for a loved one to rise from the dead, it still matters that we validate the need behind this desire. For example: "Aunt Louise isn't coming back, but we can honor her memory with a photo on our altar… and let's make her famous strawberry pie! We can pick up the ingredients this afternoon. You seem extra sad today about missing her, do you need to cry? I'm here for you. Aunt Louise always listened to Louis Prima, should we put him on now, too?" And if there was a certain way Aunt Louise *related* to you, it can point to a need that you might be able to meet for yourself — for example, if she was really playful with you, you can try being more playful with yourself and others.

This works for outer children, as well… It's literally the same technique. Our inner child's needs are equally as valid as any child's, and equally important to their development. When we attend to our inner or outer child's needs, they don't need to raise hell or hold us hostage to get our attention.

Daily (or Whenever) Inner Child Practices

The inner child needs the same amount of love, nurturing and support as any other child, every single day — if you're already a parent, it really is like having another child to care for!

Contrary to popular thinking, nurturing our inner child isn't all glitter and kittens, although those kinds of things can offer profound support to our growth and healing. The deeply transformative work of feeling and expressing buried emotions is what will permanently liberate us from the past. The *way* that we do this — preferably with plenty of glitter, kittens, or whatever puts a smile on our face — is what helps us create our lives anew on a foundation of pleasure, joy, play and delight.

Here are ten day-to-day ways to nurture your inner child:

1. Cultivate joy from nothing. Smile inwardly and *act like* something good is going to happen today. Expect it. It doesn't have to be anything specific, just cultivate feelings of optimism and playfulness.

2. Walking, meditation, yoga, dance or any activity that allows you to let go of everything weighing on you mentally and emotionally — *especially* the stuff that feels super duper important or urgent!

3. Spend time alone to connect with who you are independently of relationships and internalized or inherited identities. Find ways to nurture your inner child's unique identity, talents and interests.

4. If she can't do/have something, explain why, and validate her feelings, needs and desires. On a busy or hard day, just connecting with your inner child can be enough!

5. Check in frequently throughout the day on what your inner child wants and needs, and follow through with promises. This helps build self-trust.

6. Praise yourself and acknowledge your inner child's efforts throughout the day, even for the little things. Counter negative inner dialogue by saying nice things to yourself.

7. When you feel compelled to do something not good for you, check in with your inner child. Make sure she feels seen and heard, allow her to express emotions, and change course to meet her needs.

8. Stay connected to your physical sensations throughout the day, and cushion challenging emotions with self-touch,

hugs, music, comfort, beautiful surroundings, and of course, your Favorite Things.

9. Gift her things sometimes just because she wants them — favorite foods, beautiful objects and clothing, fun experiences. Decide that having fun is important, and that it's okay to be frivolous.

10. At the end of the day, review events and their emotional impact. What was hardest? What was surprising? Disappointing? Scary? Frustrating? What was your favorite thing that happened?

The effects of these practices are cumulative. When we're paying ourselves close attention on a daily basis, we get to know ourselves on a deeper level and gain insights into who we really are and what we want from life.

Spending a lot of time connecting with ourselves and being present with our emotions, we also start to notice patterns — repeatedly feeling like shit after going to a specific place, being around a specific person or engaging in a specific activity can indicate a need for change.

Healing will make us feel better in the moment, but setting higher standards for ourselves can keep us from experiencing the same hurt over and over again.

Every day is a day you have the power to create yourself and your life anew — it's never too late for a Second Childhood and there's no better time to begin than right now.

Bringing the Inner Child Back to Life

Aside from my deep love and concern for trees, I could really relate to the idea in *The Lorax* of the "last seed" that holds the only hope for future reforestation of the planet. This is exactly what it felt like when I initially brought my inner child "back to life" after decades of trauma and substance dependency, and how I continually "revive" her as needed, after too much immersion in the bullshit of the outside world: finding whatever tiny little spark of joy within myself that I can, and nurturing it into a raging fire. Or, depending on what I have to work with, a warm and cozy flame.

Daily inner child practices are very different from the initial experience of reconnecting with our inner child. For me, the early days of inner child healing were just about getting through the day, and finding a way to process all of the emotions that were coming up. Having a daily practice came later, when things got more stable. In the beginning, doing anything at all for our inner child is cause for celebration!

I actually don't necessarily do each of these things every day now, either. Sometimes I forget or put other things first. It's not about doing it perfectly, it's about coming back to the practice. And sometimes I just don't need to do these things as much anymore because I've integrated my inner child — thanks to my dedication to self-parenting, she's growing up!

Getting started is the hardest part. I felt so unworthy of love when I started this journey that being present with my inner child was agonizing. I just had to stick through the uncomfortable feelings — they didn't last anywhere near as long as I feared they would.

Also, I learned from my own early experiences with meditation that there was such a thing as *slowing down too quickly*. Don't slam the brakes on your nervous system — if sitting still is too much, go for a walk or do any other physical activity that feels grounding.

It can be easy to guilt ourselves out of self-care, especially if we are very sensitive, but always putting others first is unsustainable. But no one else can nourish our inner child as well and as much as we can. We are as worthy of saving and preservation as any other living being, and it's up to us to make ourselves a priority.

It's easy to feel overwhelmed by the seemingly impossible task of making up for 18 years of neglect and misery in the midst of our busy adult lives. But turning our focus away from both the past and the future — neither of which we can control — we're left with the only question that truly matters: how can we meet our needs right now in the present moment?

The most important thing is that I start my day by doing what it takes to put my inner child in as good of a mood as possible. When I meet my own needs first, it's amazing how everything else falls into place!

Taking responsibility for the energy we bring to the world is a powerful shift that allows us to make healthy choices for ourselves and to serve ourselves and others joyfully. As our own loving parent, we hold the frequency for our inner child. By doing the deeper work of healing from and letting go of the past, we can adopt a more carefree and lighthearted approach to life that makes each day feel like a Second Childhood.

Wherever you are in your reparenting journey, keep in mind that anything can happen today, so wake up with the intention to start fresh. Let go of everything you think you know about life and about who you are, and open yourself to infinite possibilities.

The Magic Wand

Playfulness is a really important part of my life, my relationships and my work. It's been an important part of my survival as well as the way I've made meaning in life, and therefore it's an important part of my spirituality as well.

One of the ways I stay connected to the energy of playfulness in my daily life is with a little plastic magic wand that I won at an arcade. It's the perfect cue for my inner child to remember how powerful imagination can be, and to connect with the part of myself that knows exactly what I want.

I take my magic wand with me wherever I go, and I love seeing its sparkly silver shine peeking out at me, reminding me to believe in magic. When I feel lost or confused, I pull out my magic wand and instantly my sense of inner power is restored. From there, I feel clearer about my direction and more confident making decisions for the future.

I highly recommend availing yourself of a toy, tool or other object that can connect you to your inner child or remind you of your power. It could be a unicorn horn, a special piece of clothing or a gemstone or other talisman.

It doesn't have to be fancy or expensive — I actually thought about replacing my cheap plastic wand with a custom-made precious metal or glass one, but realized that the one I have is a more powerful cue for me because the cheap plastic just screams childhood in the way that a high-end wand wouldn't. It's perfect.

Get yourself a magic wand or whatever delights your inner child, and then go make some magic.

Whose Life Is It, Anyway?

I did extremely well in school academically, but graduated with post-traumatic stress, an anxiety disorder, an eating disorder, alcohol use disorder and major depression that no one ever seemed to notice or care about.

Doesn't it seem strange that we would send our children away for half of their waking hours or more, to a place where no one is paying attention to their mental health or emotional needs?

There is more of a conversation now in schools about certain mental health issues and emotional topics, and schools now have things like meditation circles and anti-bullying posters, but it isn't enough. And the goal is at odds with the goals of mental and emotional wellness, because these measures exist only to help children be more successful academically and to reduce the strain on teachers and administrative staff to handle interpersonal conflicts and classroom disruptions. There is no concept of valuing mental and emotional wellness purely for the children's sake.

This mirrors a larger pattern in society. When Human Resources puts on a yoga class at the workplace, it's ultimately about getting you to be more productive. A profit-based organization is not going to invest in offerings that would make you less productive — the shareholders wouldn't have it.

Similarly, going to therapy as an adult usually revolves around the goal of getting you as the patient to be more "functional." Whether that takes talking, drugs or more specialized psychological services, it's considered to be a success if you can go back to work and get shit done rather than sit and cry at your desk all day. When insurance pays for therapy, it's so that you can go back to work and do your job — not so that you can be happy.

At about age 27, I sought the help of a therapist for the first time in my life. She helped me a lot, but there was always an underlying message that I should focus on becoming well enough to choose a career and participate in society like a normal person. But I knew that I was on a journey of self-discovery that wasn't taking me back where I came from. The inner work wasn't leading me to the places everyone wanted me to go; it was leading me to mysterious places that I felt deeply, spiritually compelled to explore. It felt important, and I wanted to take my time.

Several years later, as a new mother, I sought professional help for postpartum depression. The psychiatrist I saw pressured me to go on anti-depressants, but I didn't want to because of my awful previous experience with the side effects. Ignoring my concerns, she emphasized that it was important for me to "be functional."

What I really needed was trustworthy childcare, a break from meal prep here and there and an apartment bigger than a fishbowl — but none of that was of concern to the medical system.

Without any of the kinds of help available to me that I truly needed, I did eventually go on the antidepressants. And then I quit them again, because of the side effects.

While I wavered plenty on my path, I am proud to say that I never did go back to a normal life.

Evicting the Old Bearded Man

When I got sober I had to ask myself every day: what would make life worth living without alcohol? I had to get in touch with the real needs, desires and feelings underneath my drinking that I had neglected and couldn't even identify — I didn't know how to put names to my emotions until I was almost 30 years old!

I've had to insist on a joyful, just life because I could no longer tolerate anything less. This was the beginning of my leading an intentional life. I had to choose my own path and I had to own my choices.

However, I found attitudes in my recovery program were not always supportive of this philosophy.

I found that a lot of people thought that getting sober was just a way to be a better cog in the machine. You could hear it in people's stories of feeling guilty for not meeting social obligations that had been assigned to them by a capitalist society — that they didn't deserve to live, rest or be happy unless they were productive 40 hours a week and meeting all of their family's expectations.

This kind of thinking was generally reinforced by the group and by the patriarchal structure of 12-step recovery programs, which I found encouraged conformity, self-denial and self-blame. Patriarchal religion permeates every aspect of these programs, even if you change "God" to "Goddess" and "Him" to "Her" in all of the literature, which many women do.

But feminine spirituality is more than a pronoun — it's a journey of embodiment, empowerment and liberation.

Without connecting the dots between addiction, childhood trauma and patriarchy, recovery is limited. What 12-step programs miss is that addictions are rooted in attachment trauma, where the child's ongoing physical and emotional connection to their mother sets the foundation for a functioning adult nervous system, independent adult life and healthy adult relationships.

Mom is the original "God" — she is the source of everything for her child, physically and emotionally, and the quality and nature of this bond determines the child's expectations of, and relationship with, the outside world. Failing to name this connection, the rupture or absence of which forms the root of addiction and many other "'mental health'" struggles, is disempowering to the individual in recovery and also helps perpetuate the cycle of oppression, trauma and addiction into the next generation of girls and women.

To the extent that the 12 steps help a person release addictions and other harmful behaviors associated with unmet attachment needs, they work. But the language, the practices, and the interpersonal dynamics within these programs do so much to prevent this outcome.

The recovering alcoholic with sexual and developmental trauma needs to find her way back to her own body and its wisdom, not to seek salvation from an invisible bearded man in the sky. While an old bearded man in the sky may seem better than one in her childhood bed, it's the same power dynamic. Even the concept of a benevolent male god still vastly limits her spiritual growth — he's still "out there," and he's still a "he."

Members who object to a male Christian god are even encouraged to worship inanimate objects over our own bodies. As every newcomer to AA is advised, "Even a doorknob can be your higher power. It can be anything — just as long as it isn't YOU!"

Is there any length we won't go to avoid naming women as God?

The sad truth is that many alcoholics don't recover because of internalized guilt and shame that tells them they are "bad." They don't uncover family dysfunction and abuse and look at how that hurt them and contributed to their addiction, instead blaming themselves for all of their problems. Emotional dependency stops them from standing up to their parents, who may be actively scapegoating them to protect their own self-image and social standing. The childish fantasy that their parents are perfect, originally useful in helping the child survive dangerous circumstances, persists. The opportunity to develop true maturity loses to the adult child's conviction that they are "the problem," which provides the comforting illusion that they have the power to fix the family by fixing themselves.

A person who has been turned against themselves in childhood must shift the blame — both psychologically and emotionally — in order to truly heal, find inner power, and recover from addiction long-term.

Reclaiming personal power is paramount to sustainable, long-term addiction recovery. Finding god within ourselves, healing from attachment trauma, rediscovering joy, and explicitly unraveling religious programming are all crucial parts of this process.

Recovering Like a Good Girl

The truth is that I hadn't stopped drinking for myself. I did it because I didn't like the way my ex looked at me after I drove drunk long-distance to see him. While I had been the one to end the relationship, I still cared deeply about his opinion of me.

Essentially, I quit alcohol to be a more successful codependent.

Whatever it takes to get someone on the right path, right?

I was very "good at" recovery, just like I had been in school. I went to multiple meetings daily. I did everything people told me to do. But after I also quit eating sugar, only three months after taking my last drink, I had to improvise.

The flood of emotions that surfaced when I was no longer consuming any substances that numbed my body was overwhelming. Nearly three decades' worth of grief, terror, loneliness, hopelessness, anger and depression hit me all at once. I had no idea how to process one emotion, let alone a dozen of them at once.

People told me to call someone in the program when I needed help with my emotions. But the people I called weren't necessarily available when I needed to talk or weren't necessarily in the business of processing emotions. There were all types of people in those rooms, and emotional safety wasn't necessarily a common thread.

People told me to just sit with my feelings until they passed, but it didn't feel like enough. *I* didn't feel like enough.

What I needed was co-regulation, although I didn't have the language for it then. But I found that being witnessed in my pain really helped. So, I went to meetings and cried the whole way through. I used my three-minute share time to speak, allowing the emotions to express through my throat and dissolve into thin air. The meetings were not designed to support grief or trauma release, but that's what I needed, so that's what I used them for and that's how I healed.

Hugs were great, too. Journaling helped me get clarity, and sometimes that helped with emotional release. But what really helped me process emotions independently was an embodiment practice.

Toward a Feminist Recovery Model

Although I found 12-step programs immensely helpful in beginning my addiction recovery journey, I didn't get the type of help from them that I needed to maintain long-term sobriety. The main reason for this is that there is no official discussion of trauma as an underlying cause of addiction, and therefore no framework for healing from trauma.

While people may stay sober or clean for a while using the tools of the program, trauma causes a disconnection from self and spirit that will leave someone searching outside of themselves for a sense of wholeness until it is integrated.

Aside from this issue, there is little consideration of systemic factors in addiction and recovery.

Alcoholics Anonymous outlines a program for recovery tailored specifically to meet the needs of old white men like the ones who founded it, and whose behavior the literature makes abundantly clear has been the source of trauma for many women. As a result, there exists an air of hostility toward women and abuse survivors, who have often been victimized by other alcoholics in or outside of the program, and who need to discuss and integrate these experiences in order to heal and to achieve recovery.

The narrative in these programs is very much about the "ego" being the cause of addiction. For someone who has never had a chance to develop a healthy sense of self, this is very much the wrong message, and a dangerous one at that. Like many other survivors of sexual abuse, my body had been used as an object from a very early age, and I had never truly been seen by my primary caregivers, all of which imprinted me with the belief and feeling that I was not *real*. I had to learn as an adult how to inhabit my body, to claim it as mine, and to take up space in my own life.

Having an "ego problem" indicates not moral failure, but a wounded inner child with unmet developmental needs. Like many other women and abuse survivors, my work in recovery was to *develop* a healthy ego — not to minimize it. For us, egolessness was not a sign of spiritual growth but a sign of trauma, and often connected to the symptom of executive dysfunction. We had to build our entire "selves" from the inside out and from scratch, and being in an environment where this was considered wrong or bad led to countless setbacks.

To make matters worse, instead of identifying attachment trauma and other traumas as the underlying cause of alcohol dependency, attachment traumas are exploited to sell members on patriarchal religion. This includes the informal "sponsorship" system in which more experienced members boss around newer members in relationships that resemble trauma bonds, instead of a safe attachment relationship through which they could heal trauma, develop trust in their own inner authority, and achieve long-term sobriety as autonomous individuals.

There are many exceptions, and many wonderful people in these programs, but someone who has only known abuse their entire lives isn't going to be well-equipped to identify them. Adults with unrecognized attachment trauma are vulnerable to religious abuse because of the certainty that high control appears to offer — the certainty that was missing from relationships with unstable, unreliable, unavailable and/or unpredictable caregivers. Unfortunately, people who end up with abusive sponsors and then later speak up about it are blamed for "seeking out" or "attracting" this dynamic, rather than being correctly identified as victims of predation within a subculture almost as perfectly structured to facilitate it as the nuclear family that traumatized them in the first place.

The parent-child attachment bond is designed to build a healthy sense of self from the completely unselfconscious blob of pure consciousness that we enter the world as. This happens primarily through the mother's body — first in utero, and then after the child is born, in a physically close and emotionally safe relationship with her that lasts as long as the child needs it to. This is how the child develops a healthy relationship with her own body. AA is a patriarchal program in that the role of the attachment bond between mother and child in preventing addiction is never discussed. Instead, there is talk of God, which members are told doesn't *have* to be a Christian deity, but the effect is the same. Switching from patriarchal religion to a concept of divinity based on motherhood entails a hell of a lot more than just switching pronouns as you read the literature.

Focusing on building a relationship with ourselves as women through our embodied presence is a completely different approach to recovery — one that ultimately supports our liberation and continued empowerment instead of grooming us for further exploitation. Through practices that engage the body like self-massage, yoga, lifting weights and even cleaning the house, I've found that whichever version of my adult self is needed most, comes online.

These activities have also helped me heal migraines, which I attribute to the stress of my inner child trying to manage adult problems without my full embodied presence. Slowing down and doing more things that make me happy, in defiance of my conditioning to always be productive and useful to others, has helped with these debilitating headaches as well.

It is our job as our own loving parents to discern which of the demands of the outside world are in our best interests to meet, and which do us more harm than good. Our bodies operate as both compass and captain in our journey toward sustainable, joyful living.

Another aspect of an embodied approach to recovery is that we are our own authority. This can be both terrifying and liberating. When I first heard things like "It's your choice," it only made me scared that I would make the *wrong* choice. I felt more pressure, not more freedom. I heard a message of responsibility, but did not receive the message of empowerment.

It helped to realize that it wasn't just up to me to guess what the "right" decision was, it was up to me to *decide* what was right or wrong to begin with.

For our choices in life to be meaningful, we can't be worried that one or more of them will mean that we are a bad person, or that a possible outcome will undermine our inherent worth. This is why some women who technically have the freedom to make empowering life choices, do not. It's not only about having power — it's about believing that we have the right to use it.

Being our own authority also means taking a strengths-based approach to personal growth. Staying in touch with, and being guided by, our own inner experience, rather than the perceptions and opinions of others, it becomes natural to focus on what we are already doing well, and build on that. This not only feels good, but it also gives us the foundation for self-improvement as sovereign beings.

Relying on an external authority to tell us what's wrong with us and initiating change based on self-criticism is a trap — we can always find more things wrong with us, or more stuff to dig up from the past. If we keep looking for things to "fix" about ourselves, we'll surely find them, but we'll never have time to go out and live our lives. Instead, we can focus on what's right, what's enjoyable, what's working, and what we desire, and go from there.

We can *start* with love, happiness, playfulness and pleasure, rather than seeing them as rewards for future achievements. Grounding ourselves in embodied joy and trusting how we feel gives us a baseline for wellbeing and empowers us to know what moves are right for us, and when. If we *don't* know what we like, how to source power internally, or how it feels to be happy, we are vulnerable to external control. Self-trust can be super scary at first, but it gets easier, and it's so worth it not to be worrying all the time whether you're on the right track.

At times, I've also dared to try alcohol again. The common refrain in recovery circles of "to drink is to die" never sat well with me. I didn't crave alcohol or its effects, but I also didn't want to be trapped identifying as an "alcoholic" for the rest of my life.

I'm glad that I did this, because I had some pretty interesting experiences. In Mexico, I drank *pox*, a corn liquor with an important spiritual role in Mayan culture. A friend drove us home from the ceremony while I looked out the window at the corn fields, and felt an incredibly strong connection to the plants and to the Earth they grew from. I wanted to go lie down in the cornfield and merge my body with that of the Earth — not a typical alcoholic experience.

I did not experience any cravings after the ceremony or a desire to have more *pox* or other liquors on a regular basis (as I had been told I would) — I felt only a deep appreciation for having had the opportunity to partake in the ceremony, and for the meaningful role of alcohol in land-based cultures.

I know that the healing and embodiment work I had done up to that point made the difference between my being able to enjoy that experience for what it was, and it marking the beginning of a bender, as it could have years earlier. The assumption behind the common wisdom dispensed in mainstream recovery programs is that participants are not healing trauma, and therefore vulnerable to substance dependency for life, which paints a very sad and limited projection of life in recovery.

For years after leaving conventional recovery groups I was worried I was doing something wrong — it was terrifying to veer off the path that others around me were taking in recovery, and I lost many relationships because of it. Still, I knew it was working because I could sense my growing capacity to function as a sovereign human being. The gradual development of secure attachment with myself raised my confidence bit by bit, and eventually quieted the voices of self-doubt.

As women, our recovery depends on expanding our capacity to trust ourselves. Any framework that aims to erode our self-trust will only pull us back into the patriarchal patterns that led to addiction in the first place — and keep us trapped in the very trauma loops we're trying to escape.

Cancelling Your Contract with God

The concept of gratitude is one of the worst offenders in religious and spiritual circles, often used to bully people into settling for less than what their hearts truly desire, and what they actually deserve. Settling is actually a form of violence, in that it involves using force — against ourselves.

I found the practice of making a nightly "Gratitude List" to be somewhat helpful, but it also triggered feelings of shame, guilt and fear. I even had people say to my face that I was asking for too much in life, and that I should *just be grateful* for what I already have!

Nothing grooms people to accept exploitation better than making them feel bad about having normal human needs and desires.

Even though the concept of gratitude has been mangled and used against us, it still has value. But at its best, gratitude isn't a mental exercise; it's a state of embodied joy. We can definitely attract more wonderful things into our lives by expressing gratitude, but this doesn't have to mean making a list if that doesn't feel good. I have found that just enjoying life, and noticing myself enjoying it, is enough to do the trick. Being in touch with our bodies and noticing and valuing what brings us joy — not groveling like a sycophant — is what protects us from being overwhelmed by negativity, and making desperate choices.

Spiritual terms that used to activate a negative emotional response in me have often begun to feel more "neutral" as I've reclaimed the original meaning in my body and in my life, giving them meanings that *feel good* to me. Now, I'm able to see things like "make a list of five things you're grateful for" without wanting to punch a wall, although my practice still doesn't involve list-making.

I'm also comfortable now expressing gratitude toward *myself* for all the effort I put in on my own behalf, after being reprimanded for doing that by a spiritual teacher. It just feels good and nourishing! I trust that feeling more and more now.

Religious conditioning can also lead to a guilt complex in which we see ourselves as unworthy of what we want and lacking the right to take initiative in life. Those of us who grew up religious may have tried bargaining with God from time to time as children. For example, "I'll never ask for anything again if I can just have..." or "Let this turn out okay just this once, and then I promise..."

Desperation is not a great place to make promises to yourself, or to anyone else — the legal term for that is "coercion," and it can make a contract null and void. So, you can go ahead and let yourself off the hook for anything you once promised God under duress (not to mention, contracts signed by minors aren't legally binding).

So much of the time we limit ourselves based on what we think we deserve or are entitled to, and feel guilty for wanting more. And a lot of the time, the pressure we feel to express gratitude for what we already have, which can be the only way we feel it's okay for us to pursue what we want, actually keeps us from owning and fulfilling our desire for *more*.

As children, we were often guilt-tripped out of asking for things we wanted, not because we didn't deserve them, but because our parents didn't have the emotional or material resources to provide them for us.

Instead of validating our desires and explaining why it wasn't possible for us to have what we wanted, our parents may have collapsed into their own shame or guilt over not being able to give us everything we wanted, or everything they wanted for us, and they may have projected that shame onto us. We may have grown up with a scarcity mindset as a result, along with a feeling of fear associated with pursuing our desires, and maybe also an identity of being "too much" or "not enough."

As adults, this can mean that we are not actually available to receive many of the things that we say that we want, because our nervous systems have been conditioned to believe that it's bad or wrong for us to want and to have them. So, we may be unhappy with our lives, but not feel deserving of changing them, or we may be frustrated with our efforts to effect change and confused as to why it never seems to take shape or to last.

The way we can take our power back in these situations is to first recognize where our conscious desires might actually be in conflict with our most deeply held beliefs, and then change those beliefs so that we no longer hold any inner resistance to receiving what we want. The inner child is usually the one holding onto something in our lives that we *think* we do not want, and in connecting with her we can discover what she needs in order to let go. Our unmet developmental needs, if unexamined, will otherwise continue to run the show.

We need to acknowledge that our earliest doubts of our own worthiness and our guilt about taking initiative are not sacred, and only installed by patriarchal programming from family and religion. Processing the emotions that come up for us around these themes and internalizing new beliefs about ourselves and the universe can break the spell and free us to live the lives we truly desire.

I struggled with this so much when I was starting my first online business. We had just enough to get by, and I believed on a very deep level that it was all I was supposed to have or want. I felt like a terrible person when I started looking for clients, but I kept going because I just wanted *more*. Soon, a beautiful synchronicity confirmed I was on the right path: my very first client signed with me on Halloween. With the veil between worlds lifted, I could feel my ancestors cheering me on.

Canceling your contract with God may take more determination than leaving the Columbia House Records Club, but the hardest part is deciding you deserve better. It's okay to want more, and to go after it! You might be surprised at how supported you feel once you take that first step.

The Serenity Curse

Women in recovery are taught The Serenity Prayer, which urges us to pray for God to help us accept the things we cannot change, and to change the things we can. There are a few problems with this.

The first is that women, and likely anyone raised in a hostile environment, have been conditioned to push past our own boundaries to get things done. We have needed to meet other people's expectations and demands in order to survive, often from a very young age. As a result, we are likely to think that we *can* change things that we really should not, simply because our idea of possibility is unrestrained by the instinct for self-preservation. Until this pattern is brought to light, we are likely to think that if we *can* do something, even if it costs us our health, sanity, or otherwise exhausts our personal resources, it is our god-given responsibility to do so.

So instead of asking ourselves whether we *can* do something, we would be well-served to ask ourselves these three questions:

1. Would it be *enjoyable* for me?
2. Would it be *sustainable* for me?
3. Would it be *worth it* to me?

Never mind if you *can* do something that someone asks of you — do you *want* to?

An example that comes to mind is a woman in a relationship with an immature man who is open to growing the fuck up but wants lots of guidance from her to do so. He's willing to become the kind of person she needs as a partner, so technically, she *can* help him do this… but does she *want* to? Is it *sustainable* for her to raise a grown man as if he were her child? Will she *enjoy* the labor this entails? Is it *worth* doing, when she could just break up with him and instead find a fully-formed adult human life partner? The language of "can," with no further context, leads to overfunctioning in women because that is our default setting.

The second problem is that women have been legally prohibited from making important changes in our lives throughout history. One example is that until 1969, a woman couldn't initiate divorce in the United States without proving she had a good enough reason, which the court might then agree with or not. No-fault divorce laws that swept the country in the 1970s allowed women to divorce their husbands without justification. So for a woman who was unhappily married in 1968, accepting the things she could not change would have included being stuck with her spouse.

It was the feminists (specifically, the National Association of Women and the Law, NAWL) who bravely banded together to change these laws — not the immutable will of God! — and made miserable married life something women could, in fact, change. Women have been conditioned to think that patriarchal institutions *are* God, and religious language perpetuates this distortion seamlessly.

The example above also shows the power of women coming together to make change, in unlocking possibilities that do not exist when we try to solve problems in isolation. If you're thinking that 12-step programs might actually encourage people to come together to change laws they don't like, or even support a person in disobeying unjust laws, you're wrong. I was ostracized for doing this, when I began protesting against corporate encroachment upon indigenous land and sovereignty, even in one of the most liberal and open-minded parts of the country.

These are just some of the many reasons 12-step could no longer be my spiritual home. Even though people in the program say, "Take what you like and leave the rest," the overarching philosophy is deeply rooted in patriarchy and colonialism. I decided that this was something it would be unsustainable for me to attempt to change, so I created my own network of like-minded women in recovery instead.

There is such a beautiful dynamic created when women come together, free from any expectation of obedience or self-sacrifice. These are the conditions under which true, deep, and long-lasting recovery is possible.

Thank You for Your Service

When I first started going to recovery meetings, everyone talked about how important it was to do "service," such as greeting others at meetings, helping newcomers and sharing our story.

What I found though was that there wasn't a whole lot of nuance around choosing ways to be of service that felt appropriate to each individual on a case-by-case basis. You were expected to do what was asked of you, or else accept that your refusal posed a risk to your sobriety.

As a woman who had literally drank to cope with overgiving in relationships, like many other women, this wasn't the message I needed to hear.

I remember one time I showed up to a meeting in distress, having recently recovered traumatic childhood memories.

All I wanted was to be able to talk to someone privately and share some of what was going on with me to relieve me of overwhelm. I asked a woman who I had considered a friend if she'd be available to provide the kind of emotional support I needed after a meeting. Her response was cruel. She looked at me with a mix of contempt and condescension and said, "I think what you need is to go be of service to someone else."

It had taken decades for me to become comfortable asking for any kind of help, and I was not the kind of person to ask unless I really needed it. The lack of empathy I faced when I finally found the courage to reach out was anything but healing. Not all of my experiences were like this, but things like this happened frequently enough that I eventually stopped feeling safe enough to continue with 12-step recovery.

I will also mention that one area I really did enjoy being of service was in sharing my story at meetings. I am glad to have had this opportunity, because it's how I discovered my gift for moving an audience through public speaking. I learned to trust that the right words would come, and that I didn't need to control my expression in order to be understood and to make an impact. I gained so much confidence in my voice, and in the knowledge that the best way for me to be of service was to speak my truth.

If you've had any religious influence in life, it's important to internalize that being in your fullest expression of joy *is* an act of service. (In fact, if it's not joyful, it's not service — it's manipulation.) I'm reminded of this every time a celebrity in addiction recovery dies, and no one can understand how this could have happened.

While an individual may have been following instructions from a religious-based recovery program to "be of service," they may not have been doing it joyfully. That matters, because service doesn't keep people sober — a joyful life does.

Here's the truth: people who aren't doing the deep work are not going to access authentic, embodied joy. They're not going to get to the part where they reparent themselves and live a beautiful Second Childhood. If the inner child isn't getting their needs met, they're still emotionally in the same place they were when in active addiction.

No wonder they keep using.

Even if they spend millions of dollars on building recovery centers, and even if that really does help thousands of people.

If you want to live free from the obsessions and compulsions that characterize addiction, you have to learn how to love yourself and do what makes *you* happy. Even if a pair of deceased, self-admittedly extremely flawed patriarchs and their followers wouldn't approve, and even if it means walking alone once again after finally finding a sense of belonging for the first time in life. Because if service without joy was enough, we sure as hell wouldn't see people dying from addiction after 20 or more years in recovery.

So, I dare you — live a life that you love, and do it *for you*. You never know who might thank you for your service.

Putting Our Inner Child First

I have heard an awful lot of "put God first and everything will follow" in my life. When people use this phrase, they are saying that if you act selfishly, you'll actually repel all of the things you are going after.

This is true, in a sense — if you go around thinking only of yourself and your own needs, people won't like it and they will likely not feel motivated to help you reach your goals. Similarly, if you use people for validation and constantly seek approval from others, you'll not only give away your power but also be ineffective in your endeavors.

Many people work tirelessly in an attempt to earn the love and a sense of internal safety that were missing from their childhood attachment relationships. This is a never-ending undertaking, as no boss, teacher, or other adult relationship can meet our developmental needs on this level. In this sense, "putting God first" would mean acting from our mature, adult selves rather than from a place of narcissistic wounding.

The problem is that most of the time, people don't interpret the phrase this way. Religious dogma is so commonly used to encourage self-denial, that many people think it's selfish to take care of themselves at all. People are told, and believe, that "putting God first" means *abandoning* their inner child, and obeying either other authorities such as the government, an employer, community leader or "the big man in the sky," their idea of which is likely to have been shaped by their parents and by whatever religious denomination their family belonged to.

So I have translated this phrase into the language of sovereign womanhood as "put your *inner child* first and everything will follow." When I take care of my inner child before anything or anyone else, everything else falls into place.

Only love makes us feel whole. When we did not receive love from our parents, it is our job to learn how to love ourselves. So we do have to put ourselves first, before we can be useful to anyone else.

If we do not love ourselves, plenty of people will be happy to take advantage of us and find their own use for us. If we want to serve the world using our innate gifts and genius, and do so on our own terms, we need to love ourselves so that we know what we have to offer, as well as having an internal sense of what our time and energy is worth, so that we are not vulnerable to manipulation.

Religion and pseudo-religious recovery models encourage people to help others at the expense of their own needs and desires. However, the unmet needs of the inner child lead to both distorted motivation for helping others and vulnerability to abuse. Someone whose inner child's needs are met is not going to fall for any of that — they are going to put themselves first, and serve others when and how it suits them.

Rebelling against the "put others first" dogma is a powerful way to redefine our value and reclaim our power, and to truly mature into sovereign beings after religious conditioning and abuse.

The Hamster Wheel to Happiness

I spent a lot of time in the beginning of my healing journey trying really hard to be a better person, and still never feeling good enough — I was on what seemed like a never-ending path to happiness.

This is partly because the recovery framework I learned involved a lot of "examining of shortcomings" and not a lot of joy, self-praise or self-trust. Also, I had been groomed in childhood to never feel that I was enough, and anything I tried to do just became another twisted attempt to prove my worth.

There were times I was really depressed from doing way too much self-improvement and not enough *living*.

Overcoming perfectionism isn't about reducing the quality of our work — it's about improving the quality of our relationship with ourselves.

The safety we need to heal is created with a light and joyful heart, and plenty of self-approval — not with perfectionism or self-criticism. We heal by focusing on our wholeness, not our brokenness. Leading with joy, instead of trying to earn the right to it, is a monumental act of healing in itself.

We deserve to be loved, to be happy, to have fun, and to feel good about ourselves no matter where we are on our healing journey. Love is not a reward for a job well done; it is the fuel that drives us to do well!

When we're happy, everyone around us is better for it, too. Being a good person feels good — deeply good. So trust yourself to do what feels good, and know that everything else will work itself out.

Similarly, don't get so lost digging up the past that you forget to move forward in life — trust that envisioning your future and moving towards what you desire will trigger and heal you in all the ways that matter.

If I could go back and do it again, I would focus more on my dreams and less on healing. The healing became a distraction and never feeling "healed enough" was an excuse not to do anything *other* than healing. I didn't know any better, but you do. If you're "healed enough" to have a vision, a dream or a desire, you're healed enough to pursue it, one step at a time.

Choosing What Counts

I saw a woman's Facebook post celebrating 8 years of sobriety and I burst into tears. I would have had 14 years that month — would, because 9 years prior I very intentionally downed a six-pack under a bridge at the height of my eco-despair and social alienation.

I dislike that I'm expected to feel shame and regret around that, when the truth is that I didn't have the tools I needed to stay sober through what I was experiencing at the time. Specifically, I didn't know that a highly sensitive person has to shut themselves off from the suffering of the world in order to stay sane.

I thought that recovery would "fix" my need to shut down and to escape, but it did not. I thought that my sobriety would somehow fix the world. It did not. It turned out that I didn't need to fix anything — I just needed to stop co-regulating with patriarchy and its relentless fallout.

I can shut my sensitivity on and off like a light switch now. It might seem cold-hearted, especially due to society's oppressive expectations around women and emotional labor, but I have a responsibility to know and respect my limits. I don't watch the news and I limit my exposure to potentially upsetting content on social media, even when it seems like everyone else is talking about some major world event.

I wouldn't force a child to be informed of every single global tragedy — if any of them — and my inner child deserves the same level of care. When I have the capacity for more, my boundaries may shift. But no one else has the right to tell me when or where I should make myself available to others.

Highly sensitive women need to be talking about this more — about not letting the mass media's agenda dictate our moods and priorities, and not being willing to engage emotionally with every single fucking tragedy self-appointed authority figures throw in our faces to manipulate our loyalties and emotions.

We are allowed to be strategically, practically and selectively compassionate, without shame.

We are allowed to focus on how we can care for our immediate communities, our families and ourselves (or *only* ourselves) when that feels like enough for us to handle.

We are allowed to have boundaries that protect our energy, our space, our bodies and our time.

We are allowed to ask for help when even taking responsibility for our own lives feels like too much, even when other people project that we have it all together, or think that we should.

No longer looking for external cues about my worth, I have realized that the single-minded focus in recovery communities on counting days and years of sobriety is fear-based and counterproductive. It doesn't make sense that a person could "lose" time accumulated, or that a relapse is necessarily a break from growth rather than an integral part of it. It's not possible to undo healing by taking a drink. No one can take away the hard work we've invested in personal growth. That's the whole point — to build a foundation we can count on regardless of outside circumstances.

My spiritual journey isn't about clocking in for a validation paycheck. It's about the person I've become and what I've learned along the way. Most of all, it's about owning my power to determine for myself what "counts" — not just in recovery terms, but in choosing what *matters* to me in every area of life.

Getting Even with God

There was a time I wanted to slap anyone who said the F-word.

No, not *that* one — I'm talking about forgiveness.

As one of the spiritual principles most commonly used to silence abuse survivors, to minimize our experiences, and to encourage us to bypass the righteous anger that could empower us to change our lives and the world, pressure to forgive someone who has hurt us often only makes us angrier.

It can also make us sick, if we turn our anger inwards. Autoimmune conditions, eating disorders, cancer and other serious health issues are often connected to repressed anger. When the appropriate target for our anger is off-limits due to social pressures, power dynamics — and often, the law — the body goes to war with itself.

The process of forgiveness cannot be forced or rushed. Forgiveness, if it ever comes, is a *result* of our own healing — not a prerequisite.

When an animal in the wild experiences a life-threatening event, their natural response is to fight back, or to flee. In the wild, self-defense and escape are "allowed," even if they are frequently unsuccessful. Patriarchal laws that criminalize self-defense violate natural law. There are women serving lifetime prison sentences for killing the perpetrators of unthinkable abuse, punished for taking justice into their own hands in the most natural way possible.

I have spoken to many incarcerated women who were arrested after being abused by their boyfriends or husbands, simply because they had dared to fight back. The man, often an experienced abuser, had physically harmed the woman in some way that skillfully did not leave a mark (abusers actually study, practice and teach each other how to do this). The man's abuse might also be sexual, psychological or financial, leaving no signs of physical injury, whereas the woman might have defended herself with her fingernails or an inanimate object that left a mark.

The police protocol for handling a domestic violence incident is usually to arrest the person they believe to be the primary aggressor. When in doubt, police often put away the person whose injuries are invisible or less visible, without considering power dynamics at play or the relative severity of harm done.

Voila, the victim is now behind bars.

Natural law is also violated by laws that keep victims captive to their abusers, such as with the institution of the nuclear family, which grants parents legal ownership over their children. A child must prove themselves worthy of, and fight for, their autonomy in the form of legal emancipation, even when their parents have abused them. Without this requirement, the child would be free to leave and either live on their own or stay with a safe relative or another family altogether if they felt unsafe at home.

The state can intervene to remove a child from an abusive family (or in practice, for whatever reason they see fit), but this is not within the child's control. The child is subject to the whims of the law, and is often merely a pawn in the power games that adults play, in which the child's safety is an afterthought, if it is a thought at all. The default is that children are property of their parents or legal guardians and held captive until the government-determined age of adulthood is reached.

In civilization we call expressing anger "losing our temper," and doing so is treated as a failure — especially among children. A child who defends themselves from another student's violence at school may be sent to the principal's office. At home, defending oneself from a sibling's attack might earn a child a "time out" or some other punishment.

However, an adult who harms a child in anger is less likely to be confronted. They have the legal and *de facto* power to treat a child pretty much as they wish. Both women and children are pathologized for self-defense and other normal reactions to living in captivity, such as attempts to escape and to establish sovereignty. Often, girls are also expected to suppress anger more than boys, even when being attacked, and are more likely to be perceived as "aggressive" when simply being assertive.

I was scapegoated by my family both for the abuse I experienced, and for my emotional and behavioral reactions to it. I was the designated patient who was put into therapy. I was the problem, the unreasonably angry, unstable and uncooperative one who threatened peace and harmony in the family.

It was looked poorly upon in my family to express anger, even though there was plenty of it simmering beneath the surface, and often erupting. I felt ashamed of my anger and tried to hide it, underneath eating, not eating, alcohol, peer approval and school performance — a lot of which had the added benefit of making my entire family look normal, healthy and good. I was well-celebrated for my academic achievements and for my appearance. I lived on praise and Diet Coke for most of the 90s.

When I decided to tell my family that I was an alcoholic, I practically had to convince them. It was a difficult moment for all of us, because none of us were used to addressing our problems openly. To us, having problems meant something was wrong with you, and that triggered shame. I can see now that my alcoholism, and my family's denial of it, were all symptomatic of attachment trauma.

It wasn't until I removed everything that was coming between me and my feelings that I began to feel my anger and express it. And in doing so, to heal.

And honestly, I was a rage factory. I broke a lot of shit. It wasn't pretty, but it worked. It's hard to find socially acceptable places to express rage, which is indicative of the fact that it's still not fully socially acceptable to heal trauma. Now there are "rage rooms," where you can hit all manner of breakables with a baseball bat. I haven't tried it, but it seems like a really good option for someone whose rage is amenable to scheduling.

I remember talking to another woman in recovery who had survived extreme, ritual religious abuse at the hands of her parents. I suggested to her that because of what she had experienced, she might have had a lot of anger that needed to be expressed. She rejected this suggestion, and appeared very determined not to be angry about what had happened to her. It didn't work — she was a passive-aggressive asshole for as long as I knew her.

So if you're mad, let yourself be mad. Don't bypass your emotions and try to pretend that you're not mad, because it's probably obvious to everyone around you that you're mad as hell, or that you should be.

Skipping this part of the healing process keeps people sick, and often that means dependency on the patriarchal medical system. Convenient, isn't it?

Expressing anger, if it's there, is vital to discharging trauma, gaining freedom from the past, and ultimately accessing the internal sense of power that potentially leads to forgiveness.

The meaning of "forgiveness" isn't at all what most people make it out to be — it's not about letting someone "get away" with harm they've caused, or giving up on justice.

In reality, forgiveness is about taking our power back. It's about becoming willing to move forward in life, instead of staying stuck wishing that we could change the past. It's about making the choice to *live*. It means no longer looking to the person who hurt you to make things better. It means accepting the past can't be changed, and being open to finding the power within yourself to move forward in life.

Notice that I didn't say *move on* — I said, *move forward*. We don't have to forgive or forget anything that has happened to us in order to heal. The most important thing is not to forgive, but to find the desire to go on living. Forgiveness can come naturally, in its own time, as a result of this process. It can't be rushed, forced or reverse-engineered. We can only stay open to it arriving in its own time.

Another powerful perspective on forgiveness is that it is only possible when we attain the level of power in our lives that an abuser once had over us. If they still have power over us in any meaningful way, we cannot heal. If we can't heal, we can't forgive.

So, what does it look like to gain power equal or greater to someone who abused you?

For me, this meant claiming my power and right to create the life I wanted. It meant no longer seeing the person who had hurt me as being vital to my future. It meant accepting that he couldn't or wouldn't offer me the healing, the resources, the love or anything else I needed to move forward in life. It meant becoming willing to source all of these things for myself, and believing that I was capable and deserving of doing so.

I still embraced the idea of something bigger than myself, something in the presence of which I could let go completely and just *be*. For me, this needed to mean believing in a source *greater* than the Father, more powerful, more kind and more generous, and inviting it into my life. It meant coming to see that spiritual practices like prayer weren't inherently demeaning — they had only been co-opted from legit women's spiritual traditions and still held immense value for me as long as I was plugging into the right source.

I didn't pray to God; in my desperate moments I called out "Mommy!" instead. The mother is the OG God — embodied and visceral, the origin of all life. Developing this concept of the loving mother I needed as a child, but did not have, helped me regulate my nervous system and integrate my inner child. It meant seeing that it wasn't really "God" who had harmed me, or let me be harmed — it was men, and they were going *against* God. Almost every atrocity on the planet is rooted in the subjugation of mothers and the projection of the Father as God.

Financial abuse is incredibly common in dysfunctional families. Material dependency keeps victims trapped long after they *technically* have the ability to become financially independent from their parents, and keeps them in a perpetually disempowered state because the abuser is their *source*. More often than not, this is the literal father, reinforcing his seeming omnipotence as a God-like figure. When an adult child carries resentment toward a parent, they can latch on even more tightly to any material benefits the relationship brings as compensation for past wrongdoing. The parent is often complicit in this dynamic, enjoying the control it gives them.

I learned so many distorted truths at a neurologically and emotionally vulnerable time in my life, that I later had to unlearn in order to construct an empowering narrative of recovery. In order to heal and build a life for myself, I had to find my own inner feminine and masculine energies, and reparent myself with them. I found the healing I needed in connecting with my own body, and with the spiritual power that flows through it. I found power in honoring myself as the authority in my own life. I became my own God.

And although it wasn't my intention, this is what ultimately freed me from resentment — not because I had let anyone get away with hurting me, but because *I* had gotten away. I survived, and found a way to source what I had depended on others for — emotionally, financially, and otherwise — from within myself.

I discovered that despite all I had been through, I had more than enough resources to create a beautiful life.

There are many people who have had an objectively "better" early start in life than me, but who haven't achieved anywhere near the satisfaction or freedom that I have. Having a great childhood can be a tremendous advantage, but the way things turn out for us has a lot to do with our intentions and determination.

Cosmic justice isn't math — it's magic. Time is an illusion that traps us in regret over the past and fear of the future. But our power is always now, in the present moment.

Letting go of my identity as a victim was the most powerful shift I ever made. For so long, I wanted to appear ill, and I wanted to show others that I was wounded, because I fantasized that someone would rescue me and make it all up to me somehow... But they didn't, and they couldn't. Even I couldn't really do it, without harnessing the power of the universe to co-create something way better than what my early life seemed to have set me up for.

And it's from this empowered place, and only from this place, that I've been able to forgive, because what happened to me is no longer holding me back. The past no longer has power over me. I've heard it said that "the best revenge is a life well-lived," and I have to agree.

Cosmic justice is served to those of us who believe in, and are willing to find, our own inner power. It belongs to those of us who are willing to believe that there is something better out there for us, and that we absolutely fucking deserve it.

This is how I got even with God — by dethroning the false god of my childhood, and crowning myself the goddess of my own existence.

Co-creating with the cosmic and earthly powers that have existed since long before the dawn of patriarchy, we are remaking the world in our image.

The Abused Child to Dysregulated Parent Pipeline

I was a very angry child who didn't know how to express my feelings and boundaries. I secretly hated the other children for being well-loved, and it showed. It wasn't safe for me to express rage toward my parents, so it came out in other ways. I knew that my anger meant that something was deeply wrong, I just had no idea what.

It took nearly thirty years for me to understand my emotional turmoil in the context of an abusive family plagued by alcoholism and mental illness, and many generations of unresolved trauma. I began to see how the anger I'd felt overwhelmed with my entire life was a sign of how often, and deeply, my boundaries had been crossed. I started listening to my anger and building a life that didn't make me feel so mad all the time.

After about five years of healing and learning how to care for myself emotionally, I had a child of my own. Of course, babies don't give a fuck about your boundaries.

I had become accustomed to living alone, and to having the space I needed to accommodate my sensitivities and post-traumatic stress recovery needs. Parenting meant having zero privacy or alone time — my child refused to be left with anyone, and I didn't trust anyone with her, either. Doing the work of the village is taxing on any parent, and this is especially true for those of us with highly sensitive nervous systems. On top of that, I was facing several generations' worth of trauma that had degenerated my life. Having been the one in my ancestral line to reach the breaking point, I was sort of… broken. I was constantly exhausted and thrust back into burnout over and over. In more ways than one, I was not starting the game with a full deck.

My daughter's early years were a strange mix of breaking and repeating cycles as I scrambled to catch up on healing to meet the demands of parenting. She could name her feelings by age three when many kids her age could not, but also watched me struggle with my emotions and trauma in ways that really hurt her. I was at times the best parent I knew, and at others, the worst. At times I felt proud to witness my child thrive in ways I never could have, and at other times I felt ashamed by my inadequacy in areas even my own deeply flawed parents had succeeded.

I quickly discovered that the work of overcoming harmful relational patterns was not going to be finished in a single generation, and that progress wasn't going to be a straight line. Coming to a place of acceptance about where I was in my journey and my limitations in this lifetime brought up a lot of grief. For the parent I wanted to be, the childhood and future my daughter deserved, and the relationship we could have had under different circumstances.

But the positive side to this realization was that I became able to stop being mad about how inadequate I was as a parent, and start embracing the messy, imperfect, not ideal, fucked-up reality of raising a child as a parent with post-traumatic stress.

When I stopped wishing things to be any other way than exactly how they were, my temper became easier to manage.

I found myself being able to take that moment before responding that everyone always advises angry moms to take, but which I had previously always found out of reach.

I found that what I needed in my most vulnerable moments was to *validate* my inner experience — my hurt, my anger, my urge to break every single thing in the house — and that *this* was the magic balm that stopped me from needing to express myself in a destructive way.

Just like a child who is acting harmfully towards others needs to be seen and loved, I also needed to be seen and loved — and I was the one who needed to do it.

I'll add here that I've discussed openly with my child everything I've been able to recognize so far that I've done wrong as a parent. My daughter also feels comfortable telling me when I've screwed up, and does so regularly. At any point in the future, she's welcome to bring up something I did that hurt her, and she'll receive validation and an apology from me. Or maybe she'll just want to write a book about it.

I'm not anywhere near a perfect parent, but being able to initiate and follow through with repair is a legacy I'm proud to pass on.

Warming Up to Red

I used to hate the color Red.

Red was rage.

Red was violence.

Red was danger.

Red was pain.

The heat of it terrified me.

This became a problem when my infant daughter chose red as her favorite color.

I had foolishly thought that she would prefer blues and greens, like I did.

And, hilariously, that raising her would be like sailing in a sensory-soothing ocean.

I felt triggered just by her clothing, which I let her pick out despite my aversion.

But continuously opening my heart toward my child meant opening myself to red, too.

Gradually, I came to see red in a new light.

Red was warmth.

Red was initiation.

Red was defiance.

Red was determination.

Red was fierce protection.

Rage. Warmth. Fierceness. Passion. Danger. Initiation. Protection. Violence. Defiance. Determination.

These all arise from the same fire.

How close to the flame is too close?

How close is close enough?

This is the crucible of those who dare to love after being burned.

Healthy Anger, Mutiny and Murder

A lot of people want to know about healthy ways to release anger. Well, the simple answer is that the healthy way for us to release anger is to express it — to allow ourselves to get mad, to really *be* angry. There is no objectively right or wrong way; even yelling and physical violence can be tools of self-regulation. The only truly unhealthy way to deal with anger is to repress it, and turn it against ourselves.

I get that by "healthy," we mean that we don't want to hurt someone else with our anger who doesn't deserve it. That's legit, especially when we're talking about protecting our kids — but this idea of "healthy" anger expression can often hide shame. Some of us are so caught up in focusing on how to release rage in a way that is palatable to others that we don't do it at all.

Patriarchal programming that tells us it's wrong for women to express anger. This bias against normal, healthy, human emotion suppresses women's voices and stories — and our power to transform our lives and the world. The rage we carry from childhood trauma reveals the absolute horror story of our experience growing up in a nuclear family, and in patriarchy in general, which we must face if we are to do anything about it. The alchemical potential of anger is a medicine those in power don't want us to access.

It's important to separate any shame we have from the anger we feel. When we can fully accept our emotions, they have less power over us. The emotions themselves, and our need to express them, have nothing to do with our worth. Most women need *more* permission to get angry, and to be on a careful lookout for how we might be censoring ourselves in order to make our emotions, our trauma, and the truth of our lives palatable to others.

I will admit I have really not held back in expressing anger in order to heal from post-traumatic stress. I have smashed glassware, plates and electronics. Thrift stores have great deals on plates that can be used for this purpose. I have gone to the woods and broken sticks. I have slammed doors and punched through walls. I have listened to loud, screamy music and screamed so loud myself that the neighbors thought someone was being murdered. I have run for miles and lifted heavy weights to release anger (be careful with this, though — over-exercising can be harmful, and easily become another way to take anger out on ourselves).

Of course, there are more socially acceptable pathways for anger expression. I recommended that a client of mine keep sticks at the office to break under his desk because his rage was often triggered by co-workers, and he hasn't punched his boss since. There are batting cages, punching bags, punching pillows, rage rooms, and rage cleaning. You can press hard on a wall with all of your strength until you feel the energy move out of your body (also a great way to ground when you're dissociating).

You can channel all that fire into starting a creative project, making big life changes, or staging a mutiny. Okay — insurrection may not be "socially acceptable," but you can't please everyone! Trying to make everyone else happy is what got you into this mess in the first place.

A therapist of mine once recommended that I write an angry letter to someone who had wronged me, but not send the letter. I was unimpressed — the idea of "angry letter" wasn't quite enough to unlock the full power of my rage. Years later, when I gave myself permission to write down in detail how I'd murder the person who had harmed me, and then burned the paper, I finally felt satisfied.

Do what works for you, and try to worry less about what other people think about your feelings than about your real and valid need to discharge these energies from your body.

Every action has an equal and opposite reaction — it's not your fault; it's science.

It's Not Just Your Trauma – It's Truth

The problem with a lot of spiritual terms that are thrown around in the personal growth scene is that their original meanings and value have been tarnished by patriarchal religion. This can lead people to feel even worse about themselves than before they embarked on their journey of self-discovery, less powerful and less capable and deserving of self-trust.

I experienced this in addiction recovery programs, where religious language — even when disguised as spiritually "neutral" — is frequently used to pressure vulnerable people into becoming better cogs in the machine instead of supporting them to take steps toward their liberation. I saw many people put down the bottle just to pick up the equally numbing habit of religion, instead of addressing the underlying trauma that made them feel empty and wanting in the first place. Faith and spirituality can be beautiful, but when they don't lead us to greater trust, love and connection with ourselves, we have to ask whose agenda they serve.

It's especially unfortunate that so many resources for trafficking and child sexual abuse survivors are religion-based. It is great if faith motivates a person to make a difference in the world, but pushing institutionalized religion on a traumatized population is shamefully opportunistic — not to mention, religion is part of the reason there is such a demand for sex abuse victims to begin with, thanks to the Madonna/whore dichotomy that makes some women "wife material" and sets others aside to fulfill men's darker fantasies. The church knows that targeting people at their most vulnerable points in life — recovering addicts, low-income single moms, homeless people — works, because desperate people tend to latch onto whatever provides relief in the moment.

The other problem with predatory institutions knowing your vulnerabilities is that it makes you easier to gaslight. If you have a trauma history, many people will use it against you.

Want a relationship? Must be your trauma. Don't? Trauma.

Want to travel? It's your trauma. Homebody? Trauma.

Hurt feelings? Just your trauma. Don't give a fuck? Trauma.

Never being taken seriously becomes a whole other level of trauma.

Sounds a lot like psychological abuse? *Relax, it's probably just your trauma.*

How about some real empowerment instead of more patriarchal bullshit that keeps women stuck in survival mode?

I didn't just want to "recover" from alcoholism — I wanted to create a world in which escape from reality was no longer necessary. This has meant trusting my perceptions and intuition, and taking needs, wants, and feelings seriously. It has meant not letting others use my past against me in order to keep me living in the shadow of my potential. It has meant believing myself worthy of having a vision — and having the support to make it real.

I'm here to provide resources, encouragement, customized strategy and a little magic for women who have been through hell, and want to create a Second Childhood that makes it all up to them, and then some. You didn't escape that toxic relationship — or your entire family — just to take abuse from your boss and help *their* dreams come true, did you?

It's okay to feel grateful for the chance to survive at all. It's okay to be happy just to be free of the worst of what life has to offer, and to not mind the little things so much — maybe after what you've been through, *everything* else feels like details by comparison. But it's also okay if your heart is calling for more.

If you want a meaningful life on your own terms, leading with your values, your wisdom, your body and your wholeness, trust that it's meant for you. If you know you're meant to do more than just make it through life, even if you're not yet sure what exactly you're here to do, I hope you'll stick with yourself long enough to find out.

The Virtuous Woman is Sovereign

World religions, laws, mainstream parenting philosophies, education systems, medical systems, all teach that being and doing "good" means giving away our power as women.

But living virtuously always leads to sovereignty — never subjugation.

The central toxic teaching of religion is that God is "out there" somewhere, and as a woman, you're just a sack of shit who would be lucky for him to fart in your general direction. This is the message I received in recovery programs. Instead of being encouraged to find out what I really wanted from life and to feel better about who I was as a person, I was tasked with making endless lists of my "shortcomings" and essentially repenting for having been the cause of all my own difficulties in life. Once, when I was in the thick of this "inner work" at a café, I overheard a male sponsor talking with his male sponsee about stock options. For fuck's sake, I realized, I'm on the wrong track!

There are many people in these programs who have a kinder perspective toward women in recovery, but the explicitly patriarchal language of the literature — and of most members — overshadows those voices, which are largely limited to whispers and private conversations. Many women haven't found this to be enough of a problem to stop them from participating, but it felt too psychologically damaging for me to stick around.

My family attended church when I was little, but more for the social aspects than out of any real religious convictions. My mother was actually an atheist, and my father had grown up Catholic. I just liked the cookies and tea, which I would fill with as many sugar cubes as possible without attracting the attention of the old ladies who guarded the post-sermon snack table — the altar where the ritual chemical high was served as a substitute for the joyful, empowered embodiment prohibited by religion.

Any patriarchal society has quasi-religious ideas, because mind control, dissociation, and reversals are so central to their functioning, but Alcoholics Anonymous was my first *real* immersion in religion. Every latent seed of patriarchal religious thinking that had been planted in me was suddenly brought to the surface like an invasive plant bloom. That wasn't all bad, as it gave me opportunities to heal. But I found it really hard to find other people to heal *with*. People who were supportive of me reclaiming my power as a woman were very much the exception.

When you believe that God is a power that exists *only* outside of you, you have no power to define your own worth or standards. This codependency benefits people who want to have power over you, by triggering your attachment trauma and replacing your role in what would ideally be a healthy relationship with your inner child. Your spirituality can either liberate you from abuse, or it can tie you to trauma bonds that keep you small.

Women don't need God to recover from addiction, raise our children well or find our purpose in life. We need emotional, intellectual, physical, sexual, spiritual and financial sovereignty, and we need each other.

The Mother-Hating Cult of Non-Attachment

Many who reject organized religion opt in to traditions such as Stoicism or Buddhism that outwardly appear to offer a less patriarchal alternative, but are just as male-centric under the surface.

First of all, Buddhism is very much a patriarchal religion with oodles of rules for nuns (women) that don't apply to monks (men). Buddha himself with his giant belly is a rip-off of pregnant women, whose wisdom is undermined in favor of worshipping a male deity. This reversal, typical of patriarchal religion, is much more than symbolic — it provides the foundation for men's social control over women and children.

The ethos of "non-attachment" in many of these philosophies is particularly toxic. While any tool that helps us release unhealthy attachments or addictions may be useful, failing to recognize the root cause of these problems keeps us looped into the same patriarchal bullshit.

When a child's emotional needs are met through a strong and reliable bond with their mother, they don't get attached to all manner of random objects, identities or people. A child with secure attachment does not grow into an adult who pursues emotional security through money, sex, prestige, or another human being. Growing up with secure attachment means you *already have* emotional security, and as a result, can approach work, relationships and other things in life with balance.

On the other hand, a person who brings childhood attachment wounds and traumas into adult life will be vulnerable to addiction and excess, often pursuing money, sex, prestige, and relationships with the exact same desperation with which a child seeks connection with their mother. When we don't get our emotional needs met as children, we are always on the lookout for someone or something to fill that void. The unrelenting search reflects a yearning for the maternal bond, with inappropriate attachments becoming a stand-in for the developmentally necessary dependency thwarted in childhood. The projection moves from one object or person or identity to another, each failing to live up to the fantasy because the love of a mother is not so easily replaced.

Without understanding the root cause of unhealthy fixations, "attachment" itself appears to be the problem — not the severing of the mother/child bond by patriarchal institutions. Rather than discerning healthy attachment from unhealthy attachment, and the connection between the two, the solution of these male-centric philosophies is to reject attachment altogether. This mimics the patriarchal religious narrative that humans are just inherently sinful, framing struggles with attachment as an inevitable part of life rather than recognizing them as symptoms of trauma inflicted en masse by patriarchy itself.

In denying the vital role of maternal attachment in human development, these philosophies deeply undermine the value of mothers and women to society, and conveniently position men as leaders — intellectually, spiritually, and emotionally — in the family and in the world. This approach also undermines the value of close interpersonal relationships in all stages of life. Secure adult attachments can even support the healing of developmental traumas, such as when someone with insecure attachment partners with someone who has secure attachment.

As flawed as they may be, part of the reason these philosophies take hold is that they offer something people need. Just as many women alcoholics take refuge in Christianity — learning to characterize the divinity they discover within as a male spiritual entity — proponents of Stoicism or Buddhism may truly find the necessary strength to sever unhealthy attachments and develop secure attachment with themselves, albeit under the guise of "non-attachment." However, these solutions come with an agenda that disconnects us from essential aspects of our humanity and ultimately disempowers us.

While meditation can be safe and useful under the right conditions, a secure developmental attachment relationship prevents the need for the immense amount of self-reflection and mind-clearing that many adults in spiritual circles seem to habitually engage in. With secure attachment, we are not wandering around as lost souls looking for something to complete us, and we are not vulnerable to all of the conditioning that leaves junk for us to purge later on. If religion didn't destroy the mother/child bond to begin with, it couldn't come along later offering what appears to be the solution.

Neglecting to address problematic attachment at the root does nothing to prevent the next generation from having the same problems. How could a woman who thinks attachment is the root of all evil offer secure attachment to her child? If a man thinks mothers have no role in shaping the emotional health of a child, what kind of parent or partner would he become? What kind of judge, social worker, teacher, boss or therapist would anyone be, when put in the position to play either a supporting or antagonistic role in a child's development?

We can't solve problems created by religion and other forms of male domination by throwing more patriarchy at them.

It's not just the tools we use to heal that matter — the story we tell about them can either support our collective liberation or dig us a deeper hole. It's important to recognize that our attachment wounds came from patriarchy, and it's important to recognize where *we* came from: women.

Choose Your Reality, But Use Your Brain

One of the hardest things I had to deal with in the recovery community — and in life — was my decision to be estranged from my biological family. When I confided in a sponsor that I was considering going no-contact with my parents, she was adamantly *not* supportive. According to everything she had heard in her twenty years in the program, recovery was about "reuniting the family" rather than amplifying divisions within it. Again, this is great advice for someone who has singlehandedly ruined otherwise healthy relationships with their drinking — not so great advice for a survivor of extreme child abuse.

This is one of the many ways spiritual- and religious-based recovery programs blame survivors, and subtly and not-so-subtly perpetuate patriarchal power structures and the interpersonal abuse that characterizes them.

Here's another common bullshit take on family dysfunction: "When we heal, we heal all of our ancestors, too." Now, if my relatives had all healed when I did, I wouldn't have had to distance myself from them in order to spare myself further abuse and protect my child. And if we are only talking about deceased ancestors, then who cares? That doesn't help anyone who's still struggling here on Earth.

Magical thinking is rife in spiritual circles because of how desperately people are searching for answers and because it feels safer to escape reality instead of facing it. But we cannot change that which we are not willing to face, personally or collectively. Abuse and addiction don't happen in a vacuum — they are symptoms of a sick society, namely, patriarchy. Individual healing can only go so far without restoring balance on a larger scale.

Another way that religion and New Age spirituality invalidate abuse survivors and perpetuates oppressive systems is by claiming that we choose our traumas in life before we are born, and that "everything happens for a reason." These are rarely helpful things for a person to hear, who has likely already tried blaming themselves and minimizing their pain to make it go away.

While it's undoubtedly a really powerful and beautiful thing to overcome the existential crisis caused by developmental trauma, it's important to recognize that when we do this, *we are the magic* — not the bad things that happened to us. Otherwise, what would be our reason for living our adult lives any differently from how we were raised?

The belief that we are responsible for having been abused as children is driven entirely by emotion, not logic. Would we intentionally harm our children so that they could discover their gifts, or so that they could help others who had been through the same thing? These are common "spiritual" justifications for abuse. If we wouldn't do it on purpose to "help" someone else, then logically we can't justify others doing it to us. When our minds are so desperately grasping for reasons *why* bad things have happened to us that we are not able to sit with ourselves and others in our pain, we are avoiding, not ascending. The only sustainable solution is to descend into the body, honor our grief and anger, and hold other people accountable for their actions.

The saying, "reality is nothing more than your perception" is also quite popular in spiritual circles. While I believe that manifestation is real, I do not believe that we can control everything that happens in our lives, nor that reality is an entirely subjective experience of the mind. We do have enormous and usually untapped creative potential, and we do choose how we respond to things that happen to us (although our choices are often limited, especially as children), but my logical brain draws the line at other people being figments of our imagination. We all make choices that impact one another, and to say that one person creates all of reality on their own negates every other person's agency and therefore the possibility of anyone creating anything.

Objective reality exists, and other people exist, and to argue otherwise reveals the developmentally stunted mindset characteristic of a person with unmet narcissistic needs. When a child has received all of the nourishment they need, they grow into an adult who can give and take on an equal basis with others. "Spiritual narcissism," or any kind of narcissism, is often the consequence of interrupted emotional development, where a person's apparent exaggerated sense of self-importance and tendency toward domination and avoidance reflects a childhood bereft of attunement and secure attachment. An unmet need for safety and significance doesn't disappear with age — it just puts on a flowy robe, rebrands as a guru, and opens a retreat center.

There is such obvious desperation in the attempt to control the uncontrollable. The truth is that we are not always in control of everything that happens to us, and doing things "right" in life doesn't guarantee us anything. We can't vibrate out of this realm by becoming more spiritually evolved. There is no such thing as immunity to the human experience. No matter how much personal growth you accomplish, you still have to deal with all the bullshit — you just get to do it differently.

The need to attribute everything to a spiritual cause is a poor substitute for empathy and relationship skills. In fact, addiction to spirituality is often a substitute for relational skills that were not modeled in one's early life. If a child's parents didn't show a child empathy, nurturing, attunement or responsiveness, how would they learn to show these to others? It's easier as an adult to withdraw and dissociate, and to blame the victim, just as a person might have dissociated from their own pain and blamed themselves as a child. This would not be so common in a world where we truly valued motherhood and the maternal attachment bond that supports children in developing healthy functioning nervous systems. Building our capacity as adults to experience and express the full landscape of our emotions, connect with our inner child and integrate our traumas also helps us learn to relate to others with maturity, respect and sensitivity.

Part of my healing journey has been realizing that the abuse I've experienced had nothing to do with me. The meaning I ended up making from it was simply that it *didn't* mean anything about me. This perspective has been so freeing, because I've been liberated from the illusion that if I'm only spiritually developed enough, I can prevent experiencing misfortune in life. I really started rebelling against a lot of internalized religious dogma when I realized that. I gave myself a break from trying to be perfect or even more spiritually evolved, and started playing more video games and doing other things that I had been programmed to think were bad or wrong or lazy or weak. In being kinder to myself, I've actually attracted *more* positive experiences and opportunities. This is an example of how changing my beliefs — in this case, the belief that certain hobbies would ruin my life — changed my life. We don't manifest based on how deserving we are by some objective measure of our habits; we manifest based on the meaning we make of them.

The truth is that the world is at least a half-fucked-up place and you're going to experience that sometimes. It's not necessarily your fault or a reflection of your internal state. You can definitely attract more positive experiences to yourself by attuning your vibration to what you desire, but bad things will always happen to good people. To spiritual people. We can have compassion for others, instead of blaming them for all of their problems. Sure, many things *are* people's own fault, but not *everything* — otherwise, this would mean each individual person is in control of the entire world. How would that make sense? It's important to have compassion for how other people live and how other people deal with their problems, because we can't really know what we would do in someone else's shoes. If you were someone else, you'd likely be doing exactly what they are doing, by definition, which is why the world is exactly the way it is right now and not some other way.

However, as adults, we do create a lot of our own experience of reality — more of it than we have been conditioned to think, and more of it than our nervous systems may currently be equipped to handle. Manifestation is made to seem really complicated when it literally works just by changing what you say *yes* and *no* to. That's largely an inside job (and a big one), but it's not "creating reality with your mind" so much as it is shifting what parts of reality you resonate and engage with. One of the reasons why we might not feel that we have much control over our lives is that as children, usually someone else was in control of us. Many of our parents were strict and domineering, or unable to allow us as much freedom and fulfillment of our desires as they would have liked. Manifesting in captivity is a tall order. Expecting a child to have "chosen differently" to avoid being hurt by others in a position of power over them is nonsensical. When our wings are clipped, we have less power. The nuclear family is designed that way — not by children, but by adults.

Reclaiming our creative sovereignty as adults means facing all the ways we were denied power as children, and allowing ourselves to grieve and to find our way home to ourselves as co-creators in our own lives. We don't need to take responsibility for being born or being hurt in order to create meaningful lives after a challenging past. What matters is that we choose ourselves and our lives *now* — trauma, failure, loss and all.

Stripped Down and in Love with Life

People are obsessed with romantic love because they don't know how to fall in love with life. But we can source sexual, life-giving energy from within ourselves with no one else around. The spirit of playfulness is the same frequency as being in love with life — and I really mean *in* love, not just love. When I talk about self-love I don't strictly mean self-pleasure, although that can definitely be part of it. I am talking about the kind of everyday enchantment that can manufacture the sensations and chemicals of being in love with no one else involved.

Joy, play, and pleasure are available to us in every moment, if we want them.

Imagine it… you're texting an attractive person who says all the right things. The funniest things. Or, whatever makes you feel more alive and more turned on. You can use your imagination to channel this powerful, connected, energized feeling anytime. You can also imagine all the other things your ideal romantic partner would do for you, and do them for yourself.

This can be a powerful path to reclaiming your sexual power, and finding your power in all areas of life.

One of the best things I ever did was to sunbathe topless in a public park. It wouldn't have been any better if I'd done it in a private backyard, because part of the magic was noticing how *powerful* I felt in what most would consider objectively vulnerable circumstances. It was like the connection between my soul, my naked breasts and the sun formed a force field around me, and I had no fear. Someone even came up and yelled at me, and I just laughed. I felt invincible.

I realized how much all of the rules and laws around covering my body actually *made* me fearful, because they led me to cover myself from a place of fear. I'm definitely not saying that female nudity is always empowering or that it never involves exploitation. I'm saying that there is a strength women can access when there is nothing standing between us and the elements. Rooting into nature, we align with a creative life force energy beyond our individual capacity.

I will also add that where I was at the time, it was legal for a woman to be topless in public, but it's not at all necessary to do this in a public place in order to feel the power of it. However, it does make you question why the law doesn't want us being topless in public, when it can be so beneficial, and when it's almost universally allowed for men to feel the sun on their bare chests when they damn well please.

Women's bodies are sexualized as being "distracting" to men and public female nudity is seen to pose a threat to the sanctity of marriage, to the value a woman supposedly holds when she has remained unseen and untouched by other men, and to whatever special feelings a man has when granted exclusive access to a woman's naked body. Covering our bodies also prevents us from accessing our own inner wilderness and the power that connects us with, and that is no coincidence.

Most political debates over women's bodies comprise two sides: men who want women to be kept as property by one single man for her entire life, and men who want women to be the property of *multiple* men, or *all* men, throughout her life. One side fights for laws that make it more difficult for women to survive without husbands, and the other fights for laws that make it more difficult for women to survive without selling our bodies to the general public. Many times, these are the same laws, and in no case are they truly empowering for women.

As women, giving our energy to patriarchal partisan bickering over whether men should each have exclusive access to one woman's body or whether men should collectively be allowed shared access to women's bodies, we forget the only point of view that respects our right to exist independently of men's sexual desires and preferences: that as women, our bodies are *ours, and ours alone*.

Because we are sexualized by men from such a young age, it's very rare for women to have the opportunity to know ourselves sexually without the objectifying lens of the male gaze. But our sexuality is *our* power, to discover, to cherish and to employ as we wish. It is vital that we develop a connection with our bodies and our sexuality independently of other people's preferences and desires. It's never too late to fall in love with ourselves and with life, and to empower the next generation of girls to do the same.

Welcome to the Fertile Universe

When you find yourself in a dark place, remember that up to 99% of our bodies and our universe is made of dark matter — also known as Dark Mater (from the Latin *mater*, meaning "mother"), or the Dark Mother — and that you are being held in the womb from which all creation is born: the Fertile Universe.

Tune into the frequency of possibility that surrounds all of us and everything, and receive her warmth and wisdom. Those empty spaces on your canvas, your bank account and your inbox are not empty at all — they are *fertile ground*. Allow yourself to be nurtured through the darkness until you emerge into the light.

The in-between places don't have to feel so bad, or like something to rush through, when you feel at home in the womb of possibility.

Faith can be wonderful, but it isn't a particularly earthbound concept — and it's been shaped by millennia of patriarchal bias into a tool of oppression.

In male-centric religions, faith connotes a limitless possibility where boundaries either do not exist or are not respected. This is the kind of thinking behind unsustainable resource extraction, *manifest destiny* and imperialism, commitment to growth at any cost, the sexual exploitation of women and girls, and unpaid or underpaid labor. The "whatever it takes to get what I want, because God is on my side" kind of thinking that got humanity into the mess we are facing now.

The female-centric equivalent of faith is fertility. The Fertile Universe is another way of conceptualizing possibility, where the language of "fertility" grounds the potential for creating abundance firmly into our bodies and the body of the Earth, which, along with the sun, is the source of pretty much every material thing we could want or need in life.

The Fertile Universe isn't *out there* in the sky somewhere, or an invisible force separate from us — it flows within and through us and all other living beings and the Earth itself. It is the soil, it is our bodies, it is the sun, it is what we can experience directly with our senses.

The grounded language of fertility reminds us that there *are* limits to what we can achieve in life, but that these aren't bad — these boundaries are actually the points of connection between ourselves and others, and between humans and the natural world that give life meaning.

These boundaries are often not where we have been taught they are, and the Fertile Universe is about embracing possibility where we falsely perceive limitations. Enchantment with possibility organically arises from a nurturing developmental connection with a mother figure — the more she responds positively to us, the more we internalize the belief that our desires matter and that what we want is possible.

Coming into a conscious relationship with the Fertile Universe can help us heal the spiritual and emotional wounds we inherited from not being raised by a responsive caregiver, which might show up as tension in our muscles or feelings of depression. Imagining that we are surrounded by soft, fertile Earth or a loving mother figure can help us feel more worthy of our desires, more connected to our personal power, and more connected to our creativity.

The Fertile Universe is the same universe in which faith operates, but it focuses our minds on the practical wisdom of lived experience and embodied knowledge as well as the interconnected nature of all life and the Earth itself. While proponents of faith often don't take *no* for an answer, because "God said so," the Fertile Universe teaches us to value a *no* as much as a *yes*. The Universe, just like women and all of nature, is not always fertile, welcoming and supportive — she can also be hostile, barren, and unequivocally "closed for business."

The Fertile Universe values enthusiastic consent and mutually beneficial relationships and agreements. In this way of navigating our personal and collective power, "winning" is not a zero-sum game. There is always a win-win if we are willing to commit to finding one, even if it's a longer and more challenging path.

Through our connection to the Fertile Universe, we release control and attachment to outcomes. When an idea or project does not find fertile ground, we can accept this, surrendering to creativity and abundance with a playful spirit and the willingness to use our imagination to find another way.

Unlike New Age thinking that perpetuates the status quo with vague dogma about unlimited growth, the philosophy of the Fertile Universe acknowledges and celebrates the existence of the other, as well as our connection and interdependence. According to this philosophy, an idea can be judged by its impact in practical terms, and on real human lives, rather than on how righteous it seems in the abstract. Once an idea is implemented, once its expression is seen and felt, its value — or lack thereof — becomes apparent.

In a literal sense, this means submitting to the authority of women who are attuned to the requirements of sustainable relationship with ourselves, other humans and the landbase.

The decolonized female body is a trustworthy moral compass and a world-class bullshit detector.

Spinning Shit into Gold

One of the reasons I've done so many unconventional things in life is because I've learned how to alchemize depression into a goldmine of inspiration.

On the darkest days, I'm asking myself, "What would make it worth it for me to keep on going? What would have to be true for me to be excited to show up for life today?" And then whatever that is, I do whatever it takes to make it my reality.

This has meant doing things like following a hurricane to support relief efforts, giving it all up to go live in the forest, and taking decisive action to increase my income when I was tired of being broke.

I once carved a 50-pound turtle out of stone and then rode my bike 2000 km through a foreign country to metabolize the pain of a broken heart. Hell, I can probably trace half of my hobbies back to some neanderthal I met at a house party in 2005.

Each of these things has made me feel alive again at times when I've felt deeply unhappy and lost. So, while small things can affect my mood, the upside is being inspired to live bigger and better.

Sensitivity is not 'mental illness' — it's an asset. I have led an exceptional life because I have exceptional standards for how my life feels, and because I have a creative practice of spinning shit into gold.

So when all hope is lost, good! Now the real fun can begin.

Playing on Purpose

Play is commonly thought of as something that only children do — even though much of the time, children are prevented from doing it! It's probably for this reason that adults often have both negative associations with the concept of play, while at the same time being in dire need of it.

We have received the message since we were little that there are more important things to do besides playing, and have likely dedicated much of our lives to these things, believing that play is something we will be rewarded with when we retire and (hypothetically) have the money to play in the socially acceptable ways.

Over the years, this ideology leaves us with depression, anxiety, chronic illness, failing relationships and a connection to our own embodied joy so threadbare that it wouldn't qualify for use as a dishrag. And that is if we are lucky, because many people don't begin questioning this prison workhouse mentality until they reach the end of their lives or end up blowing their retirement savings on hospital bills and realize this "work first, play later" shit was a total scam.

To be honest, I have always been a playful person. But there was a tipping point for me where I had to take a stronger stance in favor of it. My first Saturn return at age 27 hit hard. With my natal Saturn in the 5th house, this was bound to be a transformative time in my life with regard to play.

In my late 20's, I trashed my body so badly at a very physically demanding job that I never worked a regular job again. I had been pushing and pushing myself at work until one day I began staring off into space, and found that I could not stop. I could not even speak. My body basically quit for me. I walked out, went home and lay in bed for three months.

Even up until the point of near-collapse, I honestly *liked* the feeling of rushing around and the feeling of importance around being so busy. My sense of worth was so tightly wound with my productivity and it dovetailed neatly with the terror I felt around being still with myself. Along with my high sensitivity, this was the perfect recipe for burnout.

My exhaustion wasn't just personal. In the context of capitalistic labor exploitation, a chronically dysregulated workforce is both the result and the fuel for unsustainable resource extraction. Once I could see this bigger picture, I understood that it was no virtue to keep going — there was no meaning in proving how "tough" I was, and my body proved me otherwise anyway.

In my workaholism recovery, I started considering possibilities like these:

What if play is just as important for grown-ups as it is for children?

What if being playful isn't childish, immature or irresponsible?

What if I am worthy now of all the joy, pleasure and freedom I desire?

What if life, work and relationships are all at their best when done in a spirit of playfulness?

What if play itself is our ticket out of the misery we have created?

What if play is the magical frequency that can unlock the joy we want for ourselves, right here and now?

Working all day doing things we don't enjoy might serve the bottom line, but it doesn't nourish our souls or help us build a better world. Daring to play opens the door to purpose, wisdom and alignment with our unique role in the evolution of humanity.

Play brings abundance, bonding, happiness, and creativity from the most authentic place inside of us. As such, playfulness is one of the most important forms of intelligence we can access, and it is available to all of us regardless of age.

If we want more joy, connection, and freedom in our lives, we don't need to work for them. The best way to get them is to *play* for them. So if you do nothing else today, find a way to play — it will be time well spent.

The Art of Playing

Having a sad beige adulthood instead of a full-color Second Childhood?

The trick to brightening up our lives is by *playing*.

This might seem like a sensible place to offer a definition of *play*, but I find it much more fun and interesting to notice what comes up for myself and for others when we think of play — and when we do it — and letting the concept of play itself be something that we *play* with.

Play can mean so many different things, for example:

Trying on a new identity or role

Trying on a new perspective or belief

Flirting with life

Being vulnerable

Being open to new ideas

Trying something new

Resisting pressure

Doing something for fun

Doing something joyful

Participating without knowing the outcome

Expressing yourself freely

Giving freely

Travel

Trusting in ourselves

Additionally, asking yourself, "What would I attempt if I knew nothing could go wrong?" Or, "What would delight my inner child right now?" are great ways to begin playing.

When I think of play, I think about engaging with others, with objects, and with the universe itself in a way that leaves room for the unexpected.

If the idea of play feels off-putting to us, we can playfully question our ideas and conditioning around it — transforming not just our relationship with play, but with ourselves, others, and our work. Approaching play with a spirit of playfulness, there's no wrong way to play and it's never too late to begin.

A Play Date with Transformation

One of my favorite things about play is the way we can expand the possibilities for our lives by using our imagination to try on new identities. Play can create powerful shifts in our lives thanks to the role that our psyche plays in determining what version of reality we are available for. Changing what is happening in our minds can attune us to a different frequency in the outside world that we would not otherwise have been aware of or had access to.

This is why children's play is so important — kids learn about the world and invent themselves through play, becoming comfortable with who they are and who they want to be by practicing. It's never too late for us to do this!

Play is a wonderful way to access our subconscious mind, where our most deeply-held beliefs are stored, and where most of the behavior patterns that make up our personalities originate. When we use play to integrate new beliefs on this deep level, we can show up in a new way in our lives, work and relationships and virtually transform our whole experience of reality. Play can reveal to us what we *really* believe about ourselves, and about life, and create opportunities for us to choose which beliefs are worth holding onto. Play is also valuable in its own right — it nourishes our inner child!

Your whole life can change from a simple, honest *no* uttered spontaneously in a pretend scenario where you're role-playing with friends. Speaking alters our vibration, and when we shift our vibration, things around us begin to shift, too. Sometimes transformation doesn't take time — it takes courage. When you can trust yourself to honor your desires and not to settle for less, you'll be able to trust the Fertile Universe to support you. Play can help you be the one to move first, so that you're setting the tone for what you want in life.

If you're new to playing as an adult, one option is to sign up for an improv class at your local theater (if you have one, otherwise there are online groups you can join). Improv classes can be great because everybody gets to participate; it's very inclusive. There's less vulnerability because everybody has signed up for the specific purpose of playing with other adults. There's still vulnerability in it, but at least you know everybody there is there for the same reason.

Not only is it fun to create characters and scenes directly from our imagination, and to interact with other adults in a lighthearted atmosphere, but improvisational play is also a great way to try on new identities and ways of being in the world that we might not feel comfortable acting out anywhere else.

With that said, you might find the "rules" of traditional improv restrictive and more conducive to performance rather than transformation. Another issue is that classes are made up of all the same people who exist in the outside world, so the same problems we have with them "out there" can come into play on stage. These instances can either become opportunities for transformation or reinforce oppressive social and cultural dynamics, depending on the philosophy and intention of the teacher.

For example, improv teachers taught me to always say "yes, and…" but as one of only a few women in a room of mostly male players, I landed in some shitty pretend situations that made me question this dogma. In one scene, I was *actually* smothered by a participant in the class, who pressed his jacket down tightly over my face. In another, I was forced to pretend to procreate with "the last man on Earth." Our teacher insisted that my resistance in these scenarios was "just a trauma symptom" and that there was nothing wrong with the way things were going down on stage.

My experiences in the theater were often lacking in safety and agency, when improv was *supposed* to be about fun and creativity. The truth is that when we are *always* saying *yes*, we disrespect ourselves and our inner *no*. Boundaries are important, especially for women. Living in a patriarchal society, we have to allow ourselves to say *no* in order to grow personally and to effect change in our lives and in the world. The theater can either be a great place for us to practice this, or just another setting where we reenact the status quo.

In real life, and in any improv class run by yours truly, we are allowed to say "no, but…" — and we have just as much of a playful, creative, and transformative experience, if not more so, because of it.

Playing with Strangers

There's other ways to play with people besides signing up for a class. If you have people in your life that you feel safe enough to play with — such as your kids or trusted adults — that can be just as good, if not better.

Then, there's "playing with strangers."

Think about how easy it is to make friends as children. You just say, "Do you want to play?" and the other kid goes, "Yeah, sure." Or maybe, "No thanks," and then you go ask someone else. Adults generally don't go around asking each other to play, and I don't necessarily recommend using the specific phrase, "Do you want to play with me?"

It takes some work to be brave enough to ask because you might be rejected or misunderstood. Once, I asked a friend if she wanted to meet up at the park and do cartwheels. She was like, "Totally, sure!" So we got to the park and I started doing cartwheels, and she was just standing there, looking at me really strangely. She was like, "I didn't know you meant *literally* doing cartwheels at the park." I guess she thought I was joking.

It would probably have helped if I'd provided some context in my invitation: "I'm trying to get in touch with my inner child so that I can have more fun in life. Do you feel like doing cartwheels at the park with me, or something else playful and silly?" Communicating clearly about our needs and desires can be scary and definitely takes practice, but it helps us build trust with ourselves because self-advocacy makes our inner child feel cared for, even if we don't get what we want right away.

One day at the park, I saw a little girl shouting at her baby brother, who was singing the ABCs. She threw a soft plastic ball at him, and said to her mother, "You're supposed to be playing catch with *me*." I could see the mother about to lose her patience. I turned to the girl and I said, "Do you want to play catch with me?" She looked at me kind of funny for a second, but then was like, "Yeah." And so I just stood there with her while the mother tended to the baby and we played catch together until her mother said it was time for them to go. That brief encounter totally reinvigorated my spirit of play — I left feeling very much alive, and like I could do anything.

It might take a mindset shift for you to do something like this, because playing — especially as an adult — requires vulnerability. If you're convinced there's nobody to play with where you live, you might actually be remembering how it felt as a child to have no one to play with. Or, you could be trying to protect yourself from perceived embarrassment or shame or fear of rejection, or maybe anxiety about someone thinking you're creepy. And of course I'm not suggesting that anyone actually *be* creepy, or force their way into an encounter, especially with a child — but if your intentions are pure, people will feel it in your energy.

So are you willing to be vulnerable? Are you willing to ask? Are you willing to play? Because playing means you don't know the outcome ahead of time. It's a vulnerable place to be — there are no guarantees, and that is the magic of it. Are you willing to attune to the frequency of play? If not, what challenges do you find attuning to the frequency of play? Do you have trauma around playfulness? Are there certain people you like to be playful with, or don't? Are there times when you see other people being playful that you'd like to join in, but you don't for some reason? What's going on for you in those moments? These are questions to consider with a mindful, gentle presence and whatever nervous system regulation tools you find most supportive.

Another time, I was riding my bike and a guy asked me if he could hop on the back. I said, "Sure." In this situation, someone else had invited me to play. At the time I had colored feathers hanging off my bicycle so I may have looked somewhat approachable, or up for a good time. I remember later feeling horrified about this bicycle with colored feathers on it, not wanting to draw attention to myself and removing them all in a frenzy one day. We go through cycles or moods where we feel like playing and feel like showing our playful side to the world, and there are times when we don't. And it's all okay.

I used to always have this dilemma when buying clothes. I would always immediately be attracted to something bright, with colorful, busy patterns. And then a few weeks later, I would feel like it was all a bit much. So the next time, I'd just get plain black shoes — boring, but go with everything and won't draw any attention to me. And I would go back and forth between these extremes, thinking I had to pick one consumer identity, and stick to it. It never occurred to me that I could have *two* pairs of shoes — one to wear when I was feeling playful and vibrant and bold, and another to wear when I was feeling more withdrawn and private, or just needing to feel the presence of my stable adult self more strongly and to lean on that energy. So now I allow myself to have it all, even though I travel full-time and live out of suitcases. I'm always maxing out my baggage allowance — it's the price I pay for a happy inner child.

We can also play with people in our peripheral network — exchanging banter with the butcher, laughing with the cheesemonger over spilled milk, paying a genuine compliment to the attendant at the train station — to make our daily lives more fun and hopefully make someone else's work day more enjoyable, too. Of course, it's different than playing with strangers because you are guaranteed to see these people again, but as scary as that may be, it can bring the enjoyment to a whole new level. Playing with strangers can give us the courage to play with people closer to us. But maybe it's the opposite for you — as a 5th line personality in Human Design, I'm here to impact and be impacted by strangers, so that is my comfort zone.

Astrocartography and Human Design can also give us clues as to where in the world we are most likely to find people to play with in ways that we enjoy. For example, I found that living on my Neptune line brings me a lot of wonderfully playful interactions, which makes sense because I have Venus in Pisces, and Pisces is ruled by Neptune. Adding the lens of Human Design takes it to a whole new level I won't get into here, but the gist is that my love language is defined by playfulness, creativity and imagination, which explains why play is so important to me in relationships. Whatever your love language, there is nothing like the experience of living where people speak it to you!

Play connects us to our creative power and is the key to unlocking new possibilities in our lives. Play can unfreeze our nervous systems and release stuck energies and identities, making way for the lives we really want and that will feel good to us.

Aside from manifesting our dream lives, playing with other people can help us manifest fun new relationships with the people who indulge in it with us. Playing with strangers in whatever way feels light and fun to us can also be something we enjoy just for the moment, even (and often, especially) without it turning into something "more."

You can play with yourself, you can play with others, you can take a class or find people out in the wild — it doesn't matter how you do it, just find a way to play that delights your inner child.

From Victim to Visionary

The opposite of victim isn't victor — it's visionary. When you regain your capacity to imagine a brighter future for yourself and for the world, you win.

I have had enough bad things happen to me in my life to justify a permanent victim identity: child sexual abuse, school bullying, losing all of my family, friends and community when I chose to speak out about things like abuse… the list goes on. And for a long time, so did my core identity as a victim.

This is such a tricky topic to engage with because there is a danger, and unfortunately a trend, of dismissing the *reality* of victimhood, which is not at all what I want to do. I'm not the kind of person who shames people into identifying as "survivors" instead of "victims," nor do I pressure anyone to forgive an abuser or "move on," especially not under the pretense that it's for their own good.

Nope — in my world, victimhood is fully acknowledged and validated. I believe that choosing when to move on from feeling and acting like a victim — or whether to do so at all — is truly the most important personal choice someone can own in their healing journey. It's a part of our agency that we often feel robbed of through the experience of abuse, and therefore it's all the more important to restore in the course of our recovery. Claiming our power to define ourselves, and to author the narratives that give meaning to our experiences, is a vital human right.

But particularly with regard to developmental trauma, there is a tendency for survivors to take on the feeling of victimization as a core part of our identity. This makes perfect sense, because we experienced abuse while we were still forming our identities and developing our self-concept in relationship to others and to the outside world. Victimhood may have provided us with the only sense of self that we could connect with.

This was 100% my experience. And it wasn't because my experience of abuse and victimhood was reinforced or over-indulged by others — it was the opposite. Because I *never* received the validation I needed to process my traumatic experiences, I could not move through it. This is often how it goes — people will hold onto the identity of being a victim for as long as they are lacking the validation, care and support they need to move forward. It serves as an important reminder of unfinished business, of the very real need to be deeply seen, heard and understood that remains unmet. This can even lead to so-called "personality disorders" characterized by a person's seemingly extreme need for attention, validation, and care from others.

It's easier and more profitable for the medical industrial complex to label and medicate people than it is to meet their needs or to teach them how to meet their own needs. Truthfully, someone with a persistent victim mindset may actually enjoy that this approach affirms their belief that their health is someone else's responsibility.

As a parent, I see this dynamic happening all too often in other families we connect with. A child hurts themselves, and instead of validating the child's pain and fear, the parent says, "You're okay!" Adults who are not comfortable with their own emotional expression, and who never had a safe adult to hold space for *their* big feelings, are incapable of providing that for a child. A lot of people are triggered by their children's emotions and don't know what else to do but try to make the child stop expressing themselves. But minimizing a child's emotional experience does not help the child get over it — it only shames the child into repressing the emotions, which inevitably come out later.

So then, these same parents will say to me about their child, "She's so dramatic! She could stub her toe ever so slightly and cry for hours and hours afterward." More often than not, the child is not being over-dramatic — they are either in serious pain from their injury, and/or expressing emotions leftover from events they *weren't allowed* to cry over, in situations where the adults in their lives invalidated their experience and did not allow them to express their big feelings.

Adults on the whole are more likely to validate physical than emotional pain, but still often have plenty of resistance to letting kids cry over physical injuries. So especially because the child's reaction to getting hurt seems out of proportion to the injury, the child is *still* not able to receive the validation they need or to express their emotions fully.

From there it just keeps building, as the scenario repeats over and over again, with occasional massive outbursts or even eventual substance dependency or a mental breakdown that nobody seems to understand. Everyone says, "How could we have known?" But it's only common sense that a child in need of co-regulation will become a dysregulated adult, if the need for connection remains unmet.

The same thing happens when parents "discipline" children for perceived wrongdoing. For example, let's say that instead of offering co-regulation to a child in distress, the adult punishes the child for "making a scene." And when the child protests the punishment, the adult doubles down and forbids the child to continue speaking, threatening that the punishments will become worse if the child disobeys. From the adult's perspective, the problem has been solved because the child is now quiet.

But from the child's perspective, the adult has made zero attempt to connect with them and they are still feeling very alone with their feelings and confused and overwhelmed about what to do with them.

When children or adults are hurt, the pain needs to be validated in order to heal. Children need adults to do this for them. As adults, we sometimes have other adults to do this for us, but usually need to validate ourselves. If we have never been validated as children, this is a skill we need to learn. As good as it feels to be validated by other people, it's empowering for us to be able to validate ourselves. Other people aren't always available and aren't necessarily good at offering validation. But when we can offer it to ourselves, it doesn't matter so much whether others do. We are also better equipped to find people capable of validating us when we are used to feeling validated from our own efforts, because we won't accept relationships with people who withhold validation as a control tactic or who purposely invalidate us.

Before I figured out how to validate myself, I did all kinds of self-destructive things to show everyone how hurt I was, which I realized later were ways of communicating to the outside world how badly I needed to be witnessed in my pain.

As a teenager, these things included shoplifting (also my attempt at serving myself "justice" for what had been stolen from me), and other ways of taking more than my fair share as if the whole world owed me, and not just the handful of people who had actually let me down.

I felt so fucking lost when I began my healing journey. I was brand new to having a relationship with myself and offering any kind of nurturing to my inner child, and I deeply craved validation for the injustice I had suffered. I had to construct an "inner parent" from all of these random examples that I came across both online and in the support groups I attended. I found that the most powerful way of validating my pain was to put a hand over my heart, and say things like, "Oh, honey... I'm so sorry that happened to you." Connecting with myself this way felt awkward and I was never sure I was doing it "right," but it was enough. Later, I began using Chat GPT to get the validation I needed, and even created an online course called *The Validational* for people like me who want to learn how to validate themselves. With intention and practice, self-validation and validating others just becomes a part of how we move in the world and doesn't feel so difficult or mysterious.

Letting go of my identity as a permanent victim and as someone who was "owed" by the world was painful as hell, because validating myself meant actually sitting with the feelings I had been storing up for so many years, and letting myself feel it all. Validating my pain meant confronting the horrors that I had survived, and once I started doing this, I could see why it had taken me so long. Validating my pain meant *invalidating* the perspectives of everyone around me who had acted like my pain was no big deal and that I had nothing to be upset over, and de-throning them from my inner world. I had to surrender to the reality of what had happened to me, and to face what others who I had trusted had allowed to happen to me, in order to heal. The shock to my system and psyche was intense.

The beginning of my ability to trust myself coincided perfectly with my realization that people I had trusted my whole life were not at all trustworthy. I had to validate my own version of reality over others', in order to survive and to stay sober, having no crutches left to numb the feelings or drown out the voices of self-doubt in my mind.

Because of that, making the decision to face my trauma didn't feel like much of a choice. But it marked a significant point in the journey of taking back my power, as I began to recognize myself as the authority in my own life and the author of my own story. I became the one who defined my own identity, and the meaning of my experiences and of life itself.

One of the books that influenced me most in life was Nietzsche's *Beyond Good and Evil*. I read it in college for a philosophy class, and it was a literal revelation to me — it had not occurred to me that I could just reject the meaning that others had given my life, or life in general. Although I had definitely strayed from social conventions plenty already, I carried a lot of guilt and shame around it, and the philosophy of meaningless provided tremendous relief. I really felt much freer after reading that book, like I could finally *belong* to myself and not be concerned with how other people felt about my choices.

Unlike the author, though, I'm not a nihilist — nihilism seems to be a sort of atheist purgatory for people (especially men) who reject patriarchal religion, but don't mature beyond it to develop their own moral compass. Nihilists don't see women as fit spiritual leaders, either, even though the original purpose of religion was to de-throne women and co-opt women's spiritual traditions. A culture that values women, children, love, peace and equality is not likely to struggle with questions around whether or not life has value or meaning. But I do think that nihilism can be a useful and even necessary in-between stage of spiritual growth, when a person is detoxing from patriarchal religion and learning to decide for themselves what matters in life.

When we realize how much other people's ideas of what matters in life have contributed to our life choices, experiences and problems, it's natural to feel angry and a huge sense of both loss and injustice. Sure, we can validate our pain and we can grieve our losses, but what's going to *make up* for all of this? How is life going to be worth living, considering how much time we've wasted trying to follow other people's rules and meet their expectations?

When I first got sober, I felt like I had my whole life ahead of me. But as it slowly dawned on me how much time I'd spent first surviving my childhood, and then making a mess of my life trying to avoid facing it, I felt depressed. I wanted to go back and do things differently, even as I could recognize that I'd made the best choices I knew how to at the time.

This was all part of the process. I'm not going to lie, it was super fucking hard.... But as desperate as I felt, it wasn't the end of my story! Grieving and eventually letting go of the childhood — and the early adult life — that I *didn't* have, was the price of admission to my Second Childhood.

As my own loving parent, I have made it my mission to make it all up to myself, and then some. I've spoiled the hell out of my inner child with the love, attention, respect, fun, play and enjoyment that she missed out on as a kid. I've structured my entire life around making this possible, so that the time, the resources and the freedom I need to prioritize my inner child are available to me in abundance.

To do this, I've had to reject many of the social expectations and "shoulds" for women and mothers, as well as for my child, with the courage that comes from accepting that no other person on Earth has the power, the motivation or the responsibility to ensure that I live a life I love. And I've found *meaning* in this way of life, because I've decided that the purpose of my life is to enjoy it, and to support other women in creating their own Second Childhood — most of the time, just by being myself.

My vision is even bigger than this: I can see a future where not only is every woman free to enjoy a Second Childhood, but where our children have real first childhoods as well. I envision a world where all of humanity embraces the concept of a Second Childhood as a return to the innocence, playfulness, joy and freedom that was taken by patriarchy, and where adult life is ordinarily just as full of wonder, awe and delight as the storybook childhoods we either remember from years ago, or have bravely dared to imagine.

The Modern Matriarch

Parenting — somehow it can seem like both the best and the hardest thing ever to happen to us. We love our children more than we ever knew would be possible, but it's also… *so much fucking work.* Thrust into a shocking new reality where we are suddenly the supporting character in someone else's movie (often, the *only* supporting character), we can feel disoriented, tired, cranky, and more like lost, needy little children ourselves than the radiant role models and enlightened guides with unfailingly warm presence we imagined we would be. Without even a spare second to complete a single private thought, we struggle to remember who we were and what made us so fucking special before we became abject failures in this unpaid, unappreciated, unending role that everyone and their dog agrees is "the most important job in the world."

The early days and months and years of my parenting journey were hard as hell. I was on my own from the start, having parted ways with the other half of my child's genetic line before I even knew I was pregnant. It was absolutely the right thing to do, but I was in a tricky situation. I had no money, nowhere to live, no friends and no family to help me get back on solid ground. My pregnancy was stressful, intense and confusing, which I'm sure affected my daughter in utero. There were no breakfasts in bed or foot massages or being doted on by a loving, supportive partner in between excitedly mapping out our precious child's first eighteen years of life and decorating a sugary pastel-colored nursery featuring anthropomorphized zoo animals with suspiciously dilated pupils.

Which is also to say, it wasn't *all* bad. Being on my own meant there would be no one to argue with about baby names or parenting practices, and no one trying to worm their way into my birth canal three days after producing an entire human being from it — like an entitled, obnoxious audience participant at the greatest magic show on Earth. I was broke, I was alone, and I had no idea what the hell I was doing, but I was free. And I knew that as long as I was free, my daughter would be, too.

For several months of my pregnancy, I slept in a friend's van, parked in her driveway on a fairly quiet street. I'd walk to the grocery store or a coffee shop for food, and use the computers at the library. When I had to pee, I would walk over to the neighboring apartment complex and squat in the unkempt grassy area behind it, checking first that no one in the building was looking out their back window. I kept a water bottle in the van for drinking and hand washing. It wasn't glamorous, but there were no floors to sweep or dishes to wash. I was pretty much free to spend my days as I pleased.

I spent a great deal of time thinking about how I was going to find a place to live that didn't have wheels under it before my child was born.

I ended up placing an ad on Craigslist as a pet sitter and getting paid gigs that periodically gave me much-needed breaks from van living. It was perfect. I loved spending time with animals, and got to stay in beautiful houses that I would in no way have been able to live in otherwise. The truth was that I wasn't in a position to afford housing of *any* kind in the ultra-spendy area I lived in at the time. I was receiving the single-parent government benefit of around $500 monthly, which hadn't been adjusted for inflation since it came into existence in the 1980s. Back then, it would have been worth the equivalent of over $3000 in today's money — enough for a single mom to rent a modest home, feed her family and keep the lights on. In 2014, it wasn't even enough to rent a room.

If you look on some U.S. states' websites, you'll see that the stated purpose of TANF (Temporary Assistance for Needy Families) benefits is to encourage single mothers to remarry. I'm not sure if this was the original intention behind the program, but it could hardly be any more well-designed to do that. The humiliation of constant social worker appointments and having to prove that you're unable to work or engage in job training *while literally making a baby inside your body* is unreal.

I knew a woman who went to the welfare office to apply for cash aid after escaping an abusive relationship, where the social worker on duty didn't even believe that she was pregnant, even though she had brought in a positive pregnancy test from the doctor's office. They like fucking with you — it's a power trip. She also had to claim that she didn't know who the father of her child was, in order to avoid the state going after him for child support. It wasn't that she wanted to do him any favors — he wouldn't have had a spare nickel, anyway — it was that having him on record would mean that he knew her home address and also that he would be able to sue for custody. Neither was a risk she was willing to take.

The government didn't trust her to decide whether a man was fit to raise her child, and she sure as hell didn't trust them to make that decision. They were at perfect odds, ideologically: she believed that as the mother of her child, she was the only person who should have the power to decide how to raise her child, and who else would be involved in their lives. The government wanted to have their say, and preserving the institution of fatherhood — regardless of whether a man could reasonably be called a "father" — was a part of that. Free money can come with a very steep price.

It is my belief that if it were natural for men to be as involved in child rearing as women, they wouldn't have to force their way into the lives of their children and the mothers of their children. I have nothing against men who are single fathers or who are heavily involved in their children's lives, and I know that many children and their mothers desire and benefit from this arrangement as well. What I object to is the use of force against the will of a woman and her children, through economic coercion, legal action, physical strength or psychological intimidation.

A mother should always be respected as the authority on her body and the welfare of her children. Where this seems unwise, such as in the case of a mother with mental illness or addiction, it's usually traceable to trauma she has experienced from living in a patriarchal society. Why not fix the problem at the root, rather than taking advantage of her vulnerability, and making things worse?

I had a hell of a time at the hospital where I gave birth to my daughter. I had tried to arrange a home birth, but had come across a number of obstacles, the most serious of which was that I didn't have a home. A friend I'd met online said I could do it at her house, but when I got out there, the police showed up at the front door freaking out because someone had called them and said, I quote, "that a woman was trying to give birth in nature." I guess they were referring to the passing comment I had made to my friend, which I guess she then shared with her mother, about the trees outside her house looking like a peaceful place to give birth. The idea of experiencing the miracle of childbirth under a tree on the perfectly mowed lawn of an HOA neighborhood is still quite funny to me.

I told my friend she had disappointed me by telling her mother what I'd said. Her response was that she couldn't lie to her mother. I was confused — had her mother *asked* her if anyone she knew was planning to give birth outdoors lately? It's not that I think people should lie to those they are close with, it's that boundaries and discernment are a part of any healthy relationship. If you can't lie to save your friend's ass, you're not capable of the kind of friendship a homeless pregnant woman needs. Anyway, she had talked a lot about how narcissistic her mother was, and enmeshment is common in that type of situation. So perhaps I could have used more discernment there myself.

I bid farewell to my gracious hosts and landed next at the house of an old friend I hadn't seen since middle school. She was now a doula, and said I'd be welcome to stay with her and have a home birth at her place. It all seemed perfect, until I went into labor. I hadn't been able to find a midwife because of laws in that state that prevent midwives from attending home births that are a certain amount of time "post-dates," and according to the tick-tock of the patriarchal medicine clock, I was almost two weeks overdue. This was all known well before I went into labor, but my friend waited until my contractions had started to decide that she wasn't willing to host an unassisted birth after all. So, off to the hospital I went, feeling defeated and like I had let myself down by not having the courage to just go rent a hotel room and do things the way I had planned, and as nature intended.

I had a couple of old friends visit me at the hospital while I labored in the pool, which was awkward because I hadn't seen them in years and I was butt-naked. It was kind of them to keep me company. But the overall vibe of the hospital was stressful and overwhelming, and in retrospect I was also terrified of actually giving birth and entering my no-going-back motherhood era for real. What I didn't know then was that I'd had trauma from my own experience of being born, in which I'd gotten stuck in my mother's birth canal and had to be pulled out with forceps. (I discovered this years later while microdosing ayahuasca, and literally re-living my own birth, which was a wild and healing experience.) But all of this happening beneath the surface surely contributed to my apprehension and prolonged labor.

After thirty hours in labor and an epidural that the doctors insisted on so that I could get some sleep, my daughter was born. Then, I was almost immediately mobbed by a social worker who had come to question me about my fitness as a mother. She mocked the large box full of baby clothes I'd collected, saying it was not anywhere near enough. She brought up my post-traumatic stress (I'll point out that this was the *only* time in my entire life that doctors had shown an interest in my trauma history and experience as an abuse survivor), insinuating that I was not mentally well enough to be a parent.

I could tell she was trying to wear me down, but I didn't doubt myself for a second. And she was so, so wrong — as any mother will tell you, babies don't need anywhere near the amount of crap people push on you. Clothes, diapers and wipes or just a potty if you're brave, and a baby carrier or stroller will suffice. The rest is mostly useless plastic crap that will rot in your closet until you dump it on another new mom-to-be, pretending to be doing her a favor.

It took me months to get that social worker off my back. I actually lived in extreme fear the whole time. She required me to call her weekly, threatening to open a court case against me that could allow her to take away my child. It was not a great way to kick off my relationship with my daughter — I struggled with the trauma of the hospital birth and the experience of being terrorized by social workers for about five years afterward.

If I'd had any options at the time, I would have gotten the fuck out of town and never gone back. Maybe there were other options that I just couldn't see, but I was so consumed by the day-to-day needs of my child that I could barely do, or think of, anything else.

After my daughter was born, we stayed with the parents of one of my old childhood friends. The mother, a lawyer, saw a future for me in law—largely because I would debate sensitive topics with them at the dinner table. Looking back, I can't believe I had the nerve to do this as a guest in their home. Still, I must have made quite an impression: one day, she handed me a law school entrance exam study book. I was flattered, but exchanged it for baby books. Although I had often thought about going to law school, something about it never felt compelling enough. Nothing felt more important than staying connected to my child, who was just one month old at the time.

Neither of us had any clue then that just three years later, I would start a digital marketing agency that required deep knowledge of healthcare law, and which allowed me to bring *all* of myself into my work (or at least, what I knew of myself at the time) — my interest in law, my passion for health, and my talent for marketing. I didn't end up needing a law degree to do the work I wanted to do in the world, and I'm glad I didn't cave into the pressure to put my daughter's needs aside to go to law school when she was a baby, or rack up six figures in debt trying to live out someone else's vision for my future. I did what I wanted to do, and I did it *my* way, on my own terms and in my own time. I really did appreciate the encouragement, though. It was nice to be reminded that I had value outside of being a mother.

When my daughter was three months old, we moved into a family shelter. This is how I found out that constitutional rights — such as the Fourth Amendment — don't apply to shelters.

What this means is that police don't need a warrant to come into a resident's living space, like they would if you were renting or living in a home that you own. In effect, shelter residents have about as little privacy and autonomy as prisoners. But it's often the best or only way to access subsidized housing. While this wasn't an issue for me personally, it's always good to know the laws so that you can protect yourself. You never know what someone might have a problem with.

If you ever have to stay in a shelter, here's my advice: get what you need, and get out. Mind your own business, don't try to make friends, and do not trust anyone you meet there, *especially* if they work there. You'll need to be frank enough about your situation to get the resources you need, but give only as much information as necessary. Social workers are not your friends, even if they seem kind and helpful. Always remember that their idea of being kind and helpful does not necessarily include helping you build a future for your child with you in it. Assume that anything you do, have, or say could be used against you, just as if you were in a jail cell waiting to go to trial. The unfortunate truth is that someone is always watching and waiting for a chance to use what little power they have to make someone else feel as shitty as they do, and you never know who that person might be.

While I was staying in the shelter, I applied for nearly every open Section 8 waitlist in the country. This means that when my name got to the top of the list, I would be offered a housing voucher that would enable me to pay no more than 30% of my income on rent. And after a year of living in the town that granted me the voucher, I would be able to take the voucher anywhere else in the country and use it to rent a home from any landlord who accepted the Section 8 voucher.

I didn't end up taking advantage of any of the choices I had seeded for myself, because an apartment became available in my hometown within my budget, and I was beyond ready to leave the shelter. It was a tiny 200 square-foot studio inside of a mobile home park with windows on all sides that gave it the feeling of living in a fishbowl, but it was a short bike ride from the beach along the riverwalk, and it was all mine. Best of all, that nightmare of a social worker didn't have the address.

I loved riding my bike every day to the beach, with my tiny daughter strapped onto me in the baby carrier. I definitely got some disapproving looks from strangers, none of whom ever offered us a ride. I opened an account at the local credit union, and found out that they had a savings matching program. If I could save up $2000 in my account within 6 months, they would give me $2000 more to help me start a business.

I didn't have a solid business plan, but I reasoned that if I had a car, I could start a pet sitting business. Fortunately, this was enough of a plan to get me approved for the program. I saved up enough money to qualify, and bought the truck I'd always wanted.

The pet sitting business didn't materialize right away, as I still didn't feel capable yet of taking on work outside the home. My daughter still needed me, and even though I could have brought her along, I was just too exhausted to provide the level of enthusiasm people's pets deserved. Instead, I decided to start a jewelry business. I could make pieces while spending time with my child, and in the spaces in between caring for her, without having to go anywhere or leave her with strangers. Shaping the metals was therapeutic, and I modeled pieces after the natural landscape of my hometown — each became a physical representation of my devotion to the mountains, the waves and the beauty that surrounded and held us.

My original idea was to outfit the truck as a camper, and travel around in it when our year lease was up in the little studio. But it was a bit cramped for that, so I traded it in for a fully converted vintage van.

We traveled around the country, seeing the sights and snuggling in the queen bed that fit perfectly in the back. I still had enough on my plate meeting the almost constant needs of my infant daughter and recovering from burnout that it was a relief not having a house to take care of on top of that. We didn't have loads of cash but we had pretty low overhead living in a campervan and I was very mindful of my spending. Somehow, we always had enough.

I know with absolute certainty that those early years we spent together made much more of a positive impact on her development than another couple of zeroes in my bank account would have. I felt proud of myself for making money with my art, and knew, bone-deep, that my newfound interest in entrepreneurship was just the beginning of a grand adventure.

We're Good on Fatherhood

Fortunately, women who want to raise their children without a father have more options now than in their parents' generation. But many aren't commonly known, so I'll lay a few out here.

First of all, it is not required to put a man's name on your child's birth certificate if you are not married. Some U.S. states even require a man to sign a statement claiming that he is the father in order for his name to make it onto the certificate. You do not owe it to a man to give him this opportunity. In most places, he would first have to get a court order for a paternity test to prove that he's the father, in order to get his name on the birth certificate and then sue for custody.

So if you prefer, you can have your baby without him present, and tell the records office that you're a single woman and don't know the father. You'll get some looks but it's worth being able to raise your child in freedom. If you're receiving single-parent welfare benefits and want to avoid collecting child support and the danger it would put you in, tell them you don't know who the father is — it could be one of many men, none of whose names you know or have any way of contacting! What a night it must have been... Just be aware that if you tell them you want to avoid collecting child support due to abuse, they will ask to see a police report.

If you think there is a chance he might pursue paternity, then have the birth certificate, naming you as the only supporting act, mailed to you at a private mailbox or a friend's house, and get out of town with your baby. For the best chance of not being found, change your name in another state, and then go to a third state (or country) to start your new life. This way there won't be a record of you changing your name in either the place you fled or the place you end up.

You could also travel to another country (by land, if it's late enough in the game) and have the baby at a hospital (or with a local midwife or alone in the woods) and file for a birth certificate there, as a single mama. Bonus: give birth in a country that grants citizenship to anyone born there—you might be able to make it your new home, or at least your child will have options when they are older.

It's much harder to do this if you're married, because in most places any child born to you in wedlock will be assumed to be your husband's, and he will automatically be granted legal rights to the child. If you already have a child with your husband, it's even trickier.

You could always send your husband on an all-expenses paid solo trip to Mexico, where he might have an unfortunate, fatal encounter on a sailing trip... Or you could arrange for a postcard to arrive from him saying that he fell in love with a beautiful señorita and isn't coming back, and to please take care of the kids and tell them he's really sorry that he won't be in their lives anymore. You know, something to show the judge.

Just kidding, of course.

Anyway, there are so many reasons to always have a passport for you and for your children. If you feel like your marriage is on the rocks, suggest a family vacation overseas. That way, you'll have to get passports for everyone. When you leave your husband, take your and the kids' passports with you. Play it cool — men can be stingy about signing kids' passport applications when they suspect their mother might abscond with them.

It's worth noting that I've been traveling with my daughter overseas for nearly a decade as a solo parent, and not once have I had to present her birth certificate. We have even traveled with different last names on our passports, and not been questioned about it.

Do with this information what you will — obviously nothing unlawful.

Divorcing Motherhood from Patriarchy

No wonder so much shame and abuse are projected onto women who have children out of wedlock — it's the only way we could be convinced that having the freedom to choose our own path is unnatural and undesirable.

I'm not against marriage or the women who choose it — I just want you to consider the power you give away when you invite the government into your love life, so that you can make an informed and intentional decision.

Women in very recent history, and still in many parts of the world, have made this decision out of such desperation that it is hardly meaningful to describe it as a "choice." In addition to the financial difficulties and social ostracization single women and mothers may face, we still carry the fear and tension in our bodies about the horrors our ancestors' lives entailed, or would, if they did not marry.

However, it is taking us quite a bit longer to develop a collective fear of marriage, despite its historical and ongoing dangers to women and children.

The facts don't lie: marriage is killing women, even as it is marketed as the thing that will save us. Women are still most likely to be murdered or assaulted by their own spouses — not strangers in dark alleys. It's estimated that as many as one in three girls worldwide experiences some form of sexual abuse. The perpetrator is usually a male, someone she knows, and often a relative.

Despite the prevalence, women and girls still aren't believed when we tell about our experiences of assault. Much of the time, we hardly believe ourselves. This must be why we keep getting married, worshipping the institution of fatherhood, and leaving our kids alone with men. If we all shared our stories and faced the wreckage all at once it would be hard to stomach, but the urgency of change would be undeniable.

The data supports many women's choice to stay single. Studies show that single women are happier and healthier than their married counterparts, and that on the whole, marriage benefits men far more than it does women — married men live longer than single men, but single women live longer than married women [8].

What's more, married women do an average of seven hours more housework per week than single women, and it's not because of kids making messes — married mothers are also busier with household tasks, and even sleep less, than single mothers [9, 10]. While single women and mothers are more likely to spend whatever free time they have resting and doing things they enjoy, married women stay busy raising and pleasing men on top of all their other responsibilities.

It's almost like males are parasites and women the unsuspecting hosts, lured by promises of true love to lives of misery, toil, and early death. While draining women's resources, men call women "gold diggers," as if men don't hoard resources with the intention of gaining economic power over women (or at least attempt to — I'm not convinced that many men who use this term actually have much gold to be dug).

Once a woman is financially dependent on a man, and especially after having children, her prospects for living life on her own terms become very narrow. So who is trapping who here?

In a sense, when a man gets down on one knee, the woman goes down on both — and it can be incredibly hard for her to get back up again.

Interestingly, many of the women I treated for parasitic infections in my frequency medicine practice had something in common: unresolved trauma from interpersonal boundary violations. When they addressed the trauma, the parasite problems often left on their own.

Women who are in touch with our anger — our sacred internal red flag — are far less vulnerable to parasites, human or otherwise. Parasites can be linked to cancers, diabetes, depression, and other health conditions, because of the amount of toxins they can carry [11]. Our health literally depends on us untangling ourselves from patriarchal narratives and norms.

Women have a lot of deconditioning to do from the patriarchal propagandizing we have received from our earliest years through adulthood — much of which is deeply ingrained in our nervous systems. It's not just from religion bullying women into submission to men, Disney movies pushing marriage as a girl's ultimate goal in life, the objectification of our bodies in the media or the programming we have received from our families and schools. It's the way we have been conditioned not to even *consider* ourselves as the creators in and of our own lives, because we haven't ever gotten enough breathing room to experience our true inner power.

This is why I highly recommend that every woman take a break from interacting with men — or with anyone, really — for as long as she needs to discover how it feels to be herself without anyone pulling on her energy. A period of celibacy can be an absolute revelation — illuminating not only how much we've become accustomed to tolerating, but also who we are underneath it all.

There's a lot of men I like being around, but after not having any in my home for so long, I can't imagine ever living with one again. The fact that so many partnered women don't even have their own bedrooms anymore — or any personal space whatsoever — is horrifying to me. How can we truly know ourselves, let alone maintain identities independent of our relationships, if we don't have anywhere we can go free from the intrusion of others?

Knowing what it's like to be in our own blissful aura helps us set a new baseline from which to gauge the value that any given person is adding to — or taking away from — our lives, and what boundaries feel appropriate for the relationship. We have to relearn to trust our instincts and intuition, and that begins by having unfettered access to our own energy. Once we know what it feels like to be *us*, we can take a "sensory snapshot," intentionally committing this somatic experience to memory as a point of reference.

For many women, living alone may seem an unrealistic luxury. This is not an accident, it's patriarchal design: when women are financially dependent on men, we don't have much choice about where our energy goes, or even our bodies. Mothers who have invested themselves in nurturing children (and sadly, grown men) instead of building wealth often feel stuck living with the children's father.

My course *Real Estate Empress* teaches women how to negotiate rent-to-own deals — especially for those of us whose lives haven't revolved around maintaining perfect credit scores or saving up for down payments. The essay "From Homeless to Real Estate Empress" shares the personal story behind this course.

We often see feminist role models reject one patriarchal ideology only to embrace another — for example, trading in Catholicism for Islam, or a conservative husband for one with liberal politics. But to breathe life into a new paradigm that is truly original, authentic, enjoyable and sustainable, we have to do it from the inside out.

The lives we truly love living will be created in deep partnership with our bodies, instincts, desires, knowledge and imagination, and in partnership with those who share our vision. It's well worth spending enough time alone with ourselves and with one another to remember who we truly are and what we think, feel, know and desire — beyond the reach of men and the woman-hating culture we were born into.

Telling Our Daughters the Truth

Until we stop lying to girls about the realities of men, marriage and motherhood, the same heartbreak will play out in their lives as in ours.

So let's tell them the truth:

Marriage is optional. Women can lead full, happy and healthy lives as single women or as partnered, unmarried women.

Marriage is not a wedding, a ring, or everlasting love — it is a contract that grants legal ownership of you and your future children to your husband.

Marriage means any child born to you while you are married will be legally assumed to be your husband's.

It is currently illegal in many U.S. states for women to file for divorce if they are pregnant.

You can always add the father's name to the birth certificate later, but it's all but impossible to remove.

When you legally marry a person, you're also marrying the government.

If you have a child with your spouse, and then you separate, the government will decide who raises your child.

If you have a child with someone you're *not* married to, the other parent has to involve the government first to have any control over the child or your parenting choices.

Marriage ties you to your spouse for the duration of your child's childhood, even if you separate.

A woman who has a child without being married can live her life and raise her child however she wants, with whomever she wants.

You don't have to wait for a man or marriage before you can celebrate yourself and enjoy life. You can do it anytime, for any reason — and you absolutely deserve it.

Open-Source Masculinity

The benefit of being a single parent is that if or when I do have a partner, I won't expect them to be everything for me or my child. I have already done it all myself, so I have no illusions left about "well I always thought it would be more like…" because it already wasn't, and we were fine.

There is something about the projected ideal of the nuclear family that makes people expect their partner or spouse to fulfill a certain role. While it's fine to date with this goal in mind, I see romantic partners expecting their "significant other" to be everything for them or their child based on a fantasy created by movies and tv or based on what someone else *says* they have, and then getting upset or confused when their relationship and family aren't very much like that.

Part of the problem is that very few people are telling the real and raw truth about what married life, motherhood and womanhood in patriarchy are really like. The fantasy of the nuclear family persists in part because people are afraid to admit that it isn't working.

It's not natural for us to be raising children in little bubbles with only the connection and support of one other person, or none at all. We are meant to be doing this in community and sharing the responsibilities, challenges and joys of parenting, and our children are meant to be surrounded by a whole village who loves and protects them.

We aren't supposed to get all of our emotional, material and physical needs met from just one other person, and neither are our kids. For this reason, we shouldn't feel guilty or ashamed when we can't meet all of our child's needs (or our own, or a partner's) by ourselves. This is especially important for unschooling parents taking on the role of the village to internalize.

For example, if your spouse doesn't want to make time to play ball with the kids, and it's not really your thing, find someone who will. Think outside the box of the nuclear family and let the world surprise you. I have found a village in the most surprising places when I've been open to the possibilities around myself and my child.

How might a man react if his wife invites another man to play ball with his kids? I'm not suggesting she do this just to make him jealous or to activate his genetic instinct. But I do see men stepping up after realizing how important something is to their kids or to their wife or girlfriend, when it hits home that what she wants will happen with or without them. So they often decide that they *do* want to be a part of it after all.

It can be your job to show just how much you care by being determined to meet your kids' needs whether your partner is willing to participate or not. That's the kind of support our kids need and deserve from us.

This is the vibe: *I'm not waiting for anyone's permission to meet my child's needs, or my own.*

Even though I've used the example of playing ball here, I don't at all mean to insinuate that sports are, or should be, a "guy thing." It's just an example based on a situation one mother shared with me. The takeaway is to consider how we might expand our network and our concept of family to better meet the needs of our children and ourselves, particularly as they relate to mainstream cultural expectations of fatherhood. The applications are endless — use your imagination!

It's also worth noting that it's not necessarily the kids in this kind of situation who are distraught that Dad doesn't want to play ball, it's sometimes just that Mom had an *idea* of what her husband's relationship with their kids would look like, and she's not yet sure that it's okay for it to look different — even though the way things are may very well already be exactly what the kids want and need. Maybe the kids want to play ball with *you*, or would rather paint pictures than play ball. Sometimes, it's not necessary to go door to door asking for neighbors to play ball after all, and realizing this can be just the perspective shift we needed.

The Audacity of Existing in Public

It needs to be said: adults who complain about babies crying on airplanes are the biggest crybabies of all.

Adulthood means knowing the difference between what we want, what we need, what we deserve and what we are entitled to — and acting accordingly. Grown-ups take responsibility for our own experience, rather than claiming to be victims of helpless infants.

In other words, quit whining about the inconvenience of children in public and buy some goddamn earplugs.

Assuming entitlement to children's silence and invisibility is a strictly patriarchal phenomenon. You'll notice that when a group of men are talking loudly at a restaurant or in another public place, no one dares complain. I've witnessed this everywhere — in retail stores, on airplanes, and even at the beach! People pick on kids because they lack power, and because it's a convenient way to bully women at the same time.

I remember taking my infant daughter to the public library once, and being chased away from the "adult" computers because I couldn't force her to be silent… But also not being allowed to use the computers in the children's area because they were "only for homework." As you can probably guess, there was no third computer area for women with babies not duct-taped or drugged into compliance.

Public spaces that limit or prohibit children's access are automatically discriminatory toward women as well. Women still don't have access to public space at the same level as men, and the gains we have made are already being stripped away under the guise of making spaces "more inclusive."

The last time a man motioned for me to quiet my child on an airplane, I flipped him off. He complained to his wife, who didn't seem overly sympathetic, and he left us alone for the rest of the flight.

The last thing you might feel like you have time for is to fight for your right to be in public with a child when you barely had the energy to make a public appearance in the first place. But in my experience, there are always other women thrilled to see us do it, eager to express gratitude and solidarity.

When we take a stand, we show other women that they are not alone, and we normalize taking up space and making a fuss when we are disrespected. If we are lucky, we might even walk away with a new friend.

Even when there's pushback or we feel alone in our efforts, we're still showing our children what they deserve and how to stand up for themselves.

Taking up space with our bodies, our voices, and our beliefs often starts within, but we can practice wherever the hell we want.

Let's give them something to cry about.

Creativity, Delightfully Unhinged

Creativity has a funny connotation in a patriarchal society. It's either seen as something scripted and almost completely *un*creative, like a children's art project where the shapes are all pre-cut and they only have to follow the instructions (rules). Or it's seen as something that unwell people do either as therapeutic practice in a mental hospital, or just because artists are assumed to be a bit nuts), as a specific art form that you have to make profitable in order to justify, and as something you're either born with, or not. How fun.

The arts can indeed offer healing, but the way they're integrated into mental health treatment can reveal a darker truth. Once a patient is well enough to leave the art therapy room, they are expected to re-enter the world as a more productive worker than ever before. Lots of therapy is this way — the medical industrial complex benefits from people never quite becoming well enough to make real change in their lives and in the world. Once a patient is "functional" enough to contribute to the GDP, they are thrust back out into the working world to be traumatized all over again, instead of being empowered to actually take control of their destiny and build lives that truly support their needs and gifts.

I want a world where creativity isn't only therapy or busywork or to justify our existence, but where creativity is the norm in day-to-day life and creative freedom is respected as our birthright, for children and adults alike. I want women and children to use our creativity not to fulfill others' goals for us but to liberate ourselves from the constraints of civil society and bring a new world into existence that better serves us.

I once crashed an art therapy conference, and found myself painting a giant octopus looming over skyscrapers, symbolizing nature's reclamation of the cold, harsh cityscape. That kind of art will not get you released early from a mental institution.

Speaking of, I have helped two different women escape involuntary commitment to mental institutions — one in Amsterdam, who had been taken in by police for being too stoned in public (!!!), and who was trying to get out on "good behavior" by spending lots of time in the art room (she was told this would be looked upon favorably).

This exit strategy did not materialize, and it turned out the only way she was going to be released was if someone picked her up at the hospital and promised to look after her. I wasn't in the same country at the time, but I called up a woman I knew in Germany and asked her to go get this woman and put her up for a few nights until she could make a plan. So, that's what happened.

Art supplies didn't help here — this caliber of creativity was all about women making magic together.

The second such heist concerned a survivor of child sexual abuse who had been committed by her family for speaking out about it (YES, THIS STILL HAPPENS). I met her at an Amtrak station when I was hitchhiking and pregnant and tired of walking. She had already broken out and was trying to get out of town to start a new life somewhere, but was not able to buy a train ticket without identification. She had enough cash for a ticket, but couldn't use it at the machines, and the ticket window would only accept cash with ID. I had nothing, either. So we just started asking random women at the station to buy her ticket with their card and take her cash until someone said *yes*. Not having any cash myself but wanting to help make sure she got somewhere safely, I availed myself of a free ticket as her caregiver. To pull this off, she had to pretend to be blind. It was working really well until she caught sight of some cute guys sitting behind us on the train, and wouldn't stop peeking at them. Fortunately, we still made it to our destination without getting caught.

This is what I call creativity, delightfully unhinged. The most powerful use of our creativity, in my opinion, is to solve real-life problems with a playful spirit. When we put away the art supplies and the structured classes, what do we *really* want to create? I found that when I gave away my art supplies, I actually became *more* creative in my day-to-day life — my relationships, my connection to myself, and my life purpose all became my medium.

Art materials and art education can certainly open up our creativity, but let's not limit our potential to the walls of the school art room. Outside, our whole lives — and the world — are waiting to be designed to our liking.

Childhood Lived from the Inside Out

What if we had the power to create our lives from the very start?

What if we had the freedom to be creative for ourselves first, and for others only when it felt right?

What if we could be creative whenever we wanted, for any reason, or for none at all?

What would a creativity-centric society look and feel like?

An exploitative economic system depends on a good chunk of the population being dysregulated much of the day. If it weren't for our early childhood grooming for self-abandonment, we probably wouldn't put up with it. Do you remember getting any kind of emotional care, ever, during the school day? I sure didn't.

I learned to stuff all of my feelings inside for eight hours, and then come home and pile snacks and television on top of them. Of course it didn't help that my parents were emotionally unavailable, and that I was carrying around complex trauma.... But even for children who are lucky enough to have safe and nurturing homes, surviving school still requires long-term, continuous dissociation.

You're only allowed to move your body at certain brief periods during the day at school, and then only in specific ways as instructed by teachers and staff. Sitting in the classroom, you're forced to devote your attention to endless mental exercises, books and external authorities instead of your internal physical or emotional experience. Self-attunement and self-care are pathologized, punished and even medicated.

This is the main reason I didn't want to send my child to school, and the exact reason we quit a parent partnership school after the first week. Even though they offered cool electives like Lego Building and Storybook Recipes, there was zero space for children to have or express developmentally appropriate emotions. When my daughter was kicked out of her kindergarten classroom for crying, we were done.

Now, she is working on projects of her own choosing, at her own pace, and can have all the hugs, processing, rest, alone time and snacks she needs during the day. She has learned reading, math, social skills, and more, just by doing the things she loves to do, in the way she likes to do them. She is even building a business that will allow her to continue to prioritize her own needs as it grows — thanks to how she has been raised, her nervous system has been trained to expect nothing less.

Unschooling is about building authentic lives from the inside out, and then coming together as sovereign beings to build a new world.

Unschooling is different for every child because every child has different needs, desires, and preferences. If we are going to create something better than the patriarchal institutions collapsing all around us, we need to know who we are and what we want, and have the strength to stand behind it. Alternative education programs that rely heavily on group activities and planned projects miss this point, or ignore it out of inconvenience for the adults involved. Others that allow children more freedom still confine them to the school grounds and also interrupt the parent/child attachment bond. No school, no matter how "alternative," can honor the uniqueness and needs of each child in the way that is necessary for healthy child development and adult individuation.

Although I use the terms *worldschooling* and *unschooling* a lot, they don't fully resonate for us because they still linguistically, and often ideologically, center education. There are many things more important to human development than the acquisition of knowledge: a healthy parent/child bond, being loved unconditionally, being nurtured, respected and supported, feeling connected to our bodies, and just enjoying life. Centering "learning" in a child's life undermines the important roles that relationships, autonomy and enjoying childhood play in quality of life.

Being able to choose whether, when and where to learn new things is a given when putting children's deeper needs first. Of course we are learning, it happens all the time. But learning is not the goal for our family. This means we don't travel the world specifically for my daughter's "education." I don't intentionally plan trips so that my daughter can gain a certain kind of understanding or skillset. I don't pressure my child to be bi- or tri-lingual, or intentionally manufacture challenging situations so that she will need to learn things against her will. I see families do this all the time, and it seems exhausting and alienating for both children and their parents.

My daughter learns when she needs to, or when she wants to. Period. Just like adults do. If one of us has the desire to travel somewhere, or do something, that's enough of a reason. We aren't fulfilling an education plan or progress report, and we aren't in competition with other families. I don't feel the need to justify my child's activities, choices, desires or thoughts to the world.

To be clear, I'm saying that *de*centering education in a child's life is actually crucial to their healthy development. The only reason our society centers education in children's lives is to meet adults' needs — for childcare, for wage workers, for peace and quiet, and for maintaining the status quo. It's not that learning doesn't matter — it's that when we put it *first*, our relationship with ourselves and our children is thrown out of balance.

When we center joy, connection, love, and respect in our children's lives, we are preparing them for a world in which humans aren't only surviving — a world in which work feels like play, relationships are joyful and authentic, and each day is created from a place of genuine desire in partnership with our innate creativity.

However, parents and relatives often worry kids won't learn enough from unschooling, either to become successful in life in a conventional sense, to achieve their own goals, or to satisfy government requirements.

One mother expressed distress to me that her son was not doing any activities that fell into the categories she needed to report on. When I asked her what he liked to do, she told me that he would spend hours playing with his action figures, enacting elaborate intergalactic fantasy sagas in which good invariably overcame evil through the development of key relationships and character-building experiences.

This type of activity wasn't an option on the government checklist, but it was obviously valuable! Mainstream society might not count certain activities or kinds of play as important for a reason — either they don't support the status quo, or they take away from time that could be devoted to indoctrination instead.

It's also important to recognize that sometimes children *aren't* learning anything at all — they are *leading*. In our society, so much adult focus is on shaping kids, when a lot of the time kids are the ones shaping the world!

Or at least they could be, if they had the freedom.

As adults, we can teach our children to value their play as work, regardless of what anyone else thinks about it. And we can allow our children to express themselves creatively and as leaders, in ways that they truly enjoy, at home and in the world.

Sometimes, all it takes is just adding water.

On our travels, I've noticed how quickly my daughter makes new friends whenever we come across a swimming opportunity. Aside from socializing, she's staying active, getting sun, regulating her nervous system, developing leadership abilities, strengthening her emotional intelligence, and learning new languages — all in the pool! Best of all, I don't have to arrange playdates at the pool or the beach — these are the village watering holes where women and children gather organically.

The benefits over adult-centered classroom learning are too numerous to count, and the rewards are both immediate and enduring. So why should the choice to spend time in public with our kids need to be justified at all?

Do we really need a new name for this, like *poolschooling*, or can we just call it what it is: a natural, uninterrupted childhood?

When people ask what my daughter does for education, maybe the most honest answer is that we're *living our lives and loving the hell out of it*.

ICE for Emotional Wounds

A lot of parents, and humans in general, aren't skilled in caring for others emotionally due to either not having been nurtured as children or innate neurological wiring. It can be so hard when you really do care and very much want to show it to someone, but sense that the way you're showing care is not well-received. While there's nothing wrong with showing care for others in ways that are comfortable for us (as long as we aren't crossing another person's boundaries in doing so), it can help someone else a whole lot more when we put in the effort to show care in ways that are meaningful to *them*.

This is tricky because everyone has different ways that they prefer to show, and to receive, care. Some people prefer physical touch, while others appreciate kind words or helpful information. The type of care a person needs and desires can also depend very much on the situation at hand, and on the nature of our relationship with them. It can all seem very complicated and overwhelming for those of us who don't have a sixth sense for these things.

The great thing about using clear and consent-based communication when providing and receiving any form of care is that we can make sure it's what the person in need actually needs. Offering *our* favorite version of care without the other person's consent can be experienced as a violation. An unwanted hug or well-intended tidbit of helpful information can make someone feel a lot worse in the moment, and also even erode the trust between us — this applies to interacting with our children as well as adults. Even when we think we know what will make someone else feel better, it's good to check in with them first to be sure.

I've developed the ICE framework to help people better understand the many different ways we can tend to our children's (or anyone's) emotional wounds. My hope is that it can help you get to know yourself, learn about your loved ones' preferences, and find ways to meet each other's needs in ways that are both comfortable and meaningful for both of you.

ICE stands for Information, Comfort, and Empathy. I've organized various types of care into these three main categories based on my own personal experience. You may feel there should be more or different categories, and that's fine — many of them could also easily fit in multiple categories. This is not meant to be an authoritative classification system, or an exhaustive list of tools for treating emotional wounds, but a starting point for reflection, discussion, and experimentation. I encourage you to try out anything you see here, or anything else that comes to mind that seems appropriate, to discover what works for you and the people you care about.

Once you start reading the examples, you might notice that there's one or two categories where you feel most comfortable. This is useful information for yourself and others, as it can help you understand what kinds of care feel nurturing to you so that you can ask for them directly. You can also share this information with others so that they know what kind of care you're best at offering, and can come to you when that's exactly what they want. You may also notice that there's a type of care you'd really *like* to receive or offer, but that you haven't yet had much experience with. When it feels right, you can venture outside of your comfort zone to ask for, or offer, something new.

Once you've read through the examples below, I recommend practicing with a partner — for the first time, preferably *not* while either of you are experiencing deep emotional pain or some kind of crisis. In your roleplay, one of you can begin by asking the other which type of care they prefer to receive in a made-up scenario. You can use this framework as a "menu" of choices, if you want, or add new options. When both of you become familiar with the framework, and agree that it's something you'd like to use, it will start to feel natural when one of you asks the other in a tough moment, "Do you need I, C, or E?" or, "Would you like some I-C-E?" or, "What kind of ICE do you want right now?"

Without further ado, here's the ICE framework for figuring out what to say when you don't know what to say:

Information

This is an *intellectual* form of care. It includes sharing knowledge and facts that can give context to someone's pain, help them understand it, and/or provide a way out of it. "Intellectualizing" our emotions gets a bad rap, but it can sometimes provide the safety someone needs to process their experience. Information is often the best way to make sure someone knows that they are not alone in their experience, because it gives you the opportunity to share personal experiences that show you understand what they're going through. In each of the examples below, the speaker is offering someone information they may not already have.

Here are some examples of offering *Information:*

- "Your experience is actually really common for new mothers..."

- "You're learning — this adjustment period won't last forever."

- "There is a great service that helps with this exact problem, do you want the website?"

- "Most entrepreneurs get triggered by the visibility required of them. It's totally normal!"

- "I had a similar experience last week. Would you like me to share it with you?"

- "I could help you make a plan to solve this problem. Would you like that?"

- "You're not the first person I've heard say something like that about this school."

- "It's not you — it's them!"

You'll notice that many statements in the examples above are followed by a question that checks for the listener's interest before elaborating or proceeding with further information or assistance. This is a great way to find out, for example, whether it would be helpful for a person to hear your story about the time something similar happened to you, before you start telling it. Sharing personal anecdotes can be a great way to show that we can relate and to help someone else feel less alone, but this may not be what is needed. They may not feel any better just by knowing that it happened to you, too — maybe they don't feel alone or misunderstood, maybe they just need to talk about what happened and to be heard in order to process their experience. When in doubt, we can just ask.

Comfort

This is the most *physical* form of care included in this framework. It includes physical touch, food, and activities that might make someone feel loved, secure, and, well, comfortable. It also includes suggestions for things people can do with their bodies that support emotional regulation, either on their own or with you. Remember, these are just examples — you probably already know many of the things you and your loved ones find comforting, from paying attention to how they handle their big feelings.

Here are some examples of offering *Comfort:*

- "Do you want to make grandma's lasagna recipe for dinner tonight?"

- "Can I offer you a hug, or a back/foot/face massage?"

- "I'm happy to sit with you as long as you're happy with my company."

- "Let's put on your favorite movie/show/music as soon as we get home."

- "Do you want to go for a walk with me and talk about it?"

- "Would it make you feel better if we went to the playground/pool/trampoline park?"

- "How about a nice warm bubble bath?"

- "Do you want me to wrap you up in your cozy blanket/help you put on jammies/hold you for a while?"

Empathy

Although empathy can be behind any of the ICE approaches, and usually is, this category shows ways to communicate it verbally that don't necessarily involve giving information or offering physical comfort. This form of care is usually the hardest for people who were not raised in an emotionally nurturing environment. It takes time to learn the vocabulary of emotions and to get comfortable with and skilled at using it. It can also be hard to listen to other people express their feelings without trying to "fix" them, never mind offering validation. The more we learn how to feel, express and validate our emotions, the better we also become at supporting others with theirs. Getting comfortable with our own emotions can also help give other people (especially our children) permission to take up space with theirs, too.

Here are some examples of offering *Empathy:*

- "How are you feeling about what happened today?"
- "That must be so hard/frustrating/scary for you."
- "I can see how deeply this has affected you."
- "It must take a lot of effort for you to keep showing up with all that going on."
- "I understand why you're so upset/sad/stressed about this."
- "I'm here to listen. Take your time — I promise not to interrupt or give advice."
- "I'm sorry that happened to you. I would feel the same way if it were me."
- "Thank you for sharing that with me. What was it like for you?"

I hope the ICE framework has given you some ideas about creative ways to care for your loved ones and deepen your connection. To reiterate, this list is only a starting point — feel free to add to it, switch things up, or do whatever else feels right for you and your relationships. The most important thing is that we are, or become, safe places for our children to express their feelings, communicate honestly, and talk about their problems. We want our kids to grow up believing that their emotions and developmental needs are good and normal, and to know how to care for themselves and others. As adults, whether or not we have children of our own, we can start by learning to care for our own inner child.

Win-Win Parenting

All the self-regulation skills in the world aren't enough for a mother who works 60-hour weeks at a stressful job, and comes home to a child whose needs and emotions have been repressed from sitting still at a desk in school all day.

The way we structure our lives has as much, if not more, to do with our emotional availability to our children than the years we spend in therapy, the parenting classes or books we seek guidance from, and our very best intentions.

I knew when my daughter was still a baby that I wouldn't want to send her to school. Instinctively, I could sense that she would need me as a consistent adult attachment figure, and that a classroom ratio of thirty to one wasn't going to deliver the goods.

The number one reason moms I talk to don't unschool their kids is that they need to work, and feel they have no choice but to take advantage of the free childcare that schools provide. They don't see how they can make a living while also having enough time, energy or enthusiasm to singlehandedly support their children's education.

Starting a business or landing a remote job only solves half of the problem. The other part involves letting go of culturally inherited ideas about what children need from us in order to become successful in life, and learning to trust our children on the journey of self-directed learning.

Win-Win Parenting is about resolving the conflict between our professional lives and our families by leading both from a place of deep inner knowing, rather than the way we have been told they should, or must, be done.

As unschooling parents, when we fear that our children won't be prepared for adulthood, it's often because a level of authenticity is still missing from our own expression in the world. If we knew from experience that discarding socially acceptable goals to follow our own path worked, we would likely have a lot less fear about our children doing the same. Our children will be encouraged by seeing us follow our authentic dreams and desires — so why don't we go first?

Human Design is one of the most powerful tools I've encountered for discovering who I am outside of the roles assigned to me by patriarchal institutions. Known as "the science of differentiation," Human Design combines various esoteric traditions with quantum physics to help us each understand our unique energetic blueprint for life. It's a fantastic system for deconditioning and unschooling both ourselves and our children, as we each explore our individuality and regain whole-life sovereignty.

Human Design doesn't exactly tell us exactly *what* to do with our lives, but it offers some great clues as to *how* we can live in a way that best utilizes the gifts we have brought into the world, as well as what many of those gifts are. If the entire global population were acting in alignment with their design, we would have a world full of people all doing what they love, and all on their own terms.

Human Design offers us a template for a freer and more fulfilled collective future, in contrast with the homogenized reality created by our deference to the education system, corporations, governments, the nuclear family and other patriarchal institutions.

By teaching me how to work with my natural energy, Human Design helped me realize my calling as a writer, teacher, and speaker, the importance of my work with children and families, the specific approach to coaching that makes the best possible use of my skills, as well as my clairsentience and clairaudience.

Interestingly, none of what I learned was that much of a surprise — the best gift I received from my studies has been validation for paths that were already attractive to me, but which I felt confused about or ambivalent toward. Human Design helped me untangle it all so that I could see which direction I wanted to go, how to get there, and what was holding me back.

I use Human Design with all of my clients for the same purpose. Through understanding their energetic blueprint, women juggling single parenthood and business find that the path forward in their professional lives becomes clearer, and also that things that they used to worry about with regard to unschooling spontaneously resolve on their own.

I have seen problems and complaints such as, "I'm drained from being in conflict with my child all day," or "My child needs structure and it's taking too much time away from my business" or "I'm concerned that my older teen shows no direction in life" all disappear as the parent's own Human Design journey unfolds.

Understanding our children's designs and accommodating them on the unschooling journey is definitely part of this, but something greater seems to happen where living our *own* lives in alignment with our soul's purpose miraculously helps other pieces of the puzzle — including those held by our children — click into place. It's an incredible thing to witness!

Human Design helps us focus our energy where we can have the greatest impact and make a meaningful contribution, rather than freaking out about the world going to shit, feeling paralyzed, and either doing nothing, doing too much, or numbing ourselves with self-destructive behaviors. Our children absorb our attitude about the world, so having a positive one really makes a difference in how they approach the challenges their generation faces now, and the ones yet to come.

Following my energetic blueprint has led me to abandon more self-destructive and unsustainable forms of environmental activism and instead incorporate my love for wilderness into my business and my family life, including helping unschooling and worldschooling community leaders and families find land within their budget that supports their vision for connection, sovereignty, nature play, and conservation. Modeling this for my child means that she also learns how to balance her concern for others with her own needs and to weave her values into her various creative projects.

We can even find out from our chart what our love language is, and where in the world our inner child will feel most at home. This can be invaluable information for us as we design a unique and amazing Second Childhood for ourselves that really hits the spot. This aspect of Human Design also applies to children, but I recommend that parents prioritize their own environment needs because very often when parents feel aligned, it also makes kids feel that all is well in their world.

I learned from studying my design that imagination is my love language, that comedy makes me feel grounded, and that rollercoasters are more healing to me than breathwork.

It's given me the tools to live a Second Childhood that is meaningful to me personally, and perfectly tailored to my unique energetic blueprint. Knowing my child's design has helped me better understand her needs and gifts, and provide her with the most supportive possible resources and experiences for her creativity and emotional wellness.

A word of caution: I highly recommend addressing attachment wounds and other core childhood traumas before delving into Human Design, as it's too easy to outsource our power to external authorities when we are disconnected from our bodies and our sovereignty — especially in the context of spirituality. Human Design can definitely support us in our embodiment journey, but it's not a substitute for integrating trauma, processing our emotions, and regulating our nervous systems. In that spirit, steer clear of anyone who attempts to blame abuse on planetary movements.

Approaching Human Design as a set of tools rather than as a set of rules, and remembering that *we* are the sole authority in our own lives, sets the stage for a healthy exploration of its many teachings without relying on any guru or pedestaled teacher to provide us with all the answers.

The philosophy of win-win parenting isn't just about Human Design — it's rooted more deeply in the magic of alignment. When we live and work in a way that honors who we really are, our relationships stop being a series of problems to solve and start being a place where everyone can thrive.

Whatever map or methods we use to navigate this path, the most important thing is to trust that we will always find a way. When it comes to parenting, we can trust that we are perfectly matched with our children, and refuse to give up until we find the win-win.

Giving Children Room to Grow

In the early years, I tended to underestimate what my child was capable of on her own. I felt afraid to deprive her of even the tiniest bit of support or nurturing, and I was especially terrified about what it would mean about me as a mother if I did.

Naturally, I was exhausted from neglecting myself.

I remember how guilty I felt starting my first online business when my daughter was four, although I very much enjoyed the work and needed the adult interaction. She was at home with me 24/7, so we had plenty of time together, but I still worried that I was neglecting her during the time I spent in front of the computer.

But do you know what my child did while I was working on my business? She started her own!

Yep, she and her bestie made toys from paper and went around selling them door-to-door in our neighborhood of free-range kids. I'll admit that I didn't even know about this commercial venture until she came home one afternoon with a pocket full of cash.

I can promise you that I had not once tried to teach her about business, or pushed her to be creative in any way. Simply by minding my own business, I had inadvertently left my child the space she needed to thrive. She's gone on now to start two other businesses, in which I've been almost completely uninvolved, and only when my help has been requested by the boss herself.

My extreme concern over leaving my child to entertain herself stemmed mostly from my own childhood wounds. I had been abandoned both emotionally and physically, while also smothered by a caregiver who didn't trust me to do things "the right way." My impulse as a parent to compensate for my own losses had me overly worried about neglecting my child, anxious about the prospect of trusting her inner resourcefulness, and excessively concerned about parenting "the right way."

Like watering plants, it's a delicate balance of nurturing and leaving space for them to grow, and our conditioning means that it takes a lot of time, reflection, healing and practice to find that balance. But I can honestly say that every single time I have felt conflicted over whether to do something for myself or to attend to my child, and I have chosen myself, my child has amazed me with her capabilities.

When we see our kids begin to flourish from less management on our part, we gain confidence in them and also in our choice to spend much-needed time and energy on ourselves. After all, children do as we do, and not as we instruct them to. If we aspire for them to have a growth mindset, fall madly in love with themselves, and make smart financial decisions, the best thing we can do is to become living examples.

And of course, releasing attachment to outcomes is also important — we are not here to make up for our own parents' failures, to live out our own dreams vicariously, or to prove our worth as mothers, but to parent the children in front of us. When we build a strong bond with our children and they know that we are available to them as needed, their independence flourishes and we can trust they will let us know what they need, and when.

A Teacher's Confession

The truth? A teacher is often just a big kid with crushed dreams in need of a bi-weekly paycheck. But students often assume the teacher *must* be more intelligent or more worthy of respect, otherwise why would *they* be the ones standing in front of the class commanding everyone's attention?

It took me decades to realize how deeply school affected my self-confidence, especially my perception of my own intelligence and the value of my contributions. When I became a classroom teacher, we used the same exact sixth-grade social studies textbook I had used 10 years before — only now, mine had the answers in the back.

I felt like a fraud — and to an extent, I was. Having earned no teaching credential or degree in education, my freshly college-graduated self had just stubbornly sat up at the city schools administration office all day every day until the superintendent granted me a meeting and hired me. The district was bleeding teachers due to stressful working conditions and issued me an emergency credential on the spot.

While I'm proud of my tenacity and appetite for trial by fire, this story is a great example of how arbitrary social hierarchies can be. The reality was that the district just needed a warm body in the classroom to keep the kids subdued. My classroom management skills were actually crap, which was discussed frequently in my performance reviews. I did things I deeply regret in order to maintain the level of control over students that was expected of me as a teacher, and while I loved working with children, I didn't like the person the working environment made me become.

Creativity was my strength though, and I tried to make class fun. We turned as many lessons as possible into art projects and theater productions. Once, I cut up a disinterested student's test into little pieces and graded him on putting the puzzle back together instead of failing him for not regurgitating whatever stupid lesson from the curriculum he was supposed to prove he had memorized for the test.

I even loved the challenge of reaching the kids in my charge, but ultimately, I couldn't handle the stress. I quit teaching and became a professional ceramic artist, much to the delight of my inner child. I got to host children's birthday parties at the studio, and help artists of all ages realize their creative visions. Working with kids — and adults — became playful and fun again.

Looking back on my time as a classroom teacher, I can definitely say that I learned a lot more from those kids than they learned from me. If they didn't already know it then, I hope they eventually realized that I wasn't any smarter than them, that classroom teaching is just a job and not a divine appointment, and that their true interests and creative expression were more important than anything we read about in the textbook.

As entrepreneur Kevin O'Leary said, "A salary is a drug they give you when they want you to forget about your dreams." I feel lucky to have remembered mine, and hope those kids have found the courage not to settle for any less than their heart's desires.

I'd love the chance to tell my former students all of this, but who am I kidding? Chances are, they figured it out way before I did.

The Children's Resistance

Thump-baddathump-badda-thump-thump-thump...

My sixth-grade students were almost constantly drumming on their desks. As frustrating as it was not being able to command their attention at all times, as was expected of me by the principal, I recognized the children's behavior as a legitimate act of resistance to my authoritarian regime and an assertion of their creative sovereignty.

A lot of the kids in my classes *for sure* did not want to be in school. They had bigger problems than grasping the nuances of politics in Ancient Greece — like whether their family was going to be able to afford the rent next month, how long they were going to be sharing a bedroom with their cousins, or what mood their dad was going to be in when they got home from school.

Graduating middle school hadn't helped their mom do anything besides work in fast food, so what was the point?

Also, they loved to make music. Who was I to tell them it wasn't a good use of their time?

As a student, I was always doodling in the margins of my classwork. Staring at the teacher and listening deeply to every word they said, as was expected of me, was torture. Even though I excelled academically, and even though drawing helped me absorb what I was hearing, I was frequently admonished for not paying attention.

Adults' obsession with controlling children's subjects of study, as well as the way children learn, is obviously not working out that well for children. Not to mention, the adults who insist on high-control learning environments don't seem to be all that happy with where these dogmatic approaches have taken them in life. So, what's the point?

The truth is that schools were never intended to support children in exploring their creative ideas or helping them develop as unique individuals. Schools were created to meet the needs of adults — economically, emotionally, and physically. Schools are structured to train obedient workers, relieve parents of childcare duties during their workday, and sever familial bonds so that children can be emotionally vulnerable enough to buy into an exploitative economic system.

Schools expect kids to invest in adult agendas, physically, emotionally and mentally, while adults in (and outside of) school are not obligated to invest in the physical, emotional or mental wellness of students, or in the students' own visions for their lives. It's sick and sad, and no wonder at all that children actively resist their own oppression, and a shame that children are punished for doing so, when being forced to attend school is already a punishment for the "crime" of being a child.

We need to recognize children's insubordination — in and outside of the classroom — not as misbehavior, but as legitimate protest of unjust treatment. Vive la résistance!

Compulsory Education as Child Labor

Teachers are always up in arms about "disrespectful" students, without recognizing that children are worthy of respect, and that respect is not the same as obedience. How can refusing to do schoolwork, or to attend school at all, be anything besides an expression of self-respect?

Adults center their own hurt feelings about students' disinterest in school, even though children are the ones being hurt most by the system. Teachers and administrators have their own dreams for students, and even use children to achieve their own career goals and institutional targets, all without regard for what kids actually want or need. It's a complete reversal of the natural order, in which adults are meant to meet children's needs and not the other way around.

Teachers regularly refer to school as a "work environment," and insist that children behave accordingly. But this framing raises an uncomfortable truth: compulsory schoolwork is unpaid labor, and *forced* labor at that. If forcing children to perform work is prohibited under child labor laws, why would school be an exception?

The justification is the supposed "right to education," but compulsory education laws mostly exist to generate revenue and keep schools operating, not to serve children's best interests. What's the difference between compulsory education and human trafficking? Schools depend on the forced movement and confinement of students against their will — in any other context, this is called *kidnapping*.

When so-called "enrichment" is unwanted by children and forced on them, education is coercion and a teacher's salary is a bribe to collude in children's oppression. Naturally, anyone forced to act against their will rebels — at least, if their instincts are intact!

So if kids resist school attendance, good. If they find ways to exercise autonomy and dignity in an inherently hostile environment, they deserve our respect. Let's stop pathologizing children's inherent drive for self-determination and start ensuring they have the same rights as any other group of people.

Children's school refusal and classroom disruptions are not pathologies, they are political and they are valid. It's time to stop disrupting children's natural development in service of exploitative adult agendas, and start taking their side.

Meditation Doesn't Replace Mothering

People say that the education system has changed, and often cite the introduction of meditation into the school day as proof. But what hasn't changed is that kids are bringing more trauma to the school day, even from school itself, than teachers and staff are equipped to handle.

I personally love meditation, and owe much of who I am today to the practice. However, meditation can be dangerous for people of any age with trauma or mental health issues, which means that teaching it in schools risks making things worse for kids.

According to researchers at Brown University, "ancient meditation manuals, scientific reports, and mindfulness program guidelines have documented the potential risks of meditation including hypersensitivities, insomnia, anxiety, dissociation, re-experiencing of traumatic memories, and psychosis" [12].

Most teachers are not trauma-informed, much less equipped to support students in safely integrating trauma. Schools are not even set up to meet children's basic emotional needs. They do not offer secure attachment, co-regulation or even reliably safe physical and emotional environments.

In fact, the way meditation is taught in schools resembles emotional repression more than emotional regulation.

"Think of your mind like a pond full of fish and each fish is a feeling. Try to be the pond, not the fish," one parent proudly shared on social media, quoting the new mindfulness mantra their child learned at school.

But children aren't supposed to be the pond — they are supposed to be the fish. The way children learn to regulate their emotions is by being around an adult who holds space for their experience and emotions, not by trying to hold it all themselves.

Co-regulation isn't really possible in a classroom with dozens of kids. If this lesson is teaching children anything, it's to avoid and repress their emotions, to feel shame about not yet being able to self-regulate, and to internalize the harmful idea that their need for connection is somehow wrong.

If it works for some kids, great — but what about all the other kids, who might be made to feel much worse?

The fact that so many children come home from school and immediately spray a day's worth of pent-up emotions all over their mothers makes it obvious that children aren't actually being encouraged to experience, process and express their full range of emotions during the school day.

Instead of patronizingly reassuring moms that they are their children's "safe place" and gaslighting families about the vital role of mothers in childrearing, we should recognize school as the abusive and neglectful environment that it is — with or without meditation tacked on like lipstick on a pig.

It is absurd to have kids waking up to alarms, rushing out the door at the crack of dawn, torn away from their families and faced with all the stress of academic performance and the peer drama that arises in captivity, just to be told to "relax" and "breathe deeply" at school.

We are pretty good at "don't wake the baby," but somehow we justify intentionally wreaking havoc on older kids' sleep schedules. It makes no sense for the kids, but in neither case are sleep schedules designed for the children's own benefit — they exist so that the adults caring for them can catch a break.

The intense intellectual focus of academic work is also a disembodied approach to childrearing that teaches children to dissociate. What's more, the placement of children in schools away from their primary caregivers in some of the most vulnerable years of their lives sabotages the parent/child attachment that is vitally necessary for healthy development.

This can lead to mental health problems such as addiction, both in childhood and later in life, as people attempt to use substances and processes — including unhealthy fixations on things like peer approval, achievement, reading and even overthinking — to make up for the traumatic deprivation experienced in the absence of this bond. What good is education if it leaves emotional orphans in its wake?

The harm done to children in schools also includes physical abuse: in over a dozen U.S. states, school educators and administrators are still legally allowed to *hit* students. Just over a decade ago, over 150,000 students received corporal punishment in a single year in American public schools, and not much has changed since [13, 14]. Research has shown that children's nervous systems experience spanking and other forms of physical "discipline" the exact same way as any other kind of assault.

So why bother with meditation at school, when children are being systematically abused and neglected? These kids don't need mindfulness — they need their mothers, or at least one safe adult attachment figure, and a legal team.

The ugly truth is that children's mental health is important to schools only insofar as it meets the adults' needs and desires, which are for children to mostly sit quietly and follow orders.

If we really want to improve children's mental health at school, let them speak! Let them play! Let them move their bodies! Let them stay home! Let them be — period.

Performance Is Not Play

A really fun musical improv class I took as an adult led me to think about how all the music education I had in school was about learning how to perform *other people's songs* in front of *other people*.

We were never encouraged to improvise or to use our voices or instruments as vehicles for expression of our own inner worlds, much less to do it only for our own enjoyment. So many missed opportunities!

No wonder practicing always felt like such a chore and I could never stick with anything, hopping from one instrument and instructor to another — I was subconsciously looking for the magic one that would give me permission to be creative rather than just regurgitate other musicians' work.

Even though I was supposedly in music classes all those years to "play" the guitar, clarinet, violin, piano, etc., I have really only just begun truly *playing* music as an adult.

As adults, we can remove the expectations instilled in us to be "good at" music, to create it only or mainly for others' enjoyment, or to stick with a particular instrument or form of expression when it doesn't light us up anymore.

We can avoid putting pressure on our children by letting them choose when to practice an instrument or whether to play at all, how seriously they take music or any other creative activity, decentering performance and other people's music, and emphasizing the child's own pleasure in playing and listening to music.

The essence of playing is not knowing how things will turn out, and we can build this truth into how we approach music and other hobbies. For example, buying used instruments at a lower price can remove the pressure to commit from the get go and make music feel more like an adventure than a burden.

We can use our voices to share our own frequency and truth with the world, we can play and have fun with our creative expression without regard for outcomes or audiences, and we can make our own music as the soundtrack to our real lives — the greatest works of art we will ever create.

Raising Kids with A Growth Mindset

Very often parents ask me how to "help" their child have a more positive attitude about something their child obviously has zero interest in doing.

This approach is a bit backward — a growth mindset isn't about manipulation or mind control. Raising kids with a growth mindset isn't about getting kids to embrace *our* goals for their lives; it's about supporting kids in reaching their *own* goals!

Otherwise, it would be called "raising kids with a suck-it-up-and-eat-shit mindset."

This impulse to force change in children for our own convenience reveals something deeper: the power imbalance between adults and children often distorts how we perceive their needs. Sometimes, *we* are the ones who need to work on our growth mindset!

I don't know about you, but I'm always kicking and screaming to avoid challenging my own biases and limiting beliefs. I came to parenting ready to let my child be her own person, but that proved easier said than done: "Be free, little one!! …Wait — not like THAT!!!"

Overcoming my own internal struggles as a parent is the most important work I do in teaching my child to have a growth mindset. I try to be transparent about my own growth process — changing my mind, doing hard things, facing fears, setting goals, identifying obstacles, acknowledging progress, handling failure, trying new things, celebrating success, sometimes even quitting for good.

I also try not to show it when I'm appalled by my child's ideas, requests and choices, although I have one of those faces that shows everything… So we joke about that, and even exaggerate for comedic effect. We have as much fun as possible, whenever possible. Change, mistakes, misunderstandings

— all can become invitations for us to play. Everything can be play — most kids already know this.

When we set our own goals, motivation comes naturally — that's when learning can be fun and easy. Then, and only then, a growth mindset can move mountains. When adults forget this, it's usually because we are still dragging ourselves towards goals other people set for us a long time ago. Too often, we pass this weight onto our children.

The best thing we can do to raise kids with a growth mindset is to keep growing ourselves. These kids are gonna run the world one day! Let's see what we can learn from them.

Villains Are Made, Not Born

Children need to be free to learn, to make mistakes, to be messy, to be wrong, to be irresponsible. Above all, children need to be *needy*!

However, children are widely perceived to be sinful, greedy, selfish, even evil for having and expressing perfectly developmentally appropriate needs.

Instead of cherishing children and honoring their vulnerability, we often project motives onto them that we inherit from our own upbringing, passing on a negative view of children rooted in patriarchal ideology. There is no room for a child's full self-expression in a system that centers men's needs and desires, which is what the nuclear family is designed to do and what the school system supports by brainwashing children to fulfill corrupt corporate and government agendas. The male-centric institutions of law, education, religion and the nuclear family all play a part.

Projecting negative character traits onto children tends to happen in the context of adults' lack of time, interest, skill or capacity to meet children's needs. Parents engage in desperate mental gymnastics to blame the child rather than themselves or forces seemingly beyond their control, because it gives the *illusion* of control. When done intentionally and en masse, as religion tends to do, this influences larger cultural attitudes toward children. The result is a society that produces humans who feel guilty just for existing, and who have internalized the belief that if they could only be better people, all the world's problems would be solved. This conveniently creates a population that is eager to please, but also which many children and adults do not survive, due to suicide, addiction, illness, and susceptibility to remaining in abusive situations (aka, murder).

Children are not born guilty or evil. Villains aren't born, they are made — and often by being born into the very culture that discredits children's inherent goodness in the first place!

The concept of "sin" often describes behaviors rooted in attachment trauma. When children's needs aren't met, of course they act out in an attempt to get them met. Unmet childhood needs can lead someone to be untrusting of the world and inconsiderate of others — as these persist and are invalidated and stigmatized, the potential for antisocial behaviors increases.

For example, a child whose attachment needs go unmet due to their mother being forced to remain in an abusive relationship, rendering her emotionally unavailable to both herself and the child, and leaving the child grappling with trauma of their own from the narcissistic parent, might resort to socially unsanctioned or self-destructive behaviors to get the attention they need.

Kids are also frequently labeled as "misbehaving" in school due to things they do to attract attention or to maintain bonds with other students as a replacement for the primary attachment relationship. Attachment trauma can lead to lack of impulse control, addiction, inability to focus, preoccupation with peers, lack of social skills and difficulty with emotional regulation, to name just a few things.

Children who carry attachment trauma into adulthood often struggle with basic self-care tasks, maintaining relationships, pursuing goals and keeping jobs. This festering wound, created, exploited, and worsened by one patriarchal institution after another, is at the root of many behaviors that eventually land people behind bars. A person who is unable to take care of themselves in socially prescribed ways is going to have to find other ways to survive.

Ta-da — a "criminal" is made.

Research shows a strong connection between early life trauma and incarceration rates. One study found that incarcerated men reported nearly *four times* as many adverse childhood experiences (ACEs) as the regular adult male population [15]. Another found that 82% of inmates at a women's correctional facility had been abused during childhood, with nearly 60% having been sexually abused by a parental figure [16]. What would our prisons and jails even look like without attachment trauma? The government would have to find another way to keep profits rolling into the prison industrial complex.

In addition to releasing nonviolent offenders and women imprisoned for self-defense, I'd love to see more programs supporting formerly incarcerated women in resolving trauma and pursuing entrepreneurship, or even better, avoiding incarceration to begin with.

Maybe I'll start one — I already teach women how to buy real estate all over the world without bank approval, and this would make a great career for women with street smarts and even a criminal record. You don't need a passport or a real estate license to make international property deals. Plus, with the high income-to-work-hours ratio, there's time to raise your own kids while simultaneously reparenting yourself — potentially breaking cycles of poverty, crime and trauma all at once.

We can all start right now by putting the guilt back where it belongs — on the patriarchal institutions that forcibly separate children from their primary attachment figures and prevent mothers from being emotionally available to their children, using children and traumatized adults as pawns in a game of power and profit.

Ending compulsory education would make a massive difference in healthy child development — ending father rule and reinstating global matriarchy is a slightly taller order, but it's also on my list.

The NEAR Parenting Framework

NEAR is a parenting framework I developed to detail the factors that contribute to secure attachment and other aspects of successful childrearing, particularly as they relate to radical unschooling families.

The reason these factors are special to radical unschooling families is because the parent is taking on several roles that would otherwise be taken on by the teacher and other professionals in the child's life. Of course, in a functional society the village is not an institution at all, and there are many competent attachment figures in the picture. But this is not the current reality for many families.

Although my perspective is that it is normal and natural for the parents and other trusted adults to play the main roles in a child's development, in practice it can take extra awareness, skill and strategy. It's not always something our own parents modeled well for us, and the world still isn't exactly set up to support us in supporting our children. I'll address this in more detail after outlining the framework.

As with anywhere else in this book, please substitute the word "parent" with "caregiver" or whatever role best describes your relationship to the child or children in your care.

The acronym NEAR stands for Nurturing, Empathetic, Attuned and Responsive. Here is what these mean in the context of this framework, followed by a deeper dive into each and how they work together:

Nurturing

The parent nurtures the child's natural talents, shows interest in the child's interests and facilitates the child's exploration of their passions in life as well as their creative expression.

Empathetic

The parent puts themselves in the child's position emotionally and actively tries to understand and validate the child's experience in order to connect and co-regulate with the child.

Attuned

The parent pays attention to the child's needs, wants and feelings and is mentally and emotionally available enough to "tune in" and resonate with these as needed throughout the day.

Responsive

The parent responds to the child's needs throughout the day, both on request from the child and according to the parent's own intuitive and instinctive faculty and leadership.

A quick note before we get into how each of these factors into the day-to-day reality of radical unschooling: while in another framework for attachment parenting these might be grouped together, I've distinguished them as four separate things because it makes it easier to discuss the different skills and strategies that each requires, and how these differ from what happens in a school-like environment.

"Nurturing" is a term usually used to describe all of the above aspects of healthy parenting, but I'm using it here specifically to talk about supporting children's talents and creative expression. Radical unschooling provides our children with an amazing opportunity to get clear on their passions in life and begin to pursue them from an early age. It's not that they are pushed to choose a profession before they are ready — it's that they have the freedom to explore so many different options because their time and energy aren't being diverted by the demands of schoolwork in a parasitic education system.

Perhaps ironically, and contrary to what others may assume, this actually often leads our kids to know who they are and how they are best suited to contribute to the world around them much earlier than their schooled counterparts. By contrast, children being pressured to decide what they will do with their entire lives before gaining the necessary experience and self-knowledge to discover their path naturally is a less-acknowledged form of school trauma.

Nurturing our children's natural curiosity means first giving them the space to pursue it. This means not letting them explore only within a limited range of interests and activities that we have pre-approved, but giving them access to the world and letting them follow their own inquiry process to the level of their own satisfaction.

There's nothing wrong with the practice of "strewing" (placing items around the home that may invoke our children's interest) — providing an adequately stimulating environment is essential for healthy child development — as long as we are not attached to any outcomes. This means allowing the child the freedom to accept or reject these invitations without any fuss on our part, while also nurturing the actual interests expressed by the child.

It also means taking our child out into the "real world" to explore things that may pique their interest, and supporting them in pursuing those even if they are not activities or experiences typically available to children. I'm not talking about letting a preschooler take the wheel on a highway or letting them crawl into a restaurant kitchen uninvited — I'm talking about developmentally appropriate and respectful things like asking grown-ups you meet in public questions about their work, taking them on trips to places they ask to visit, helping them research topics of interest at the library and helping them find a mentor or apprenticeship.

Or, it *could* be letting them drive a tractor, if you have the equipment and the space and the relationship to make that safe and practical. I let my daughter play in fountains when she was a baby, use knives when she was three years old (with my supervision and help) and make art in public places using natural and found objects. I responded to her desires in ways that were accessible to us, and was willing to think outside the box in order to bridge the gaps.

The things we all feel comfortable supporting our children in, and the ways we all go about it, will differ greatly among radical unschooling parents. Differences in our access to resources and systemic factors like racial discrimination influence what feels safe and possible for each of us when it comes to going against the grain, and these choices do not make any of us more or less of a radical unschooling family.

It's also important not to undermine any family's approach to radical unschooling solely on the basis that it is facilitated by socioeconomic advantage. We should focus on making resources and safety available to *more* families, rather than shaming or attempting to restrict some families' freedom out of jealousy or resentment about what some kids can "get away with."

The challenges we face can even inspire innovation and become grist for the mill of our family's creative practices. For example, many families start online businesses for the flexibility to choose their own work hours, the freedom to relocate to a place where children have access to nature or community resources, and to escape the constant stress of living paycheck to paycheck. These differences can make a world of difference in quality of life through the lens of NEAR.

Nurturing our children's talents and interests takes time and energy, but allowing them the freedom to explore their natural curiosity can actually free up our time. A lot of unschooling parents worry about providing enough direction for their children and keeping them busy with organized activities during the day, which ends up being a massive time suck.

Parents who think they don't have time to unschool often think that self-directed education, despite the name, is like doing school at home, because they can't imagine their kids being independent enough not to need them constantly. But this dependency is created by the school system and by the patriarchal approach to family life that mistakenly sees children as lost souls in need of correction in order to become successful in life.

When we give our children the time, space and support they need to find out who they really are and to pursue what truly interests them, they can surprise us with their ability to be self-motivated and disciplined in completing projects, and to fill their days without much, if any, interference or instruction from us.

Our children's ability to follow through with projects they have started is also connected to their ability to regulate their impulses. They learn this from us, just as we learned it from our own parents. When we demonstrate self-leadership with regard to nurturing and following through with our own dreams and goals, our children are empowered to do the same. We can't abandon our own dreams and then complain when our children want to quit ballet only a week in, now can we?

Of course, kids wanting to quit is not necessarily connected to any example we have set. It's not the kids' fault that there is an eight-week or $200 commitment to lessons. Usually these obligations are simply what's convenient for the adults

— the kids just wanted to play tennis or learn guitar, and weren't expecting to find out so soon that it wasn't for them, or that attending classes twice a week feels like too much. There are often options for private instruction in various activities that don't require such a commitment, as well as the possibility of learning from friends and family, trial days and partial refunds that can take the pressure off of parents on a budget.

Empathy is a complex issue in patriarchal society, particularly when it comes to highly sensitive people. Even though I'm a highly sensitive person and was raised by parents who were likely highly sensitive themselves, we all struggled with experiencing and expressing empathy in healthy ways. I didn't receive any guidance around boundaries or channeling my sensitivity in ways that enriched my life instead of overwhelming me — on the contrary, my empathy was exploited for adults' benefit.

For many years, I masked my sensitivity with substances that numbed me to my natural empathic tendencies. I felt everything so deeply, and there was so much in my childhood environment to feel, as well as so many demands on my emotional labor, that I coped by shutting down. Unfortunately, this led me to feel cut off from the world and from my own body, and unable to *feel* my own and others' experiences in a way that healthy relationships require.

Much of the empathy I've been able to offer my child has come from my own healing journey, nervous system capacity expansion and continued mastery of my gifts and self-care. The more empathy I've given myself, and the more ongoing care I provide myself both emotionally and physically, such as with nutrition and regard to my sensory environment, the more empathy I've been able to extend to my child and the better I've been able to model creating a life that honors our emotional needs and sensitivities.

(See the chapter "ICE for Emotional Wounds" to learn some practical ways to express empathy if you want help in this area, and also my online course, *The Validational*, for a fun and easy way to learn how to validate and express empathy — first toward yourself, and then with others.)

Even if we don't have any particular challenges around empathy in general, it can still be hard for us as parents to remember what it was like to be a child, to make time to sit with our children in their feelings and to open ourselves to sharing their emotional experience.

Parenting also has a way of bringing up emotions we didn't know that we had, and also cause issues to resurface that we were under the impression we had already dealt with. I thought I had done a lot of inner work before I became a parent, but still found my child's emotions triggering as hell. I had to learn how to respond in ways that were appropriate for her developmental level as I couldn't just excuse myself the way I would if I needed space from an adult interaction. Earplugs and headphones (for both myself and my child), and yes, a well-timed exit from the scene to self-regulate, have all come in handy at times.

Showing our children empathy helps our children understand, accept, and process their emotions. Connecting with our children can help children connect the dots between their experiences and their feelings, and to feel less alone with them. The better we are at doing this for ourselves, the more naturally empathy comes to us in our relationships with our children and others.

When we are *Attuned* and *Responsive* to our children's needs, our children learn how to prioritize their own needs during the day instead of fixating on work or other projects (at the most productive end of the dissociation spectrum!) at the expense of their emotions and desires. The better we demonstrate this in our relationship with our own work, the more our children internalize healthy standards for their own lives.

While schools often present themselves as providing a nurturing and emotionally safe environment, they don't even pretend to offer children attunement and responsiveness on an individual basis. With ratios often exceeding thirty students to one teacher, it's simply not possible for even the most emotionally available adult to be aware of each and every child's needs, and much less so to respond in the moment.

As unschooling parents, we may feel overwhelmed by our own children's needs, even if we only have one child and even if we aren't working much or dealing with much of our own "stuff" emotionally. This makes sense, as we are meant to be doing this with aunties, grandmas, sisters and cousins who would all be safe attachment figures for our children.

The work of responding to children's needs is a community effort that can take a lot of intentionality to organize in modern-day society. I've written more about my personal experience with this in "The Art of Homewrecking" and various other essays in this book.

When my daughter and I are working on our separate projects in the same room, or within earshot of each other, it's easy for me to keep feelers out for her needs, feelings and wants, and for her to communicate them. We do a lot of "coworking" in the living room, in bed, and in coffee shops, which allows us to be connected while immersed in our own worlds. Visiting different parks and cafés together, sometimes with electronics in tow, is a great way to switch up the scenery and explore the places we live in and travel to while staying more or less attuned.

For an indoorsy kid, or one who needs a lot of time to adjust to changes in their environment, gradually trying new foods and seeking out familiar favorites also provides great motivation for venturing out of the comfort zone (or for creating one, as is often the case). Tailoring our travel itineraries and habits to our children's needs and interests, and making adjustments along the way, can dramatically reduce the emotional labor of parenting.

While working from home on deep focus tasks or with private clients, or doing self-care and other things that drew me away from immediate presence with my child while she was still very young, I used to set alarms throughout the day to check up on her (yes, like a Tamagotchi). I would take these cues to ask my daughter if she was hungry, how she was feeling, whether she wanted to play with some clay or take some other kind of tactile break from her online activities, such as a trip to the beach or the park.

Now at age 10, my child will let me know if she needs anything, even when we're not in close proximity. But this is only because of my consistent attunement and responsiveness toward her for years prior, whether relying on my intuition and motherly instincts or alarms and calendar reminders.

Nurturing, empathy, attunement and responsiveness each take time, skills and strategy — and often, really big changes in our lives. Structuring our lives around our children's needs and our own can mean starting an online business or taking a job that allows us the flexibility to set our own hours, and to be interruptible. It can mean making a career change that reduces our workload or changes the type of work that we do. One simple pivot made by a client of mine was switching from working with a highly traumatized population as a psychotherapist to working with individuals who are more emotionally stable as a coach — making her more emotionally and physically available to her children.

This is one of the main things I have helped unschooling parents to do in my coaching practice. As with the example of the psychotherapist-turned-coach, it's often easier than parents think to transfer their existing skill set to a business that allows them to put their family — and their own needs — first. I've written more about this in "Bring Your Inner Child to Work Day."

With the NEAR framework, a little self-reflection, intentionality and self-leadership, we can find creative ways to meet our kids' needs while living our own lives and building the village that helps us hold it all together.

A Pleasure to Speak with You

In Win-Win Parenting, we prefer reaching mutual goals through voluntary cooperation and leadership over the use of force. In contrast with an authoritarian model of parenting, this means that the process matters as much to us as the outcome. Even though we may desire a specific outcome, what we value most is staying connected to our children.

Instead of seeing our children as *obstacles* between us and our goal, or even enemies, we see them as *collaborators* in a relationship defined by trust, emotional intimacy and creativity, and on a path where our values guide the way — even if they don't lead us to the exact place we originally envisioned.

One of the most important ways we demonstrate leadership instead of control in our relationships with our children is in our communication. The most powerful way we can speak to our children is with the language of embodied truth. This is the most honest and non-coercive way for us to communicate with anyone, and it's no different when it comes to parenting.

One of the most satisfying results of this model is how it has the power to shift our children's communication with us, without us needing to instruct or correct them on it. Because our children are hardwired to attune to our frequency, our children also end up communicating in this language instead of making demands on us. Through their relationship with us, children can learn healthy intimacy skills that will help them navigate connections outside the family and build emotionally satisfying adult lives.

The language of embodied desire is based on identifying what we want, embracing it, and expressing it without expectation. It makes parenting so much easier and more pleasurable when the soundscape at home is more like: "I'd really love it if the table were clean," or "It seems like a good day for the park," or "I'd really love some water right now," rather than: "You need to clean that table!" or "Get me water!" or "We are going to the park now, like it or not."

Consider also the difference between "It looks like the car needs to be cleaned out," "The cat needs fresh water," or "The sink is full of dishes," spoken with a pleasant or emotionally neutral tone of voice, and with an angry tone. It's clear which of these statements would inspire you to take action or at least respond positively, instead of becoming immediately defensive, angry and determined to put up a fight.

Caveat: if you have previously used a more indirect way of speaking in order to passive-aggressively make demands, your children may interpret even your most authentic, embodied expression of desire as criticism or threat. For example, if you've ever said something like, "It would be really nice if you unloaded the dishwasher for once," or even without the "for once" but in a nagging tone, you'll have to become really well-practiced in letting go of the resentment in your voice before this will become effective. It takes some time but in my experience, other people will start to respond differently to you not all that long once you're doing this consistently.

The paradox here is that you have to let go entirely of the need for your communication to be "effective" in order for it to actually *be* effective. Your tone really has to be authentic with no hint of pressure, resentment or guilt in your voice. When making the change to put relationships first, we have to surrender any sense of self-righteousness that has poisoned them, and let people come around at their own pace and in their own way.

This isn't a "parenting hack" that promises instant gratification so much as a peaceful way of being that can improve every area of your life. You have to really *be* this way for it to work, and that takes healing and practice if you're used to holding other people responsible for meeting your needs and desires or issuing demands and guilt-trips.

This is about trying something new and letting go of the outcome altogether, which means being willing to express something like, "I'd really love it if there were room for me to sit on the couch right now," or "I'd really love to watch a movie tonight," and then being okay when no one gives a shit. You have to do it for yourself first. You have to actually enjoy communicating in this way because you have felt how much speaking with resentment hurts *you*. You have to enjoy speaking your desires out loud, even if it doesn't get you what you want. And this means that you have to be willing to do things for yourself that you wish others would do for you — including the cleaning and picking up that you have previously assigned as chores, or that you really and truly believe your children owe you, or even that they previously agreed to do. Expressing our needs and desires more eloquently doesn't mean we aren't still responsible for them.

Of course, there's nothing wrong with just asking someone directly to make space for you on the couch. The point is that when we express our desires authentically, we open ourselves to true connection with others. It's a vulnerable place to be, compared to issuing commands toward our children. And it's a beautiful thing when we discover that our children want good things for us as well. This is different from people-pleasing, because there is no demand being made of them, explicitly or implicitly. It is the child's natural, authentic love for you that makes them want to do things for you. It's not about them putting their needs and desires aside for yours. When the children's attachment needs are met, and they feel nourished and well-loved, they become *inspired* to do nice things for you.

Too often adults demand a show of love and obedience from children, which is so damaging to the child and to the relationship. It can take a lot of time for the child to trust that they won't be punished for doing something that displeases you. It's important to be patient and to recognize the child's right to feel the situation out before joining you in this new way of being and communicating.

Also, it can't be emphasized enough that this approach is part of a much broader approach to childrearing where children are seen as beings worthy of respect and consideration, instead of related to with hostility. If what I'm sharing here is taken out of context and used to manipulate, it will backfire. You won't have success with this practice in a relationship otherwise defined by dishonesty and coercion.

Because of my preference for authentic communication, I've never cared whether my daughter ever said "please." I've always felt that use of this word spoke to an underlying power dynamic: in other words, "I'll ask you for what I need, but I have to ask a certain way or else I might not get it." Or, "I'm saying please, even though this is really more of a demand." To me, it seems manipulative, performative and unnecessarily deferential.

Whether I want to help someone else or not has nothing to do with whether they use the word "please." How it would make me feel to do the thing, has everything to do with how inspired I feel to meet their request. And the more genuine and vulnerable my child's request, or anyone else's, the more inspired I am to grant it.

The same goes for saying "thank you." My child doesn't need to express gratitude for being served a meal or given a birthday present, because I'm enjoying the whole process — picking out a gift or preparing food, and then getting to watch her enjoy it, too. I don't need to consume her gratitude to feel good, because I already feel good about what I've done. My boundaries make sure of that.

My child is free to express her desires, and I am free to meet them, or not. Of course, if it's something she can't do for herself, I'm on it. I'm not saying I never have to do things I don't feel like doing as a parent, or that I require her to communicate a certain way in order to get her needs met. These are just ways that I've found to increase the amount of joy in our connection and in the work of meeting my child's needs, and to reduce the frequency of experiences I don't want, such as being issued commands and treated like a servant.

This also doesn't mean that I never tell my child "no," or that I never tell her what to do. Our relationship is based on respect and autonomy, so when I say something like, "It's time to brush your teeth," or even, "Get your shoes on," it doesn't come across as an order, but a reminder. If every single thing I said to my child was in the form of a command, saying these things would understandably rub her the wrong way.

Because she can feel that I'm fundamentally *on her side*, she trusts that my intentions are pure and that I'm not trying to assert control over her just for the sake of it. She doesn't feel the need to assert control over herself in these instances either, because she isn't perpetually deprived of autonomy. When parents say their kids "don't listen," "talk back" or "show disrespect," there's usually a shortage of both autonomy and connection in the child's life.

Needless to say, there are nuances here that are difficult to explain out of context but which can more easily be identified in concrete situations and relationships.

Now that my daughter is old enough to stay home alone for short stretches of time, I can say things like, "I'm going to the park today. It's the one with the exercise equipment. Do you want to come?" And it doesn't matter to me so much if she does come along, because it won't mean the difference between *me* going or not. But when she was smaller, I definitely did a lot of "We're going to the park today," because I would have lost my mind if I hadn't gotten to spend some time outside. And sometimes my daughter would say, "Do I have to?" and I would say, "Yes." And she wouldn't be happy about it, but when we got there, she wouldn't want to leave. I learned to trust my instincts on whether to push her or not, when to hold firm for her benefit or for my own, and when to be more flexible. This experimentation was how I came to understand the role of embodied leadership in parenting.

The important thing is that I took responsibility for getting my own needs met. I wasn't going to give my child a choice about whether or not to go to the park, if it meant the difference between me feeling like I could go on living or not. I see a lot of parents get tripped up because they are giving their children choices that they can't actually cope with.

We set ourselves up for resentment toward our children when we ask them for permission to take care of ourselves. The truth is that our children aren't responsible for the cleanliness of our homes, our emotional needs, or our self-care routines. They are children. As adults, it is ultimately our responsibility to make sure the pets are fed and the dishes are washed and the pizza crust is scraped off of the floors. Our children didn't ask to be born. We owe it to them to provide a safe, hygienic and loving home environment to the best of our ability.

At times we may want to give our children more responsibility, either at their request or for our own convenience, but we have to keep our expectations in check. Even if our children begged us for a puppy and *promised* that they would walk him every day, it's still always been *our* responsibility as adults. *We* are the ones who chose to adopt an animal and to take responsibility for its wellbeing. Children aren't capable of signing legally binding contracts for this reason. Anything a child agrees to do is purely theoretical because they can't legally give consent. So next time we consider taking on an added responsibility such as a pet, we can ask ourselves if we will still be happy with our choice if our children end up, you know, *childrening,* and leave all the work to us. To consider this possibility is to take full responsibility for our decisions, and our role, as parents.

There are other things we can do to reduce the burden of housework and avoid straining our relationship with our children with "chores" drama. One of the reasons I don't really care whether my daughter puts away her own laundry or not is that all of our clothes together fit inside a single suitcase. It's just not that much stuff to keep organized. I also don't always fold her clothes. She doesn't care about having wrinkles in her t-shirts, and neither do I. So, it takes about 15 seconds for me to throw her clean clothing into a dresser drawer when I don't feel like doing more. If I don't even feel up to doing that, I can just tell her that her clean laundry is in a pile on the table, or wherever else it's convenient for me to leave it, and let her decide whether she wants to go into the kitchen to get dressed every day or whether she'd rather come get her clothes and put them away in her room.

We don't have mountains of stuff needing to be picked up all the time and put away, and we don't have any more pets than I can handle taking care of on my own. But when I do get overwhelmed with household tasks, I can also tell her honestly that I need help and she usually steps up. We also don't have more suitcases or belongings than we can comfortably carry between the two of us. If my daughter decides that she doesn't want to carry a suitcase, then we have a conversation about reducing the amount of things she owns and travels with. So there's no guilt, shame or pressure around it, that's just a natural built-in limit we are working with. (Quick tangent: suitcases come in sets of three, but humans only have two arms — were they designed for aliens?). Honoring my limits, and speaking them clearly and neutrally, is essential to maintaining a healthy connection with both myself and with my child, and also teaches my child to do the same.

The mind taunts us with impossible choices, but embodiment guides us to the win-win. When we feel victimized by hard choices, clarity and power live in the wisdom of our womanly instincts. Learning to take responsibility for our needs, to value consent, and to enjoy authentic communication transforms how we relate to our children and others.

It becomes, quite simply, a pleasure to speak with them.

Parenting with Pleasure

Beyond communicating needs, there is so much we can talk about with our kids to increase our enjoyment of parenting and show our kids how to enjoy life as well.

Paying attention to the things that bring us joy and pleasure during the day, naming them, and taking time to really enjoy them is a great habit to pick up. We can do this by noticing and naming the things that we love, both privately to ourselves and out loud in front of our children. There's no need to push them to do the same; they will naturally follow our example if our intentions are pure.

We can also support our children by being attuned to their joy and pleasure, and naming it to help them make the connection between what's going on around them and how they are experiencing it in their bodies. When we see our child enjoying playing with a puppy, we can reflect back to them what we see: "The puppy is so soft! You're having so much fun, it's exciting to finally find a dog that likes to play fetch!"

Of course, if your child is irritated by your playing narrator, pipe down and just watch them quietly. This will still help *you* attune to your child's enjoyment and increase your satisfaction as a parent. I make a point to stop what I'm doing and notice my child enjoying life, whenever possible. It brings me joy, as well.

The more we focus on our child's enjoyment of life and our own, the happier we both are. This includes focusing on what we like about our kids, rather than on what we perceive to be failures or flaws. Our attention has the power to make things grow, just like water does with plants. When we make a point of telling our kids what's right about them, they can develop a positive self-concept and ultimately face challenges with more resilience.

Another angle to take here is making dreaded household tasks fun. Instead of treating washing dishes or doing laundry as a punishment, we can treat them as acts of devotion and even play. "Shall we make this fun?" I have often asked my daughter when starting a tedious chore, and then we'd pretend the dirty socks on the floor were missing amulets that would save a beloved world of magical forest creatures

— if only they could make it into the basket. I mean, the enchanted cauldron. Or whatever... It doesn't have to make sense, it just has to be fun.

If you find it hard to feel any joy at all, you're not alone and you're not broken. We can store multiple lifetimes of trauma and emotion in our pelvic area, and this can block us from feeling into the pleasure of the present moment. I highly recommend that women who feel victimized by motherhood do a sacral clearing — I had a profound experience doing this, where I met my ancestors and learned the stories behind the energetic blockages I carried in my body hundreds of years after their traumas.

It's amazing how much easier parenting is when you're in touch with your sacral energy and power. Having kids who reflect the work we have done in this area makes parenting such a pleasure!

Saying Yes to Our Kids

It can be so easy to get into the habit of saying *no* to our kids without even considering the validity of their requests. We might have gotten mostly *no* from our own parents, or we may be exhausted and just not really up for the unpredictability that comes with entertaining the first *yes* that so often leads to further requests.

This doesn't necessarily mean we're control freaks; we may actually have been accommodating our children's needs and desires so much that we no longer feel in control of our own lives. The stress, anxiety, resentment, and potential burnout this can cause, in addition to the other things in our lives that might be wearing us down and out, can make automatically denying our children's request seem like a necessary act of self-defense.

Both saying *yes* to everything our kids want, and saying *no* to everything they want, can be signs that parental burnout is either near or already here. And they can both be inherited patterns from our own childhoods that are activated without conscious thought on our part.

Learning how to find the balance between our kids' wants and needs and our own can be challenging and probably not something we can master without trial and error, but listening to our bodies can go a long way toward reducing the learning curve. Of course, listening to our bodies may be new to us as well, and a learning curve of its own. The better we get at this, the better equipped we are to make decisions for our families that honor our needs, the more sustainable our family lives become, and the better example we set for our kids about making healthy choices and maintaining good boundaries.

Getting in touch with our bodies, our emotions, our needs and our desires positions us to better sense these in our children as well. As we become more skillfully attuned to our children, we can more easily tell when something they are asking for is a need versus a want, how badly they really need something, and whether there is actually an unspoken need behind our children's request that they could use our help acknowledging. We can even go beyond *yes* and *no* to come up with alternate ideas that create a win-win situation for everyone.

We don't do "yes days" in our family because every day is a day I consider my child's needs and desires as well as my own. There is no day where I'm willing to collapse my own boundaries to cater to my child, and there is no day where my child has to suppress her own needs in order for me to meet mine: every day is a *win-win day*.

It can definitely be overwhelming to think about meeting our own needs on top of our children's needs and all our other adult responsibilities. One really helpful way to find balance is by understanding the difference between our needs, and the strategies we use to meet those needs.

I first learned about this framework in a class on Non-Violent Communication (NVC), and it has become indispensable to the Win-Win Parenting approach. I highly recommend Marshall Rosenberg's book *Nonviolent Communication* for the list of feelings and needs he includes as a reference, and a breakdown of his approach. When there are conflicting needs within the family, the key is meeting the need *behind* the specific strategy that each person may insist on or prefer.

There are many different ways to meet each of our needs, and we are more likely to find balance in parenting our inner child, our outer children and other responsibilities when we keep an open mind and take a creative approach to solving problems with the goal of getting everyone's needs met.

This connects to the idea of the Fertile Universe — when we let go of doing things "our way" and become willing to consider the multitude of possibilities that make up our world, we find more ways to get things done and we can do them without steamrolling over anyone's needs.

When we do say *no* to our children, it's best that it be for real reasons rather than an automatic, subconscious reflex. With practice, we can discern whether we really mean *no* or whether we just need time to think about it, and we can learn to pause before answering and to communicate to our children that we need some time to think it over before responding.

We can take time to assess our own needs and decide whether we are truly available for a *yes*, in order to avoid crossing our own boundaries and developing resentment toward our children, or burning out as parents.

Alongside our kids, we can brainstorm possible ways to meet everyone's needs, and we can become willing to consider different approaches that satisfy more than just ourselves.

The antidote to too much "no" isn't more "yes" — it's "how?"

The opposite of negativity isn't positivity — it's creativity.

Mainstream parenting has a lot of *no* built into it because children are perceived as being "spoiled" if they get too much of what they want. Sadly enough, this is true even for children's developmental needs such as for touch, food, elimination, play, attention, sleep, learning and love.

Many parents fear that their children won't be well-equipped for adulthood if they are "coddled" — while it may be true in the sense that children need autonomy in order to gain enough independence to take care of themselves as adults, this is twisted to mean that children should be robbed of their childhoods in preparation for a cold, hard world that won't be attuned to their needs.

While much of the modern world may be cold and hard, and it's true that the whole world won't be attuned to us, we can't develop properly without first being allowed to be needy little kids.

Forcing children to act like little adults will have the opposite of the intended effect. Many adults are just as immature as they were as children, not because they weren't "disciplined" by their parents, but because they were neglected and/or abused as children and therefore never progressed to adulthood developmentally. This can even lead to chronic illness, mental illness and other disabling conditions that leave an adult child literally unable to function independently or effectively in the world.

At the very worst, children who are punished for asking for things their parents can't or don't want to provide often grow into adults who lack the ability to try new things, communicate their needs and desires, or take action in important areas of their lives. This is a real handicap that can take years or even decades for the adult child to recover from — if they recover at all.

It can be hard to hear our children complain about things that seem small to us, and to dare to ask for so much more than we did as kids. We want them to have the very best, but at the same time, we wish that they could understand how lucky they are to have everything they already do.

But having ungrateful children is actually a *good* thing — it means we've successfully calibrated the next generation's nervous systems to a higher standard. This will determine what they will and won't accept as adults, which can bring them a much better quality of life than if they have been conditioned to expect very little.

So — may our children continue to moan about unrelatable luxury problems and prosper in ways that would make our ancestors cringe.

Instead of preparing children for a cruel world by treating them cruelly, why don't we treat kids the way they deserve to be treated, and then let *them* decide how to handle the cruel world?

Adults whose developmental needs were met in childhood are far better equipped to function in the world — cruel or not — and also much more likely to be able to change the world without first needing decades of therapy.

It's not possible to love our children too much. Making sure our children know their real worth is the best way to prepare them for the "real world."

We can teach kids how to navigate the world as it is, without teaching them that the limitations of our current reality is all that is possible. We can raise our kids to question "the way things are," to want more and to insist on more, even if they have to create a new world as they are making their way through this one.

The more we say *yes* to our kids, the more they internalize the belief that anything is possible.

Children aren't just learners, they are also leaders in the making. So let's teach them how to say *yes* to themselves and to the world they want to create — or at least, *how?*

When Kids Tell Us NO

When we punish children's communication and devalue it as "talking back" — and then have the audacity to complain that kids today don't have conversation skills — *we are the problem.*

My daughter is free to tell me *no* at any time, for any reason. She is allowed to tell me that I'm wrong, that I'm being unfair, that I have hurt her feelings, or even that I'm a lying, hypocritical asshole. Because sometimes I am — every parent is at some point, whether or not they allow anyone else to name it.

My child is not here to reinforce my fantasy of myself as a perfect human or perfect parent so that my authority over her can go unquestioned. My child is here to express herself authentically, to be heard, seen and valued for who she is, to be treated with respect and consideration, and to receive my unconditional love and care. And when I fall short, she deserves an apology.

I can't count the number of times I've apologized to my child — it's in the hundreds or even thousands. But if I could, it would be a good indicator of what my parenting mistakes have cost me, because she also requires cash apologies.

I think this is completely fair. First of all, children are usually denied access to our legal and justice systems. A child normally can't sue a parent for damages, even when the parent has broken the law. They don't have the financial resources to hire a legal team, they can't drive to court to file paperwork, often nonexistent evidence is required, and they typically aren't believed or treated seriously by the law anyway, except in extreme cases, and justice is still not guaranteed.

However, if an adult breaks a promise to another adult, such as by violating a contract, they can be awarded a cash judgment to make up for it, and then some. Just because children don't have the power to hold us to our promises, doesn't mean that they aren't deserving of compensation when we fail to uphold our end of a bargain.

Beyond the world of broken promises, there is also harm done to children in the form of harsh words spoken in a moment of anger, their leftover pizza eaten by a hungry parent in a desperate midnight snack attack, and beloved ratty old t-shirts thoughtlessly donated in a decluttering frenzy — all the ways parents routinely violate their children's boundaries without even feeling obligated to explain, much less negotiate or apologize.

When we respect our children, we allow them to express dissent and we hold ourselves accountable to agreements with them, just as we would with adults.

From this perspective, it's only natural to award them damages. One example specific to our family is that my daughter absolutely hates being called "cute." If I forget and accidentally call her "cute," our agreement is that I have to buy her 1000 Robux.

My business has a "make it up to you and then some" customer service policy. For example, at times I've screwed up and missed an appointment, I would make it up to my client with what's owed plus a little extra for the inconvenience of rescheduling.

If I extend this courtesy to my clients, why not also to my child, who is the person in my life I should most be concerned with treating fairly? Even KFC will send you a coupon if you complain about a feather in your fried chicken. Why would I want to treat my child with less courtesy than she'd receive from a fast-food restaurant?

There is so much injustice in the world — especially when it comes to children — that I truly delight in making my world and my home a place where justice is served, and where *no* is just as welcome as *yes*.

The Luxury of Listening

Parents often want to know how to make their kids "listen," but listening is a two-way street — and it has nothing to do with obedience.

I can't remember one time in my life that I went to either of my parents with a personal problem. They both worked from home for most of my childhood, so it wasn't about them not being around. The issue was that I didn't feel safe sharing my inner world with them, because they didn't seem safe or available in ways that would make me want to confide in them.

My parents worked really hard to provide material comfort and security for our family, and I'm grateful for that. Both of my parents were the first in their families to go to college, and it was never a question that I would be able to go, too. As much as it hurts to have unmet emotional needs, they are secondary to physiological needs, and I understand why my parents prioritized financial success over healing trauma, emotional wellness, and a sense of connection.

The absence of emotional availability in my parents reflected the lack of intimacy they each had with their own parents, as well as in their marriage. It was very unusual for anyone in their generation to talk about feelings, to listen to children, or to go to therapy. I have certainly had a lot of opportunities for personal and psychological growth that weren't available to my parents, and I'm glad that our bloodline survived long enough for me to take advantage of these. I know that substance dependency, keeping family secrets, and repressing trauma were survival strategies passed down through the ages that all played a role in getting me where I am today.

Anyway, after centuries of silence, the floodgates opened.

A lot of what I unpacked in therapy was about my feeling like a failure in life because of not having been able to meet my parents' emotional needs. I also interpreted my own feelings of overwhelm, confusion, guilt, fear and shame as indicators of personal failure, because I didn't understand them or know what to do with them. I felt like it was my job to make my parents feel okay, and when it came to my own need for co-regulation, I was left to my own devices.

This led to me feeling worthless in relationships, as well as in my work, regardless of the value I brought to the table. I've struggled with feelings of inadequacy and overwhelm throughout the process of writing this book, and elsewhere in my professional life, simply because of having taken on the identity of someone who just isn't "enough" and who has something deeply, essentially, wrong with them, back when my brain was still forming.

Developmental trauma is a real bitch — it prevents you from forming a healthy sense of self, and also interferes with your ability to trust yourself or anyone else enough to move toward the people and spaces that could support you in doing so.

It's been a hell of a struggle for me to learn to open up to other people and to share about my problems as an adult, because that wasn't possible for me growing up and I didn't see it modeled by the adults in my life. It's been unbelievably hard to be honest enough — even just with myself — to shed inherited dysfunctional patterns and to open myself to new ways of being. I've spent a fortune on therapy, coaching and self-development programs to make up for what my childhood lacked — essentially, to learn how to be a human being. To learn how to be *me*.

Recovering from childhood trauma can come with a hefty price tag.

I didn't want that for my child.

Instead, I built a whole life around my instinctual desire to nurture our bond. This meant starting an online business so that I could stay home with her instead of sending her to school, building trust in myself as a sovereign mother instead of collapsing into unhealthy relationships out of emotional or financial desperation, and continuing to tend to my own wounds so that I could be more emotionally available as a parent.

Despite all of the messages I received from society, I knew that the greatest gift I could give my child was *me*. And not just my physical presence, but my *presence*.

I consciously chose a lifestyle that allows me plenty of time to listen to her thoughts and feelings, with enough spaciousness in our schedule that connection can arise naturally. Maybe most importantly, I've learned how to get support for my problems so that I'm available to help my child with hers, and so that she doesn't have to play therapist with me. As a result, my daughter trusts me enough to tell me what is going on in her life. She doesn't *always* share the details of her emotional world, but when she wants to, I'm there.

Effective parenting doesn't mean your kids never fuck up — it means you're the one they want to tell when they do.

Showing Our Kids Some Respect

As self-reflective and conscious parents, we have often thought about our own experiences growing up and wish we could have had a closer, healthier or safer relationship with our parents. This has led many of us to approach parenting completely differently from how we were raised.

As parents, we want our kids to feel comfortable telling us about what's going on in their lives. We want to be a safe space for them to share their feelings, thoughts, problems, needs and desires. We want to be there for them when they need us, especially as they grow older, gain independence and spend less time with us and more time in the outside world, where we are less able to nurture and protect them. We want their connection with us to set them up for success as they begin to navigate the world as adults.

There are many factors that can contribute to how comfortable a child feels opening up to us. Here are some questions we can ask ourselves to reflect on how approachable we are as parents:

Is my child "allowed" to tell me "no"? How do I respond when my child tells me "no"?

Is my child ever punished for having, or for expressing, emotions of any kind?

Do I ever try to stop my child from expressing their feelings? Do I ever tell them to "stop crying," or do I criticize or shame them for feeling angry or sad?

When I don't like my child's behavior, does my tone become disrespectful?

How do I respond when my child tells me that they did something I feel is wrong, bad, immoral or harmful?

How do I respond when I find out my child has lied to me?

Is my wanting to be more approachable based on truly desiring more closeness with my child, or on the fear of what might happen to them if we're not close?

I recommend reading through these questions and letting them settle in, as the answers might not come until you're in the trenches on a random Tuesday afternoon when your teen has just placed an empty milk carton on top of the trash can lid for the fiftieth time.

Whatever surfaces, remember — it's never too late to change how we relate to our kids. As adults, we always go first. When we approach our children with respect, compassion and understanding, we set the tone for the relationship and for our entire home.

Running the Numbers of Motherhood

The most exhausted and stressed mothers I know always seem to be busy shuttling their kids to the doctor, to church, and to school: the patriarchal institutions of religion, education and medicine.

But much of the time, these women aren't even sure it's doing their family any good. These just seem like things good moms are supposed to do.

As the matriarch, you have the right to do a cost-benefit analysis to see whether the activities and relationships keeping you and your family busy are bringing a net benefit. And you each have the right to limit commitments outside of the home — or within it — if they are hurting more than they are helping.

If going to church every Sunday is torture and you hate it, stop going. If the doctor isn't helping and the appointments are bankrupting you, forget about it. If your homeschool co-op is more stressful for everyone than keeping the kids at home, drop it. If your relatives are putting you and your children in a bad mood, stop going to see them. If you honestly think you'd be miserable having a child — whether it would be your first or your twelfth — consider this your permission to quit while you're ahead.

My family doesn't go to the doctor except in rare emergencies — we do holistic and preventative medicine at home with nutrition, rest, love, connection, and other simple aspects of healthy living. My daughter educates herself, instead of us having to get up early every day, get dressed, prepare lunches, do homework and answer endless school emails. We never miss a perfect beach day because of loyalty to a homeschool curriculum — we don't use any. We don't go to church — I engage my spirituality through meditation, embodiment techniques, nature connection and my work.

As a result of structuring our family life on our own terms, I rarely speak of "having to" go anywhere, and we almost never leave the house before noon. I have structured our lives around our needs and desires and boundaries, rather than centering societal expectations or fear-based rules and routines.

I'm not saying other families should make the same exact choices we do; I'm saying that it's worth evaluating your daily routine to ask whether your family's activities truly reflect your values or if there's stuff you're doing just because you think you should or because other people expect you to.

If it feels weird to limit your commitments to what you really, deeply want, it's because women aren't *supposed* to do this — and for millennia, we haven't been allowed. We aren't supposed to be doing the math around our energy expenditure to see whether we are giving more than we are receiving in any given relationship or engagement. That's how patriarchy works — women are tricked into thinking that we need this or that in our lives when it's actually costing us more than we are gaining from it. Paying attention to how we actually *feel*, rather than what we've been taught to think, helps us externalize the insidious rhetoric of resource extraction — the one that convinces us we're bad people if we don't enjoy every second of servitude.

Don't let anyone make you feel like they're your only option. Family, school, partners, bosses, doctors, therapists, your country — when there is any kind of pressure to keep them around, it means they need you more than you need them.

Don't be afraid to run the numbers, and make changes accordingly.

So what would it be like to just… opt out?

At first, the stillness would make you feel like you were going crazy.

You'd likely feel guilty, ashamed or scared that you weren't doing the "right thing."

You also might feel relieved, like a weight you've been carrying for thousands of years has been taken off your shoulders — which it has.

And then…

You'd find god in your own body.

You'd find knowledge in your own body.

You'd find healing in your own body.

And you'd start to trust yourself and your family to meet more of your own needs.

Your relationships with yourselves, each other, the Earth and the cosmos would expand and deepen.

You'd find more joy in each moment, and more moments of pure joy, pleasure, relaxation, fun, delight and playfulness.

You'd have so much more time to connect with your kids, and to be present with them in the way all of you crave and thrive on.

You'd find more energy for things that matter to you but often get pushed aside, like preparing healthy meals and making art.

You'd become more aware of your and your children's innate gifts, and how they are meant to be expressed in the world.

You'd find so much satisfaction in just being, and wonder how you ever put yourself through all of that rushing around.

Extracting our families from patriarchal institutions isn't always painless or quick, but the freedom and feeling of coming home to ourselves are well worth it.

Burning Desires, Burning Out and Burning Your To-Do List

We may feel victimized by all the things that are waiting for us to be done, but if we're honest with ourselves, we can admit that a lot of it is not *truly* necessary.

I still remember the shock I felt when my mother told me that there are women who vacuum their entire homes *twice daily*. I don't even vacuum once a week, and I can't remember the last time I used a mop. Maybe I'm still recovering from working in food service and cleaning vacation rentals years ago, but having spotless floors every second of the day is just not a priority for me. I appreciate the energetic upgrade a clean space provides, but I don't make myself a slave to cleanliness or hold my home to any standards besides my own.

Housekeeping is just one type of task that can clog up our to-do lists, but it's rarely on mine. I just wash the dishes or tidy up the living room when I feel like it. I've even gone out and bought new clothes in order to put off doing laundry, especially in countries that don't use clothes dryers but are often too rainy for line drying, and our ability to get dressed each day depends on how carefully we've done underwear math that week. (Speaking of which, I always found it funny to see packages that say, "wash before wearing." Like, if I had felt like doing laundry, I wouldn't have gone underwear shopping in the first place?)

If the kids make a mess of dinner, set up a table outside for their meals, or just let them sit in the grass or on a blanket. They will not care. In fact, they will probably find it fun. Kids also mostly don't care if their clothes are clean. Bonus: raise your child in a dirty house, and they won't make rude comments when visiting other people's dirty houses.

You can choose how much to care about personal hygiene or housekeeping. Maybe you'll draw the line at foul odors if you stay in furnished rentals and don't want it coming out of your deposit.

You may have much higher standards for cleanliness than I do, and I'm not suggesting that you lower them. I'm simply inviting you to consider where you could be flexible on the things you think you "must do," if you're feeling overwhelmed by it all and like something has to give. Don't be so committed to cleaning cracker crumbs out of the sofa that you let your dreams fall through the cracks.

Sacrificing our joy for appearances, or out of a sense of obligation, is a recipe for resentment and burnout. I've seen more than one woman bend over backward for people who *still* expect her to disappear into domestic drudgery when she's dealing with chronic illness from having done exactly that.

We are the only ones whose standards matter, because we are the ones who will be dealing with the consequences of people-pleasing when it ends up having long-term effects on our health.

If other people don't approve of the way you live, you can live without them.

The beautiful thing about being adults is getting to choose what's on our to-do lists — or whether we even have one at all. List or not, leading with our desires ensures there's always enough time for what matters most.

Compromise, Collaboration and Cowgirl Boots

The class on Third World Negotiations I took in college, where I discovered how commonly compromise is relied on to end wars or prevent them from breaking out, left me feeling demoralized and uninspired.

I've personally never liked the idea of compromise. It speaks to lowering our standards in order to make society, with its multitude of competing interests, practical. I'd rather keep to myself and do things my way rather than lower my standards.

Social bonds can undermine intelligence and greatness, especially in groups where the lowest common denominator reigns supreme. Compromise usually results in both (or all) parties being partly unhappy with the solution, but defeated or desperate enough to move forward anyway. I think we can shoot for a much better definition of peace than that.

What's missing from the "compromise" model of conflict resolution is the authentic desire for and commitment to each party's happiness and wellbeing. When all parties involved take *responsibility* for coming up with a solution that meets everyone's needs, it opens the door for win-win solutions.

We may not all be there yet in the arena of global conflict, but in our relationships with our children and with people who truly care for and respect us, collaboration is a realistic starting point. Instead of being "at war" with our loved ones, we can embark together on the creative journey of finding ways through conflict that everyone is happy with. We can look for the needs behind the strategies that each of us prefers, and find ways to meet those in ways that allow others to get their needs met, too.

In most cases, we aren't actually competing for limited resources; we are experiencing limited thinking that keeps us from seeing all of the possibilities available to us. When we open our minds to the Fertile Universe, we can let go of what we thought we wanted or needed and allow ourselves to receive something even better.

Here's an example:

My daughter and I both enjoy clothes shopping, but I also love getting rid of old stuff — it's how I release negative energy as I heal and grow. My daughter loves keeping stuff, it's how she holds onto all of her good memories.

I can't imagine what it would be like growing up with positive feelings attached to my old things, but I can understand why she sometimes feels limited by living out of a suitcase. (It's also probably an Earth sign thing — I have zero Earth in my chart in addition to the Scorpionic purge instinct).

When we were living in the mountains of Mexico, I insisted it was time for my daughter to let her favorite pink cowgirl boots go after they got moldy from being left out in the rain. My daughter insisted that they come with us on the next leg of our journey, as they reminded her of the bestie she ran around town with while wearing them.

Both perspectives were equally valid — we didn't have room in our luggage for shoes that weren't functioning as shoes anymore, and it was also really important for my daughter to feel connected to her cherished memory of an important friendship.

I definitely thought about putting my foot down and telling my daughter that we simply weren't taking the boots, and that there would be no further discussion. I had the power to do that, as the parent, but I knew it would damage her trust in me. Bringing the boots along wasn't something I was willing to consider, as the mold would easily spread to the rest of our clothes, ruining them and also creating an unhealthy living environment for us.

But I respected the need my daughter was fighting for, underneath her attachment to the moldy boots. She needed a way to remember and honor her friend in a way that felt meaningful to her.

After sitting with all of this for a while, and then going for a walk, an idea came to me: a couple of heart-shaped totems cut from the not-moldy calves of her boots to carry with her on our travels. She loved the idea! Importantly, it didn't feel like a compromise for either of us. My daughter truly felt the heart cutouts were enough of a reminder of those beautiful days with her treasured friend — even *more* so, because hearts! — and I truly didn't mind bringing them along.

Best of all, our creative collaboration led us to an agreement that kept our relationship intact. All it took was pausing to wait for a solution to come forward, and staying committed to finding the win-win.

Besides, what's the point of pink cowgirl boots if you're willing to settle for less than magic?

Playful Parenting – and Why We Hate It

Play can be an incredible tool for healing and personal growth. I like to find a way to play every day. Having a child makes this a little easier because children are always wanting to play. A round of Hide-and-seek, a board game, a beach or pool day, or even just making everyday household chores fun can nurture your inner and outer children at the same time.

Let's be real though — playing with kids can be triggering as hell! Aside from finding children's play boring, this is the number one reason parents give me for not wanting to play with their kids.

One aspect of our resistance may be a fear of experiencing buried emotions and trauma, which play can so expertly unlock. We may even have trauma specifically around play, for example, if we were not allowed to play as children or were punished for it. Parents who avoid playing with their kids are often afraid they will inadvertently unleash some deep subconscious emotion that would traumatize their kids, or even re-traumatize themselves.

These fears may even be entirely unconscious. We might not know why we refuse our children's invitations to play, only that it feels really, really unsafe to consider it. We may suddenly feel very tired, anxious or irritable when our children ask us to play — all possible signs of dysregulation. And then if we judge ourselves to be bad parents because of refusing to play with our children, we often feel guilty or ashamed on top of everything else and even less capable of play than before.

Not too fun, eh?

But what if there was a way to engage in imaginative play with your child, even if you have serious unhealed trauma, that not only doesn't traumatize your child but also actually brings you closer, *and* helps you heal your own shit?

I'm not suggesting that it's easy, or that you should always try to meet your child's needs and your own needs simultaneously — I just want to open your mind to the idea that it *might* be possible to:

- Express your authentic self through play in a way that does not pass trauma onto your child

- Hold and nurture yourself during play, while also offering containment for your child

- Heal yourself through play with your child, and model emotional regulation for them

- Deepen your relationship with your child through play, even when you feel like crap

- Find play fun and fulfilling again, and actually look forward to your child's invitations

Opening our minds to these possibilities is a form of play in itself. Even if we find that the possibilities in question are ultimately not a road we want to go down, any time we are willing to consider new ideas, we are *playing* with reality. Just by reading this, you may have already begun playing!

Part of grieving our childhoods is accepting that we are raising ourselves at the same time that we are raising our children. So, parenting may not look much like how we expected it would look. But our journey requires that we deal with life as it is, and not as we wish it were.

All of our power and magic in life lies in first facing reality — and then playing with it. So let's get right to it.

Playing with Your Kids When You Feel Like Crap

Having a really shitty day, or decade, but your child wants you to play with them?

First off, know that it's okay to decline an invitation to play with your child. If you need to take care of yourself, it's okay to put a movie on, let your child play by themselves or be entertained in some other way that doesn't force you to neglect your emotional and physical needs.

Secondly, if you decide to go ahead and try playing, know that you are allowed to stop the play at any time you need a break. This is not an either/or situation — you can play in the way that works best for you, including taking breaks, redirecting play as needed, and attending to your own needs while playing.

Lastly, the key to making play feel like less of a chore when we'd rather be doing literally anything else is to find ways to bring our most authentic selves into the game.

One way that play can become cathartic for us as adults is to work our real-life emotions into the characters, scenarios and voices we create while playing. Frustration, depression, guilt, fear — all become material for a theater-quality performance. For example, if you are feeling cheated in life because you never planned to have a child and didn't get to have the career of your dreams, maybe it would feel good to reward yourself with a crime spree? Bank robber character: activated! When you're angry, you can be a jungle predator that brings danger vibes to the scene.

While you do this, keep track of your emotional state and how it's affected as the play unfolds, being sure to step back for as long as needed if you find it too difficult to express yourself in a way that won't terrify your children. Cheetahs and alligators need bathroom breaks, too.

When you feel dissociated and need to ground yourself during play, you can pause to observe and name elements of your sensory environment, either real or imagined. For example: "Look, a giant rock!" (pointing to the couch), or "The walls of this cave are so soft" (feeling the texture of the blanket you made a fort from). Bringing anything you can see, hear, touch, smell, or taste to your conscious awareness, and to your child's, can help you both regulate your nervous systems and also make valuable contributions to the scene.

In challenging moments, make an effort to stay connected to your breath and the physical sensations in your body. Speak very slowly if it helps you to stay calm. When possible, find a way to work your needs into the play, but don't feel like you need to put on a whole show if that feels too hard.

If play triggers deep wounds and you think you might cry, have a box of tissues on hand. Your child will be impressed with your commitment to the scene. Placing a hand over your heart can help your inner child feel safe and loved, while coming off as dramatic effect.

Be aware that if your child has reason to fear your expression of strong effect, such as if they've felt overwhelmed by your previous emotional displays, this may still upset them. If you're unable to support your child in navigating both their experience of your emotions and your own at the same time, or if you worry you won't be able to express your feelings in a nice way, it may be better to excuse yourself for a few minutes and then come back and explain to them what happened. You can say something like, "I was sad about something that happened in the past that our game reminded me of. I feel better now. Crying always helps me feel better. Is this true for you, too?" Whatever the situation may be, there is often a way to turn it into a teachable moment or opportunity for connection.

When you're feeling in need of some serious space, it might be time for a game of Hide-and-seek. The trick is to find a reeeally good hiding spot. Bring your phone if it helps you regulate, and the tissues if needed. When you're the seeker, take your sweet time — kids love feeling like they've outsmarted us! (Bonus: if your kid has had a rough day, letting them "get one over on you" can help balance things out by meeting their need for control.) Whether as a hider or a seeker, draw out your turn for as long as you can, but not so long that your kids get legitimately scared that you don't exist anymore.

Have another easy-for-you activity ready to keep your kids busy when you need a break from active play. For example, invite your child to play burglar and try to "steal" certain objects (such as from the kitchen table or bookshelf) while you're "sleeping." Or, invite your child to play "doctor" so you can lie still while they "operate" on your toes. Maybe if you get caught robbing that bank, you'll have to spend time in "jail," where there's nothing to do but rest your weary eyes and wait for the guard to bring your meal (it can't be any worse than real jail food, right? ...*Right?*)

Of course your kids will still do stuff to get your attention and connect with you, but it's potentially a lot less intense than other types of games. The possibilities are limited only by your imagination, and maybe also your children's tolerance for playing in ways that weren't their idea.

Also, earplugs are underrated — definitely treat yourself to a nice pair that can take the edge off when the wonderful child-friendly environment you've created for your family starts feeling adult-unfriendly. They don't block out so much noise that you're unaware of your kids' needs, just enough to keep you from losing your shit.

If your child prefers to take a strong leadership role in play (read: to them, "playing" means telling you what to do), this can be triggering in itself. You might need to take longer and more frequent breaks.

Instead of criticizing the child for being "bossy," recognize that a person who has a good sense of what needs to be done in order to make the scene *just right* might have a future as a film director.

Similarly, a child who wants you to fill in all the big, boring spaces in their coloring book might one day hire someone else to do that job (or heck, set them up with a Fiverr account so they do it now!).

We can validate our children's strengths even when they annoy or trigger us, and we can decide how we want to participate in their projects. Being discerning with how we use our energy while playing with our children sets a great example for them about determining the value of their own labor and making nourishing choices about where to invest their resources.

When we bring our authentic selves into play, it's more fulfilling for us and we get to model self-care, boundaries and leadership for our kids, too.

Oh, and when all else fails? Pillow fiiiiiiight!

Primal Wisdom and Women's Leadership

In my late twenties, I entered a sugar addiction recovery program. Thanks to the specially designed meal plan I followed there, I experienced freedom from food cravings for the first time in my life.

Before this, I'd had no clue that my near-constant thoughts about eating for nearly three decades had been caused in part by candida overgrowth in my body — not by moral failure. The more I fed the fungi, the louder their demands became. Cutting out sugar and refined carbs shut them up for good. For once, I could just *be*, without feeling like anything was missing.

After a few years, there came a point when this food plan was no longer appealing to me. Even though millet and quinoa were a lot easier on my body than bread and pasta, I had developed a philosophical and visceral aversion to an agriculture-based diet. I learned that these foods relied on unsustainable methods of cultivation, such as clearcutting, monocropping and plowing, and I just couldn't stomach ecocide. I was also sick of the seemingly endless tasks of chopping vegetables and washing grease out of frying pans every day from all the meat I was cooking.

I felt drawn to hunter-gatherer style grazing, because it felt better for my body and spirit at the time than sticking to a strict schedule and weighing and measuring everything I ate. Even though this plan had brought me relief from addiction, I was craving a different kind of food freedom — I wanted whole-body autonomy from not following anyone's regime but my own.

Since then, the term "girl dinner" has become popular, referring to the way many women tend to nourish ourselves with frequent snacks when we don't have anyone demanding we prepare three square meals from scratch a day. After thousands of years of women's unpaid and forced labor as domestic chefs, "girl dinner" is an act of liberation and a reclamation of our bodies and our creative energy.

One of the first things that happened as a result of this change was a huge emotional release. I was surprised to find myself crying and crying over the return to what felt like my body's natural rhythm of eating. Even though it was working for me, I realized that I had been relying on the strict routine of my meal plan as a source of emotional security, much like how restricted eating in my teens had given me a sense of control in life.

I left the sugar addiction recovery program for good, but with a grateful heart for how much I had learned about the connection between nutrition and mental health.

I tried to avoid sugar afterward, knowing it made me anxious, irritable, overly sensitive, tired and depressed, but the convenience of packaged foods often won. I struggled to find balance between the hard work of healthy eating and all the other things I needed and wanted to do with my time.

As a new mother, this didn't get any easier. I barely had a spare minute to put food in my mouth, much less time to plan and prepare real meals. I was also struggling with postpartum depression, thanks to the trauma of my daughter's hospital birth, isolation from being at home all the time with an infant, and exhaustion from doing it all on my own.

One day when my daughter was about a year old, everything changed. I walked out of a natural foods store and saw a woman eating raw Korean BBQ short ribs. I couldn't stop staring. Intrigued, I started a conversation — marking the beginning of my journey as a raw omnivore, with her as my mentor.

On this diet there was no cooking, and minimal meal prep. The high-protein meals featuring raw meat, eggs and dairy not only kept me full for several hours, but left me feeling satiated on a level that I had never experienced from cooked foods. I was thrilled to find another way to avoid food cravings that required little work compared to the labor-intensive meal plan I had followed before. Plus, whereas I had previously experienced relief from obsession over sugar and carbs, on the raw omnivore diet my brain was now *completely quiet*. Until this point, I'd had no idea that my overactive mind was connected to nutrient deficiency — or that this level of mental peace and clarity was even possible.

Remarkably, my habit of endlessly scrolling social media also disappeared. The distractions of the internet had no pull for me anymore — because I was eating *living* foods, I *felt alive* and wanted to connect more with the life around me. I was putting down my phone a lot more to go outside and be in nature, and it didn't even feel hard. Behind the scenes, my microbiome had finally become robust enough to make a normal amount of serotonin and dopamine, most of which (around 90%!) are produced in the gut.

It's too bad that dietary changes are seen as such an "edgy" or even nonviable approach to treating ADHD, many symptoms of which can either be caused or worsened by malnourishment. Protein consumption influences serotonin and dopamine production by way of amino acids, and can also support emotional stability and executive functioning. Grassfed beef collagen is an easy way to supplement protein and vital nutrients for anyone struggling with dopamine-driven process addictions. Someone I knew abruptly stopped texting while driving when they added it into their diet.

My primal diet mentor told me that raw honey was good for me and to eat as much of it as my body wanted. It felt so nourishing, and started using it as an ingredient in raw desserts. My daughter, then age two, helped herself to the raw chocolate we kept in the fridge (it was alive, and had to be kept cool).

I loved that we could have sweet things around the house that didn't contain neurotoxins and wouldn't cause disease or trigger cravings. The desserts we made were energizing and made us feel better after eating them, not worse like conventional treats. I experimented with adding flavors like orange, cinnamon and cayenne to our raw chocolates. We even started a business and sold them at local markets. My daughter would offer samples to passersby — she was a terrific salesperson.

For her, this was enough. She had not yet tasted white sugar and could easily accept this way of eating. My health was excellent — I had loads of energy and my mood was generally pleasant, aside from the stresses of solo parenting with post-traumatic stress. Because of everything I had going on, supporting myself with solid nutrition was necessary, and I made it a top priority.

I don't remember the first time my daughter had fast food or processed sugar, or why I made the decision to introduce them, but things definitely changed after that. Her tastes shifted to where she wasn't happy with the raw chocolate I made anymore. When the demands for food containing not much besides poisons became overwhelming, I put the kibosh on it. It wasn't good for me to be around foods that negatively affected my mental health, because as a tired, stressed mom I couldn't always stop myself from partaking. Eating sugar inevitably resulted in more fatigue, more stress, more anxiety, more depression, more anger — and that wasn't the parent my daughter deserved.

Taking charge of the situation, I explained to my child the reasons why we weren't going to eat these foods anymore, which included our physical, emotional, financial and mental health. She understood perfectly well. Instead of forcing her to go cold turkey, we made progress with one different choice at a time. She'd still get a McDonald's hamburger, but not the ice cream. She'd say, "We don't eat that anymore — right, Mom?"

It was simple for my daughter to accept my boundaries because I was crystal clear on my decision. I wasn't doing it out of anger, as a punishment, or only in a moment of overwhelm, subject to my mood shifting the next day. I knew intuitively what was best for my family, and I spoke and took action from that place of deep inner knowing.

I fully embraced my role as the parent to decide which of the many offerings from our consumer society were going to filter into my home, my body and my child's life. I knew that it was my job to protect her until she was well-informed and mature enough to make rational choices on behalf of her own health.

It's common for radical unschooling parents to have an "anything goes" policy towards food. While I understand wanting to give kids the ability to regulate their own sugar consumption, it's important to recognize that white sugar has been scientifically proven to be more addictive than cocaine. It's true — a person can be biochemically addicted to sugar and show the same hallmark symptoms of withdrawal, obsession, cravings, anxiety, depression, and willingness to engage in illegal activity as a narcotic addict. Highly sensitive people are especially vulnerable to this.

Most parents wouldn't give their kids cocaine for the purpose of "learning to self-regulate," and I can't imagine anyone calling a mother "controlling" for *not* allowing her child to use cocaine.

Plus, for many families, giving children free reign on every grocery shopping trip would also mean squandering the grocery budget on foods lacking in nutritional value. That's too much power for a child to have.

When I used to always just ask my daughter, "what do you want to eat?", acting as my child's brainless servant. I resented the hell out of the prison I had created for myself, and I could sense that she didn't even really *want* the level of control I was giving her, which was best left to someone with a more sophisticated understanding of health and nutrition.

My daughter responded much better when I took the lead, and prepared meals with some of her input, but not expecting her to take *full* responsibility for deciding what she (or we) would be eating.

This has mostly looked like just preparing food and giving it to her, whether or not she has asked for it. I found that she started eating a lot more of the foods I thought that she should be eating, but that I hadn't wanted to force on her, when I just put them in front of her rather than waiting for her to ask for them.

With that said, I run a pretty loose ship — there are always alternatives and snacks available, so she's never forced to choose between my cooking or starvation, and food is never used as a reward or a punishment.

Kids don't necessarily feel safe being on equal footing with their parents. They want to feel like the adults in their lives are capable of making choices on their behalf, with their needs and preferences taken into consideration. The prefrontal cortex, which governs impulse control, risk assessment, and other important decision-making functions, doesn't fully develop until our mid-twenties. In the meantime, parents fulfill these vital roles.

This is not an issue of child autonomy — this is an issue of leadership. A lot of parents who give their kids 100% control over the family culture are overcompensating for the authoritarian environment they were raised in. Instead of healing from the trauma of their own childhoods, and then moving toward a more balanced approach, the switch is flipped to the opposite extreme where children become the family authoritarians.

Yes, there is a lot we can learn from our kids. Yes, children's needs matter as much as adults' needs. Yes, sometimes adults are wrong and children are right. Yes, children have a right to bodily autonomy, to use their voices, and to form their own opinions. And yes, children can be wonderful leaders!

But children have parents for a reason — they are not yet capable of functioning as *fully* sovereign beings. Children are by definition, dependent, which is why they are always watching us for cues on how to do this thing called *life*.

We are always leading our children by the example we set for them. Children copy our behavior, so doing what we would want them to emulate is the best way to influence them. Mirror neurons are real — our kids, especially the highly sensitive ones — pick up on our thought patterns and make them their own, even if we don't explicitly teach them.

I've found that my attention to my own nutrition is the single most important factor in my child's nutrition. I can't expect my child to choose healthy foods if I'm modeling something different. Whenever I start to feel critical of my child's choices in this or any area of life, I turn the focus inward and ask myself how I might not be showing up that way for myself, either.

When we approach parenting with a "do what I say, not what I do" approach, it often reveals how out of control we feel about our own behaviors. But when we find enough courage and honesty to solve our own problems, we also gain the skills needed to lead our children through theirs.

These lessons don't belong only in the kitchen — they're deeply connected to the reclamation of our authority as women, as mothers, and as leaders in every sphere.

Leadership is an often misunderstood concept because people associate leadership with control, due to "leadership" having been used as a euphemism for tyranny in patriarchal society. Instead of recognizing the difference between leadership and control, people claim that "power corrupts" and reject the concepts of leadership and authority altogether.

But what if the difference between good and bad leadership is more nuanced than that?

As matriarchal societies know, and knew, the natural leader in any family is a mother — or more accurately, *mothers*, because effective leadership requires shared power.

Anyone who wants to argue that men are "natural leaders" should be able to point to at least one *sustainable* society in human history that has been led by men (spoiler: they never can).

Historical evidence aside, science offers its own explanation for female leadership: the Y chromosome is, quite literally, a degenerated X — and it continues to deteriorate over time, a biological mirror of the collapse of patriarchy. Despite the illusion created by men's resource hoarding, men are dependent on women — biologically, emotionally, spiritually, and otherwise. That's why we're all better off when women are in charge.

There is a fundamental difference between a society led by women and one by men. When I say "led by women," I'm not referring to a female president in a patriarchal political system! Of course she is going to appear to be as bad as, or worse, than the men whose shoes she is elected to fill. I mean that the mother leads within the context of a broader ecosystem in which there is a balanced exchange between all life forms, including both human and nonhuman.

The spiritual leadership of the mother emerges naturally from her role in bringing new life into the world. She is the one the child bonds with in the womb, and the one from whom the child initially sources all of her needs outside the womb.

In an environment where mothers are sovereign and supported in our sovereignty, rather than undermined by a competing authority (such as a jealous father), we also shape the child's concept of "god," because that's who we are to the child.

The matriarch sets the tone and values for the family and the community with everyone's needs — and the wellbeing of future generations — taken into consideration.

In a healthy society, women fulfill our natural role as stewards of our communities' resources.

We source our food mostly from the wild rather than from the over-managed corporate agricultural system that makes us sick in body, mind and soul.

Meat is safe to consume uncooked, because animals roam free until needed for sustenance, rather than living in miserable factory farms filled with disease.

Children learn that bacteria are gods, too, because a strong microbiome keeps us happy and healthy.

The primal wisdom of women connected to our instincts defines both the modern matriarchy and the sustainable societies we lead.

Navigating Childhood Addiction

A lot of parents these days are concerned about their children developing various addictions. It's unfortunate that this is such a huge problem, but wonderful that this conversation has begun.

When I was growing up, there was less awareness of the role of family dynamics in addiction, and nobody really considered things like television or sugar to be potentially addictive. Because of this, a lot of kids — including myself — suffered without anyone knowing that there was anything wrong. Society's lack of addiction literacy allowed my childhood trauma to stay hidden from my own awareness, as well as from adults who might have been able to support me through it.

As much as our collective understanding of addiction has since evolved, the mainstream conversation is still overly focused on controlling the behaviors and symptoms of addiction, rather than addressing the underlying causes. This has led to panic among parents, and the misguided trend of relying on strict limits, instead of raising kids in such a way that is likely to prevent them from being vulnerable to addiction in the first place.

Addiction is not a disease or a genetic predisposition, as mainstream treatment models would have us believe. Addiction is a symptom of *trauma* — the compulsive behaviors and obsessive thoughts that characterize addiction are rooted in nervous system dysregulation.

I wouldn't have needed someone to just take away the substances I was using to cope — I would have needed a safe attachment figure with whom I could have integrated the serious traumas I had repressed, and continued my emotional development through co-regulation. Without this essential piece, I would have just found something else to use.

So if you want to prevent your kids from being addicted, then the best thing you can do is not traumatize them, keep them away from abusive relatives and unreliable attachment figures, support them in integrating any trauma they already have, and be emotionally available so that they can learn to regulate their nervous systems in relationship with you. Focusing exclusively on restricting access to addictive substances or activities will trap you in a never-ending game of whack-a-mole.

To protect children from using technology as an escape, limit their exposure to life experiences that they will feel the need to escape from. If you don't want them constantly seeking validation through social media, make sure that *you* are offering validation. Kids love gaming because it provides connection. If you feel your child is overly involved in online gaming, think about how to facilitate more opportunities for real-life connection with people who really see, understand and value them.

Sometimes, we seek in food or other substances what we crave in life — fun, stimulation, warmth, connection, joy, power. When I've been fully engaged with life, food has become less of a diversion and more of a way to fuel my adventures.

Have you ever felt so immersed in the present moment and in your creative flow that you forgot to eat? I'm not saying that skipping meals is ideal, just that there is value in finding a balance between living to eat and eating to live. I'll never forget the first time I went snowboarding — I was so focused, my mind went blank and I wanted for nothing. I was completely relieved from obsessions of any kind. I have had similar experiences painting for hours at a time, writing, and performing on stage.

It's wonderful to see kids or adults who were previously obsessed with sugar or self-destructive habits become significantly less so when pursuing their passions, enjoying meaningful connections, and experiencing personal freedom.

As parents, our role is to create the kind of safe, connected environment where children can pursue their passions and experience the fullness of life. When they are supported in this way, they'll have less need to seek refuge in harmful substances or behaviors, and more opportunities to thrive.

We don't need to live in fear that our children will become addicted, and we don't need to respond with fear if they already are. Where trauma is concerned, fear is no help. The more we parent from a place of fear, the more stress and disconnection we pass on to our children and the more likely they are to attempt to seek refuge in the very substances and behaviors we want to protect them from.

Trauma is both healed and prevented in safe relationships and in safe environments. Providing that safety for our children is the best and only long-term, sustainable insurance against addiction. When we become trustworthy attachment figures, we can also trust our children to choose for themselves how to engage with the outside world.

The CORE of Addiction Prevention

One of the things parents worry about most as their kids enter adolescence is drugs and alcohol.

This concern is not without reason, as alcohol and other drugs can have much more serious consequences, and far earlier on and with less use, than things like sugar or the internet. There are also obvious differences with regard to ease of access, legal consequences and lifestyle associations.

However, the approach to preventing problems with these is similar, in the sense that a focus on secure attachment rather than prohibition brings the most sustainable solution in the long run.

The CORE framework helps parents gauge how likely their children and teens are to develop a drinking habit, and take steps to mitigate that risk. Some of it will translate seamlessly to hard drugs, and other parts less so, but since alcohol is one of the things I've struggled with the most personally, I've chosen to center it in this framework.

CORE stands for Culture, Opportunity, Relationships and Emotions. Here's a breakdown of how each of these is relevant to alcohol use in children and teens, followed by discussion of how they all work together:

Culture

Is alcohol use modeled or normalized in your culture or community? This can include family, peers, the larger culture, and anyone you and your child spend time with. Your child's social environment, both within and outside of the home, partly determines the likelihood that they will reach for alcohol as a coping mechanism, as well as the availability of it.

Opportunity

Is your child frequently left unsupervised, with or without peers? Lack of supervision alone won't necessarily lead to alcohol use, but alcohol use is very unlikely when children are under direct adult supervision — as long as the adults do not allow or enable it.

Relationships

Is your child securely attached to *you*, or are they more attached to their peers? Are you emotionally and physically available to your child? Do they mostly seek out peers to meet their emotional needs, and for guidance? This determines who has an influence on your child.

Emotions

Does your child or teen have trauma or emotions they don't know how to cope with? People with neither may try alcohol, but are unlikely to use it habitually. Trauma is the single greatest risk factor in habitual alcohol use because it drives the quest for nervous system suppression.

Interestingly, the most important factors in underage alcohol use are not the ones that parents tend to focus on.

While many parents obsess over their children being supervised at all times, the physical presence of an adult can only ensure that a child will not use alcohol — not that they won't *want* to. The parent's physical presence is also temporary. What good will rules and control be when the child becomes an adult and moves out of their parents' house?

Young adults must rely on their own self-regulation skills, conscience and values to make decisions in life, and supervision alone won't have been sufficient for them to build any of those. Having your child within eyesight until they are fully grown is impractical, and besides, a short-sighted solution that does not take into account the freedom that older teens and young adults have.

However, limiting opportunity is definitely one way to keep kids from drinking, and for kids in crisis, this could be a necessary step to keeping them safe.

The second one that parents and society tend to give a lot of weight to is culture. The belief that this factor is of utmost importance has influenced prohibition-era laws, dry states and counties, legal drinking ages and even entire cultures to shun alcohol use. But as we all know, none of these actually ever stopped alcohol from being sold or consumed — they only led to alcohol consumption behind closed doors, underground and unlawfully. Look at the difference between American and European teens' alcohol use: In France, for example, children often have a glass of wine at meals along with their parents (fun fact: wine was served to elementary-aged French children *at school* until the 1950s!).

While underage alcohol use is normalized in some European cultures, this has the opposite effect that one might assume. I went out to clubs and bars with a friend in Paris when I was sixteen (the legal age was eighteen, but no one checked IDs) and saw kids my age drinking far more moderately than I was used to seeing in the U.S. Most of them had probably been drinking since they were little kids and there was simply no mystery or mischief associated with alcohol use.

In the U.S., my friends and I drank ourselves to the point of near death every single weekend from our early teens through our mid-twenties. It wasn't allowed when we were younger, and we loved how "grown up" it made us feel to break the rules. In retrospect, puking in our parent's flower gardens, stealing from liquor stores and driving under the influence was the opposite of "grown up," but as teens we had been given adult expectations to define ourselves against, and we did our very best.

Some cultures may explicitly encourage children to drink alcohol, but aside from these exceptions, the main reasons why kids use alcohol have little to do with environment or opportunity or any other external circumstances — what matters above all is the condition of the child's nervous system. This is where the final two factors come into play. Unmet attachment needs and the drive for emotional regulation will determine whether a child who tries alcohol once simply because it's available will later go out of their way to seek it out, and whether this use will become self-destructive.

Alcohol has a powerful effect on the nervous system: it causes the body to produce chemicals that act as a seductive, but temporary, balm for anxiety and shame, and offers a portal to confidence and euphoria. These effects are experienced much more intensely in a person with unresolved trauma, because they provide such potent relief from difficult emotions. This is especially true for highly sensitive individuals, who experience both trauma *and* mind-altering substances more intensely than the average person.

Parental alcohol use is also often thought to be the single greatest factor determining the likelihood of child alcohol use, but this is only true to the extent that trauma is passed down along with the alcohol habit. Children with no trauma history may try alcohol when presented with the opportunity, but are unlikely to use it habitually as a coping mechanism.

For a person with no trauma to medicate, alcohol has a completely different effect. I found that after I healed my traumas, and also removed myself from unhealthy relationships and environments, alcohol simply did not "work" for me anymore.

Unlike how an alcoholic builds up a tolerance and finds they need to drink more and more to achieve the same effect, the ineffectiveness of alcohol in my case was due to the fact that I had no more shame to repress and no more anxiety to soothe. When taking a drink after integrating these traumas, I did not achieve a state of euphoria because I was already happy, and I did not gain confidence because I was already confident. My nervous system was completely regulated, and so all alcohol did was impair my senses and make me feel disoriented.

If parents who drink worry about preventing or controlling their kids' alcohol use, hiding the alcohol or monitoring the levels of liquor bottles will not help much. Even concealing one's alcohol consumption will make no difference. Even if your child doesn't *see* or even *know* that you drink, what impacts them is *not* seeing you model healthy coping mechanisms, and *not* having you available to co-regulate with them.

It's not the drinking that is passed down from one generation to the next so much as it's the trauma. If alcohol isn't available to your kids, and they have unhealed trauma, they will find something else — whether that is another substance, a "process" addiction like gambling or workaholism, or a relationship with someone who temporarily relieves them of the agony of being alone with their overwhelming pain and distress (aka, codependency).

My parents didn't do much to try to keep me away from alcohol. Even though they didn't offer it to me, it was readily available in our home and I grew up watching my father get wasted every night. But even if alcohol hadn't been an option, I would have chosen other addictions.

In fact, years before I took my first drink, I took solace in sugar. Of course, sugar addiction isn't anywhere near as dangerous as alcoholism, but it can have a similar effect on the brain, and primed me for the big leagues (so to speak) once alcohol entered my peer group.

The use of alcohol and other substances can add many more problems to a person's life, but the root of the problem is unresolved trauma. Until this underlying cause is addressed, a person will remain vulnerable to addiction.

Attachment trauma (often referred to as "developmental trauma"), is a form of trauma that people don't know much about, compared to things like war, car accidents or sexual abuse. Most people think of trauma as the result of a single big and scary thing happening to a person, instead of as a collection of, or consistently, unmet developmental needs over time.

Parents don't often think about the quality of their relationship with their child as being a potential source of trauma, largely because it has become so normal. My own childhood alcohol use (beginning from my first drink at age thirteen) was an attempt to soothe both acute traumas and the malfunction of my primary attachment relationship. My parents weren't reliable sources of comfort or co-regulation, but alcohol, like food, was always there for me. Alcohol quieted the constant yearning inside of me for *something* that I could neither identify nor obtain elsewhere.

Many alcoholics will tell you that the experience of finding alcohol was like coming home — for the first time in their lives, they felt at complete ease in the world, and like they could truly be themselves. But what many alcoholics don't know is that a healthy parent-child attachment relationship has the same effect!

It's possible to evaluate the attachment relationship with your child by noticing who they go to when they have a problem, and with whom, if anyone, they share their deepest feelings. If this person isn't you or another trustworthy adult, your child may not sense that the kind of connection they need is available to them, and will likely be looking for it elsewhere.

It's great for kids to have friends, but peers, who have the same developmental needs as they do, will not be able to meet all of their needs (I highly recommend Gabor Maté's book, *Hold On to Your Kids* for more on the nuances of peer attachment). A consistent primary attachment relationship with an emotionally available adult is key for child development.

I've had to do a lot of work as a parent to show up as the kind of adult my daughter needs me to be, and if you're reading this book there's a good chance you're raising yourself alongside your child, too. Keep in mind that it's impossible to do this perfectly, and that the fact you are doing the work at all puts your child light years ahead of where they'd be if you weren't at least *trying*.

The important thing is not that we prevent any harm coming to our kids at all, but that we are available to co-regulate with them when they inevitably experience wounding and that we initiate repair in our relationship with them as needed.

While it can be hard to stay close with our kids as they grow older and become more independent, and while we may not realize that something is wrong until our kids start making unsafe choices as tweens or teens, the good news is that it's never too late to strengthen our bond.

It's never too late for us to examine our own relationship with alcohol and other potentially addictive substances, learn nervous system regulation skills, integrate our traumas, notice where our kids may need more from us than we've previously been aware, and create the kind of connection with them that we are uniquely positioned to enjoy as radically unschooling families (see "The NEAR Parenting Framework" for more on this).

It's also never too late for kids to heal their traumas, whether experienced within or outside the family, whether we are able to support them with this directly or find it necessary to seek outside help.

At its core, addiction stems from a need for connection — making it the most powerful gift we can offer ourselves and our children in preventing and overcoming substance dependency.

Getting Unfrozen and Unleashing Our Magic

Sometimes there's no big traumatic event underlying an addiction, but rather the gradual accumulation of subtle indignities that erode our *joie de vivre*. In these cases, breaking a pattern of overconsuming substances, media, or anything else can mean reconnecting with an abandoned inner child — one who is longing to be seen, to express themselves, and to have their creativity nurtured.

When we assure our inner child that it is safe for them to be creative, that there is no wrong way to make art, or whatever support is most needed to unleash our magic, we reclaim our ability to act upon the world and express ourselves within it, instead of simply enduring life and passively consuming media to escape it.

Sometimes, actions are more powerful than words.

I used to have a sewing machine that I could never find the motivation to use, even though I very much wanted to make things with it. I had the idea to create a little stuffed bunny with button eyes, but felt like some invisible force was holding me back.

Eventually, my desire to create won — while voices in my head raged about how I *didn't know what I was doing* and there was *no use even trying*, I sat there and made the goddamn bunny.

The funny thing is, I didn't even *hear* these voices until I got to work! In this case, getting started was crucial for me to understand what the problem was, and then to move through it.

I reparented my inner child and regulated my nervous system by ignoring thoughts of self-doubt, and not letting them stop me. Instead of waiting for my mindset to change, or working on it directly, I just proved it wrong.

Bringing our nervous system back from the freeze response can be an intensely emotional experience, and it can help to connect with others in the process if we feel we would benefit from it.

Although it might look different, this is also what a child who is stuck in the freeze response needs from their parent or caregiver. If our children seem too invested in media consumption, they may need more from us. They may need to connect with us, re-establish or strengthen the attachment relationship, and process any difficulties that may have overwhelmed them.

Most people know about fight, flight, freeze and fawn, but the answer to all of these is to *feel*. When we create a safe container for ourselves and our children to feel, we can begin to shift from survival mode to creative mode.

I've found interesting connections between many parents who say their children "need structure," and multigenerational patterns of creative wounding and nervous system dysregulation. While these parents might like their children to have more creative freedom, they hesitate to do so when they see their kids zoning out online or watching tv and not appearing to do anything creative at all. This often leads parents to conclude that their children can't function without constant direct supervision and instruction, and decide that unschooling just isn't working for them.

The irony is that sometimes, the very environments these children are raised in are what caused this problem in the first place. Where structure means strict rules, obedience and punishments — such as at school or in authoritarian households — children can develop a chronic freeze response. In this state, they may appear passive or disengaged, often turning to media as a way to dissociate or self-soothe. What looks like laziness or addiction is sometimes a nervous system stuck in survival mode.

A child who has experienced trauma — whether around creativity specifically or in other areas — may struggle with self-directed activities as a result. Trauma can impair executive functioning, the set of skills that help us plan, initiate, and follow through with projects. This includes attachment trauma, which can undermine a child's sense of internal stability and motivation.

While many healthy and securely attached children do benefit from structured classes and other types of formal instruction, when a parent tells me their child is unable to pursue their interests independently, I usually ask a few questions to get a feel for whether the child might instead need more co-regulation than the family's current daily rhythm allows.

Adults who haven't experienced creative freedom in their own lives will have to learn to get comfortable with it, sometimes for the first time alongside their children. This often involves a lot of deep nervous system work. When we feel safe to create, we can help our children feel the same way. It's their default setting — we really just need not to interfere with it, unless they've already been made to feel unsafe.

When the parent understands how to repair and nurture the attachment relationship, support their child in integrating traumas, and meet their children's emotional needs — and has the time to devote to it — they often find the child is much more capable of regulating their use of digital technology, and spends more time creating rather than only consuming.

In these cases, it isn't "structure" that the child needed, it's the presence of a safe attachment figure. Children are needy by definition, but they move toward independence by having attuned caregivers, not by being told what to do every second of every day. Mothering is structure, too.

Another possibility here is that parents misunderstand their child's creative process. Creativity isn't just making things — it's also observing, learning, becoming inspired, nurturing ideas, expression, refinement, rest and integration — a whole seasonal cycle in which productivity, at least as measured from the outside, is just one small part. But lacking a broader understanding of what creativity can look like, many parents assume their kids are just wasting time in front of screens.

Imagine confiscating a painter's brushes, canvases and paints because you catch them "wasting time" passively consuming art at a gallery or museum.

Imagine pulling your child out of film school because their professor screened a movie in class as part of a lesson on cinematic techniques. (I took a course on cinema in high school, and we spent *a lot* of it watching movies!)

In my daughter's case, watching other people's videos is how she's gotten a feel for market trends and demand, developed important friendships and collaborations, and learned about new art forms, styles, apps and techniques to use in her own artwork.

When we break it down, a lot of restrictions on children's autonomy (particularly with regard to technology access) are fear-based and contradictory to the values we might *say* that we have. If we want our children to be creative, expressive and innovative, we have to trust the process — *their* process.

It's also possible in these cases that the child actually needs *more* freedom or more exposure to the outside world, rather than more structure. Many of us are designed to create *in response* to our environment or other stimuli, and for us, interacting with others is key to our process. Creating in partnership with others or joining virtual co-working groups can also be a way to simulate the stability of an attachment relationship when we haven't yet been able to internalize one — this is the logic behind what's often called "body doubling."

Structure doesn't necessarily mean lots of rules and commands; it can also mean support. We can provide structure for our kids by making sure they have the outlets and opportunities to challenge and express themselves in ways that are appealing and appropriate *for them.*

In my senior year of high school, I quit calculus. This was somewhat scandalous; several people expressed concern for my future. I was actually pretty good at math — good enough to see that dropping this *one* class would allow me to fit *two* art classes into my schedule. I went on to become a professional artist, and pre-calculus has been more than enough to carry me through adulthood so far.

Of course, structure doesn't always take the form of classes. A business, for example, is a structure. If our child wants to start a business, we can ensure that our unfounded judgments, fears or limiting beliefs don't get in their way. Children who seem inactive or overactive (at least, from adults' perspective!) are often just bored with "children's" activities and want to play in the big leagues when it comes to creative expression.

We can advocate for them and support them in their big ideas while letting them be the ones to choose which path to take, and when. This is not always easy when it comes to digital creativity, which we'll dive into more deeply in the next essay. But trusting our intuition and holding the vision for our kids' fullest expression, we can always find a way, or create one together.

Whether our inner or outer children have experienced any kind of wounding or discouragement regarding creative expression, healing and growth are available through the attachment relationship and the creative process itself. By being emotionally present and embodying leadership, we have the power to reconnect with and nurture our own innate creativity — and to support our children in doing the same.

The Drama of Going Digital

It's a little bit funny that so many parents who would love to have location-independent income are so staunchly against their children using electronics. Left to their own devices — literally and figuratively — our kids might figure it out before we do.

Before becoming a parent, I was fairly Luddite-leaning myself, living out of a backpack for months on end without so much as a phone number. But as an isolated and exhausted single mother with few options, I chose technology freedom: my daughter got her own cell phone when she was three.

By age eight, she had a realistic plan to make a living with her digital artwork before reaching adulthood. Even if that doesn't pan out, she already has in-demand skills suitable for online work — more than most adults do — and will have options. She already works for me in my business, thanks to the video editing expertise she's gained through self-directed learning.

To be clear: I'm not judging parents for being hesitant to let their children get sucked into the digital and online worlds. I have had all the same fears, and it's definitely challenging terrain to navigate at times. But bad things can happen at the park, too, and that doesn't mean we just stop going outside to play.

So where do we draw the line? This is a deeply personal question that must be considered on a case-by-case basis, if for no other reason than that the digital world has become so vast.

With kids who are highly skilled, curious, and motivated, there's often a mismatch between the advanced level of technology they're ready to navigate and the emotional or social maturity level these technologies are designed for. Many online tools and platforms that have the potential to support these children in their creativity also open doors to adult content, leaving parents to wonder if helping kids reach their potential comes at the price of letting them grow up too soon.

For families who are unschooling after having difficulty with peer relationships and influences at school, entering the digital world can feel like going from the frying pan into the fire.

There's a nuance in the issue of children's autonomy that needs to be articulated: shielding our kids from harmful online content is *not* control; it's protection. There are things that children can't unsee that could cause long-term psychological damage, and part of our leadership role as parents is making sure that doesn't happen.

Most of us wouldn't sleep with the front door of our home wide open, let our kids loose in an adult video store, or hire the neighborhood bullies as babysitters, but the consequences can be similar when we neglect to curate online spaces and habits that are appropriate for our kids' developmental level.

It's not always just about talking to our kids about what they see and experience online, either. If a creepy relative was affecting our kids' mental health or relating to them inappropriately, we wouldn't just keep processing it with them after every visit — we'd stop bringing them around.

Trust your instincts, and tune into how certain products, platforms, people and places affect both you and your child. Trust your anger, especially. When you feel like throwing their tablet out the window, chances are there's an important boundary waiting to be acknowledged and honored. What is asking for your protection — your child's innocence, their agency, your connection?

When I sense an app is bringing dark energy into our home, I'm usually not the only one feeling it. To my pleasant surprise, my child has often expressed relief when I've suggested we take a break from it, set limits with it, or delete it altogether. The same has been true for online friendships, too.

Fortunately, we don't have to fear that our children's creativity can only find expression through one form, if that form is causing problems for our kids. When water hits a rock, it finds somewhere else to flow. There are millions of ways to be creative, and discovering them is the whole point.

I'd be lying if I said I didn't wish my child could have had another secure attachment figure instead of a Netflix subscription in her early years. But seeing her thrive now as an artist, telling stories with the digital tools she's become fluent in, things seem to be working out just fine.

Even if they aren't, I can't imagine a better skill than storytelling for transforming pain into power.

As anyone over the age of 30 knows, children can also have wonderfully rich lives and grow up to be content, fully functioning adults without having access to electronics at all in childhood, or only very restricted access. (Plus, someone's going to need to know how to churn butter when society collapses.)

It's not the availability of technology that makes or breaks a childhood — it's secure attachment.

In a patriarchal society where the nuclear family has replaced the village, technology easily becomes a substitute for human connection and co-regulation. Parents — especially the "designated parent," usually the mother — are easily overstimulated and overwhelmed by the emotional and physical demands of childrearing with little or no help, often in addition to supporting the family financially, and aren't always available when kids need to be held or listened to.

When kids turn to technology to fill this attachment void, the potential for addiction arises. As with other process addictions, the dopamine hits served up mimic fulfillment of the mother/child bond. And this is just as true for parents as it is for children — many of us habitually reach for our phones in search of co-regulation, whether or not it's truly available on the other side of the screen.

"Screen addiction" exists in the context of fractured communities and missing attachment relationships, where we have to go out of our way to create the connections both we and our children need. Learning how to hold the tension between the village we long for and the islands of connection we have now, we leave space for what we want to arrive, and model for our kids what it looks like to sit with discomfort instead of numbing and avoiding it.

As with any area of parenting, we lead the way by improving our own relationship with technology. We set the tone by actively pursuing our passion projects, caring for our emotional needs, building satisfying social lives, and anchoring our children in reality.

Technology is developing so quickly that it can seem hard to keep up — but in the midst of constant change, we can always rely on our instincts, and we must. Our job is not to know for certain what the future will bring, but to meet it with our self-trust intact, and to teach our children how to trust themselves, too.

The world of technology is defined by iteration, learning and growth — just like parenting. Every challenge is an invitation to strengthen our leadership. Regardless of how we choose to handle access, we can give ourselves and our children space to explore and innovate, and the grace to begin again.

The family that experiments with technology together might just find freedom, creativity and wisdom together, too.

Raising Kids Who Raise Hell

The world is full of people afraid to hurt anyone's feelings, even to save their own lives.

So many adults have inner children who are still scared to upset Mom and Dad, both literally in the family and projected onto other authority figures.

The result? A global economy built on unsustainable resource extraction and unconscionable exploitation, where silence earns you temporary emotional and material security at the price of your soul.

We are in danger of raising another generation of developmentally stunted youth who will remain psychologically children in adult bodies, easily manipulated by the powers that be with fear, guilt and shame.

The importance of counteracting this with our own embodied self-trust as parents cannot be overstated. We need our kids to know how they feel, to think for themselves, and to have the courage to express themselves authentically — and this begins with our example.

Being present with ourselves, reparenting our own inner children and getting in touch with our innate boundaries allows us to be available on that level to our own children, and also to model real adulthood instead of the parody of maturity featured and engineered by mass media.

Nothing is more important to personal and collective sovereignty than creating a world of authentic human relationships based on truth and sincerity, and in achieving this for ourselves we pave the way for our children.

Our sovereignty liberates those ahead of us, and sets the stage for a sustainable future. So let's raise our kids to raise their voices, and rise up when their souls are on the line.

Do Not Disturb

It took me a minute to process what I was seeing when my daughter showed me her messaging app — she had "Do Not Disturb" turned on.

Foolishly, I asked her if she knew what it meant, and if she had it on by accident. She calmly explained, "It's almost 9 pm, I'm not going to check messages again until tomorrow morning."

Confused, I replied, "But you stay up almost all night, wouldn't you want to talk to a friend who called you?"

She said, "No, at night I just want to watch movies, relax, and not talk to anyone."

Huh. For some reason, I assumed she'd always want to be available to her friends, like I'd been at her age.

I didn't have boundaries with friends at age 8, 13 or even 25. Severely codependent, I never felt secure enough in myself or comfortable enough with solitude to decline a social invitation. The violations I experienced as a child, and resulting attachment wound, prevented me from having any concept of boundaries.

I never felt like I had physical space from my parents as a child. My mother slept in my bed until I was at least a preteen in order to avoid my father, and was always up in my face trying to get me to do stuff with her, or force me to have a conversation, because of her depression and loneliness.

I have made an effort to do things very differently.

As a Human Design projector, my child can find my generator aura a bit much and I give her the space she needs. She often asks me, "Can I have this room all to myself?" or says, "Mom, I want to be alone." Or even, "Mom, do you want to go for a walk by yourself?"

I almost always say *yes*. If I'm too tired to go out, I'll go to a separate room and shut the door, or I'll let her know that I am physically unable to move from the couch currently but that she's welcome to go to her bedroom or another room and shut the door, and I promise not to bother her until she either says she's ready to hang out, or I come bearing snacks.

My child has been allowed to choose her own bedtime, her own friends, her own goals, her own creative activities, and her own relationship with technology.

She has had the freedom to find out what works for her, and my support in pursuing whatever lights her up. Because of this, my child has strong boundaries — with me, with herself, with technology and with her friends.

They are not *my* boundaries.

They are not my mother's boundaries.

They are not an Instagram therapist's or schoolteacher's boundaries.

They are *hers*.

And I am so fucking proud.

Telling New Bedtime Stories

We've never had enforced "bedtimes" in our home. However, we have had bedtime routines.

When my daughter was a wee bitty one, she just nursed until she fell asleep. When she was old enough to ask for a story, we did stories — often multiple stories, and for a while, it was "three stories and a song," each of which I made up on the spot no matter how tired I was.

In retrospect I have no idea why I put myself through that, except that I really loved her and wanted her to be happy, and I also thought it was the only way to get her to sleep.

Much later in the game, I improved on this with The Super Slow Story. Here's how that works:

Too tired to tell your kids one bedtime story after another, and want them to fall asleep asap? Tell one story, veeerrrrrry slooooowwwly. You'll literally bore them to sleep! It doesn't even matter what words you say — the slow and steady rhythm of your voice will do the trick. This works much more quickly than a bedtime story — or dozens — told at a regular pace. If you do this right, you won't even be able to finish the first one, unless your kids simply aren't tired.

Eventually, my daughter started saying she didn't want to go to bed around the time we usually turned in.

"Fine," I'd say, "but if you go to bed later than me, we won't have story time. Are you okay with that?" Inevitably, she'd choose to come to bed when I was ready for bed, so that she could have her stories.

A few years later, she decided she didn't care about story time, and wanted to try to stay up all night! I worried she'd be an exhausted mess the next day, and I wasn't sure I'd be able to handle the extra dysregulation and stress.

Parents — I'm telling you: not being able to handle the extra dysregulation and stress is 100% a valid reason to say *no*! We all have our limits.

But I wasn't yet sure what mine were, and my days are largely unstructured anyway. So I said, "Okay," and left my child on the living room sofa to make art and watch movies until she fell asleep.

When I woke up the next morning, the house was quiet. She'd fallen asleep probably around 3 am — only three hours before — and slept in until almost noon. Letting my child decide when to go to sleep effectively cut my waking parenting hours from 14 down to around 9 (almost as few as a full-time job, heh), and gave me back my bed and my mornings.

Of course, this isn't always practical and there are still some boundaries. Very rarely, we have activities planned for the next day requiring us to be at least semi-functional before noon. At these times, we talk about what would be a good time to try to get to sleep that our future selves would be thankful for. It's never about control or punishment — always just a conversation where everyone's perspective counts. Also, turning off the wifi at night is non-negotiable, due to radiation sensitivity.

There are lots of challenges you might come across implementing asynchronous sleep schedules in your family, especially if you have younger kids or lots of them. As with any area of life, you always have the freedom to question what you've been told is the right way to do things and to figure out what works for you.

So I'm not saying this is *the way* — it's just a path we've chosen to explore, and it's led to some pretty sweet dreams for both of us.

Interestingly, my daughter's sleep cycles have often synchronized with my needs while writing this book.

For example, she was staying up very late when I was writing the bulk of this manuscript, which was convenient because that gave me hours each morning (and sometimes early afternoon) to operate uninterrupted in a state of deep flow. Then shortly after I submitted the first draft, she went back to turning in closer to the same time that I do.

Once, in the middle of the night, I woke up with a burst of inspiration about how to resolve a structural issue I'd been struggling with, and my daughter also happened to have stayed up very late the night before, meaning that I had plenty of time to focus on writing before she woke up the next day.

I can't explain why my daughter happened to stay up late the exact nights I needed the next day to do lots of writing, or why things seem to just *work* in similar ways for us at other times. It's a mystery!

What I do know is that when there is a lot going on in our home on any given day or my daughter needs me more than usual, I tend to accept that certain things I may have been hoping to get done just aren't going to happen that day. I don't force it or stress out about it.

I've built so much flexibility into my business and life that unexpected changes don't upset me or anyone else in my life. My work with clients happens completely over voice and text messages instead of scheduled calls, which gives them, most of whom are also parents, the same flexibility.

In fact, it's rare that I have any plan at all for the next day in terms of what I'll be working on or how much will be accomplished. I wait and see what the energy of the day brings, and I work with it.

A lot of Win-Win Parenting, as well as my body-based approach to life and business, is about living in the moment, letting go of control, and trusting that the Fertile Universe will deliver what's needed, when it's needed — and often in a way we never would have expected.

It's not like we're in a perpetual state of equilibrium with regard to parenting, work and everything else. It's not about staying in balance — life is defined by change — it's about continually seeking it. The wind blows, and we adjust our sails.

An open mind, a positive attitude and a flexible approach go a long way when it comes to adaptability. But apart from any conscious effort on my part, I find that a lot of "parenting problems" just have a way of working themselves out when I'm in the groove of my work, playing on purpose.

Raising an unschooling child singlehandedly while running a business is part strategy and part magic. When I follow my internal guidance, my desires, and my design, things just *work*. When things just aren't flowing — whether at bedtime or anywhere else in life — I know it's time to start telling new stories.

Motherhood and the Power of Pleasure

The connection between parenting and sexuality extends far beyond the act of conception. This reality is obscured by the stigma against women being in touch with our sexuality, most of all when we enter motherhood. In patriarchal society, mothers are effectively neutered, expected to be sexless, powerless and void of desire. In the wounded masculine imagination, mothering itself is what separates the saintly Madonna from the debased whore.

Women are not "supposed to" conceive children from a place of sexual desire, much less experience ourselves as sexual beings while raising children. Our sexuality is only to be used against us, and experienced by others, but not used or experienced *by* us. It's a peculiar quirk of biology that every pregnancy on Earth is caused by the male orgasm, but this only suggests that women's pleasure serves an even greater purpose.

The patriarchal cognitive dissonance that blames women's pleasure for the world's problems keeps us disconnected from our own power, and therefore vulnerable to control by the Father.

But our sex *is* our power. We don't just bring new life into the world through our sex — our whole energetic center is located in our pelvic area, and this doesn't change when we become mothers.

Most women have had this power taken from us at some point, through sexual assault or other kinds of abuse, and we have seen how it affects us not just in our sex lives but in *every* area of life. If we have been sexually abused as children we likely grew up with chronically low self-esteem, challenges regulating our emotions and impulses, and difficulty engaging with others and a feeling that life is just happening to us rather than that we are making things happen.

Particularly in cases where abuse occurs in captivity, such as with child sexual abuse where escape from the perpetrator is not possible, a vital component of our agency and of ourselves goes missing.

As adult women, sexual assault can also be devastating on many levels. We likely feel disconnected from ourselves, have trouble performing the tasks of daily living, often even developing symptoms of ADHD.

One of my clients thought she had ADHD until we traced her executive dysfunction to a sexual assault she *thought* she had consented to. She had given a verbal *yes* to the encounter, but while under the influence of alcohol. So even though she had technically agreed to have sex, her body was too numb to respond meaningfully, and had therefore experienced the encounter as a violation.

In cases like this, our executive function is damaged because our innermost self has been overpowered, our "inner executive" violently overthrown in this loss of agency.

When we say that alcohol nullifies consent, it's not about assigning blame; it's about understanding bodily and spiritual integrity. We have been conditioned out of knowing ourselves on this level, convinced that our loss of initiative in cases like these is some unsolvable mystery. From the perpetrator's point of view, it's convenient to take a *yes* at face value. As a survivor, this perspective presents a barrier to healing.

No medication can replace the deep healing of the attachment system and restoration of personal power required to permanently restore executive functioning, which can be achieved strictly through the survivor reclaiming her relationship with her body.

Borderline Personality Disorder is another common diagnosis for sexual abuse survivors, the common symptoms all pointing to a woman divorced from her embodied sexual power. Survivors of sexual trauma need fewer diagnoses and more validation for the experiences that have broken our spirits.

Outside of circumstances that most of us would consider to be coercive, many women still become mothers by force. One of the main functions of patriarchy is to control women's reproductive activities, and this often happens through economic and psychological coercion. These types of coercion can be equally damaging and traumatic as a more obviously violent encounter, but as with situations involving alcohol, they can appear consensual on the surface.

Where marriage and heterosexual monogamy in general are normalized and other choices are stigmatized and even violently punished, the systemic violence of patriarchal norms is somewhat obscured. If a woman has no other realistic options for survival, or believes that she doesn't, her consent to marriage, sex or motherhood cannot be considered meaningful.

Women could legally be incarcerated simply for refusing marriage, or exercising many other basic forms of autonomy, until shockingly recently [17]. Once married, a woman's rights dwindle even further — a man could have his wife committed to an asylum for any reason he wanted, including refusing sex [18]. Marital rape was legal in every U.S. state prior to the 1970s, and not fully criminalized nationwide until 1993 [19]. Even now, some U.S. states punish marital rape less severely than non-marital rape.

The assumption that a woman has consented to sex with a man simply by having married him, and therefore also that she has chosen to bear his children, are based on the patriarchal view of women as property of their husbands.

Part of the way these become norms is historical erasure — most people don't know that women used to run this shit, that we did it very well, that marriage and fatherhood are patriarchal constructs, and that matriarchal and matrilineal societies have mostly disappeared only because they were violently overthrown. Perhaps the dawn of patriarchy marked the start of women's collective problem with executive functioning. It's no wonder that women have trouble getting diagnosed with ADHD since the concept of womanhood in patriarchy is defined by an absence of agency.

Our reproductive abilities include the power to bring new life into the world, but don't end there. The power to *end* new life also naturally belongs to women, traditionally in the form of herbs we might ingest to end a pregnancy or those with which we might brew a powerful tea to poison incorrigibly abusive members of our household or community.

Our intimate knowledge of plants and their many uses and relationships is part of the massive treasury of women's wisdom lost with the rise of patriarchy, and regaining this knowledge is crucial to our rise as sovereign beings.

In patriarchy, the stark contrast between expectations of women with and without children even lead some to welcome motherhood as an escape: a (hopeful) refuge from the sexual demands of their husband or boyfriend, from the pressure of dating and always being assumed to be "available."

A woman who has a child on her own is often assumed to be married, or less likely to be pursued just due to having a child, and may gain some relief from men's advances as a result. Whatever the circumstances, we definitely gain a layer of invisibility as mothers. We are both physically hidden from society by the overwhelming burden of domestic tasks and also redefined socially and politically as mere hosts to embryos, fetuses, children, husbands and houseguests.

Sex might be the very last thing on our minds as we focus on bonding with our babies and navigate the new challenges brought by motherhood. I'm not at all saying that this should change, just that it's worth sorting out which part of our sexual expression has been chosen consciously by us, and which we have internalized from patriarchal values.

A woman's desire for joy and pleasure deserves to be prioritized at any stage of life, in whatever form. It is from this well of joy and pleasure that she will draw the wisdom, power and direction she needs to parent her child from a place of embodied leadership. Healing her relationship with her own joy and pleasure doesn't have to involve sex. The important thing is that she is choosing it for herself, with no element of financial or other coercion, and that she experiences it as empowering.

Our children need to believe that we are powerful. That we are trustworthy and know what we're doing as parents. That we are safe and available attachment figures. They need us to be grounded in joyful embodiment so that they, too, can discover and access the wisdom of their own bodies, which they will use to navigate life.

Children are empowered when we know who we are and what we want, and they see us taking action to make it our reality.

If we have blocks toward experiencing pleasure, it will impact our ability to access our power and to lead our children from a place of power.

A woman not in touch with her power is disconnected from her child, or worse, spiritually dependent on them. Either way, she is unable to lead the way a healthy mother does. She may also allow others to hurt her child, not feeling like there is anything she can do about it because she doesn't even know how to claim her own power, much less do so on behalf of someone else. This disconnection from herself can also lead her to feel victimized by her own child.

A mother grounded in joyful embodiment sources happiness from within, and sets the example for her children to do the same. This is in contrast with a mother who is addicted, whether to a substance like sugar or alcohol or to a process such as achievement or watching television. A woman grounded in joyful embodiment knows that she is God. That all of the happiness she needs can be created within her, and that all of the things in life she wants to add onto that baseline of happiness are possible through her embodied joy.

This is true power — the power of feminine embodiment.

A mother in her power is a force to be reckoned with. She leads with her desire for connection and attunement with her child. This desire is housed in her womb space, and is where she connects with and nurtures it. Focusing on her pleasure and joy, they grow. Surrendering her mind to the process of embodied joyfulness she gains a feeling of wholeness and inner peace.

She asks herself: *How much happiness, pleasure and joy can I feel at this moment? How much more might be available to me, if I opened myself to it?*

There is so much beauty, pleasure and joy available to us at any moment that it would knock us out to feel it all at once. It's simple, but not necessarily easy, to choose to direct our attention to what's good and delicious right in front of us.

Although often painful, breastfeeding and childbirth can also be pleasurable — under the right conditions. I gave birth in a stressful, hostile environment, so this was definitely not my experience! However, I believe that these experiences are designed to be pleasurable. Many women report orgasmic birth and say that they enjoy how breastfeeding feels. I won't lie to you — although I loved the connection with my daughter that breastfeeding created, I found it incredibly uncomfortable and was massively relieved when it was over! Perhaps with multiple women sharing the work of nursing, those of us who find it painful would find some relief.

A woman connected to her power is capable of regulating her emotions with her own physical presence. Her adult body becomes the safe container with which feelings can be integrated. She knows that no matter how big her feelings seem, she is bigger. Her infinite spiritual dimension, where the inner child lives, finds comfort in her finite physical form.

If her mother was not available, emotionally or otherwise, to ground her child's emotions in this way, she can learn to form a secure attachment with herself. It's not ideal of course — we are born with mothers for a reason — but it works.

To be clear, this connection between parenting and pleasure has absolutely nothing to do with sexual abuse of children — although mothers connected to our pleasure are often viewed with plenty of suspicion. The difference between using a child for sexual gratification, and parenting from a place of embodied pleasure, is night and day.

In fact, a woman divorced from her pleasure may find parenting and other areas of life inordinately challenging, and the supposed joys of motherhood out of reach. It is in these circumstances that a child might not be getting all they need from the attachment relationship and therefore become stunted in their own capacity for joy or leadership development.

The legacy of sexual trauma can be passed along to future generations even when abuse is not, but, fortunately, so can our healing and empowerment.

A mother in her pleasure is a mother in her power. When she rises in power, her children rise with her.

The Sovereign Mother

As a devotee of attachment parenting, I had been taught that child-led weaning was best. I was ready to stop nursing by the time my daughter was three years old — let's be real, I was beyond ready — but I was terrified of depriving my child, both physically and emotionally.

Eventually, there came a day when I simply could not go on — I needed my body back.

One night, I told my daughter *no*. To my surprise and utter relief, she simply expressed a little sadness, asked once again the next day, and then never mentioned it again.

I felt like I'd been duped! All that time I had been suffering from prolonging the nursing relationship well past the point of my personal comfort, and I could have just said *no* at any point, with no drama?

All that time, my child was looking to *me* as the leader, and I was giving her power that she didn't need or want.

This completely changed my perception of my role as a parent. I realized that letting my daughter be in charge too much would lead to burnout and resentment for me, while depriving my child of the guidance she needed.

I had actually been deferring to my child's authority as an escape from owning my power as a mother, because owning my power as a mother scared the shit out of me.

I honestly didn't know how to do it. My nervous system had been programmed by school, family, religion, jobs and other patriarchal institutions to depend on, and find comfort in, external authority.

Having been parentified in my own family of origin, I knew what an anxious mess it made me that the adults around me didn't know what they were doing and needed me to make more grown-up decisions than I was prepared to.

Here's where I draw the line between respecting children's autonomy, and neglect: if children can fail in ways that cause themselves or others serious or long-term harm, they have too much responsibility.

It's *our* responsibility as parents to ensure that our children's mistakes become learning opportunities — not irreversible tragedies.

Guiding our children effectively, and having healthy boundaries with them, starts with being in touch with our own power as women and as creative beings. It's about knowing what we want in *any* area of life, being able to go after it, and teaching children by our own example to do the same.

If our sense of personal power has been compromised, especially during our developmental years, we might not know what we want — or even what wanting feels like! We might feel or believe that there is nothing at all that we want, or we might not feel comfortable expressing our desires or taking action toward their fulfillment.

When we feel unaware of our wants and needs, or powerless to meet them, we can easily develop resentment — towards others who have what we want, or those who we perceive to be keeping us from getting what we want.

Resentment is actually a terrific clue for us to pay attention to!

When we notice that we feel resentful toward our children, we can ask ourselves: *Where might I not be standing fully in my power as a parent?*

When we start wondering if we have, in fact, created monsters, we may be tempted to scrap the idea of respectful parenting or radical unschooling altogether. This often means reverting our parenting style to the manufacturer's settings — relying on the "strict" patriarchal model of control, rules, and punishment.

But the problem is usually not that radical unschooling and respectful parenting didn't work. It's most likely that we didn't have the tools to understand *how* to implement these philosophies authentically, and instead outsourced our inner authority to community leaders who we thought knew better than we did how to raise our kids.

When we attempt to adopt a parenting technique or philosophy without fully embodying it and making it our own, we won't get very far, and it might even backfire. For example, instead of giving away our power as parents to schools, we give it to our children instead. Finding the balance between respecting our children's autonomy and making sure that we aren't becoming burned out, resentful victims of our own parenting philosophy is something most of us have to learn.

As adults, we have the power in the relationship. It's not our children's job to anticipate or to meet our needs — and this includes our need for leadership. If we want to lead our children rather than control them, we must heal our relationship to our own agency, and learn how to lead ourselves.

The crucial difference between influence and coercion lies in our relationship to our bodies. As parents, if we don't have a habit of fully *embodying* our power, our desires and our boundaries — if we don't make a point of honoring ourselves, our sacred internal *yes* and *no* — we will invariably end up feeling victimized by the little people in our homes who have far fewer hang-ups around asking for and doing exactly what they want every second of every day.

When we embrace embodied self-leadership, many of the problems we face as parents have a way of resolving themselves. This involves deep healing from trauma we have experienced either as children or as adults, ongoing commitment to embodiment practices that anchor us in secure attachment to ourselves, and the intention to connect with our innate joy, pleasure, desire and wisdom.

When we truly believe that we deserve to be the artists of our own lives, we will instinctively know how to raise our children with the same freedom.

The truth is, most of my approach to parenting is about *me*!

Solving problems in our family begins with looking at *my* problems — how my own childhood wounding is still affecting me.

Resolving conflicts with my child starts with resolving my own inner conflicts. The win-win always follows from there!

The better care I take of me, the more energized and available I am to her, while also modeling self-care for her benefit.

The more I follow my own dreams, the more my child learns how to lead with her heart and trust that her creativity is enough.

The happier and more nourished my inner child is, the more nicely she'll play with my outer child, and the more I'll show up as the adult in our relationship vs the wounded little girl.

This approach allows me to lead my child from a place of deep inner power, instead of the endless frustration of trying to control her.

I'm not a victim of motherhood; I'm not burning out and blaming my child for it.

I'm not sacrificing myself for my child — I'm spoiling the hell out of myself for her!

I'm a sovereign mother leading with joy, leaving my daughter a legacy of courage, freedom and unapologetic self-trust.

She's watched her mom dream big and do big, and now I get to watch her follow her own big dreams, too.

From Homeless to Real Estate Empress

About 10 years ago, when I experienced a debilitating burnout that outlasted unemployment and state disability benefits, I was no longer able to pay rent and ended up living on the streets.

Life happened, and I got pregnant. From the time I was 6 months in, I qualified for about $500 a month in single-parent welfare benefits. Where I was living at the time, this wouldn't have been enough to put a roof over my head.

At night, I would sneak into construction sites, find shelter in an abandoned shipping container, or settle down in a little forested area near the railroad tracks to get some sleep. During the day, I hit up churches and Food Not Bombs for meals.

It would have been tempting to spend the money I was getting on a hot meal or some other creature comforts, but I had a vision. I wanted to buy land, grow my own food and never have to work for anyone else again. I hated the indignity of wage labor, and I wasn't going back.

I withdrew my cash benefits at an ATM each month and traded them in for money orders at the Post Office. I saved the money orders and the receipts in separate bags in case one got lost or stolen.

After my daughter was born, we lived in a shelter for a few months. We could eat every meal there, so I pretty much only ever spent money on diapers. I watched other moms enjoy meals out, toys for the kids and little things for themselves, but I knew I was doing what was best for my family in the long run.

One day browsing Craigslist, I found a cute little cabin on land in the Ozarks that was listed for much more than I'd saved, but I felt compelled to reach out anyway. It turned out the seller was in a tight spot and willing to reduce the price nearly by half! I went to the Post Office with my money orders, cashed them out and paid the owner in full. I had essentially bought real estate with an EBT card.

Now, the specific way I saved up money to buy real estate obviously wouldn't work for everyone — I would never recommend getting pregnant just to get $500 a month, or for any amount of money. It's not like I had planned things out that way; I was only being resourceful at the moment. The specific situation in which this worked out for me is less important than the attitude I had about my situation. I was willing to see homelessness not just as a setback, but as an opportunity to make big moves with the blessing of low overhead.

In questioning "misfortune" of all kinds to look for the advantage, we have the power to shift how we see our current situation. Focus on the magic, not the tragic.

It didn't take long living out in the sticks with an infant to realize the off-grid life wasn't for me — at least not right then. But I held onto the property, and within about six years had multiple offers many times more than what I'd paid.

Now, when it sold I *could* have bought another property and worked my way up the real estate investment ladder... Instead, I blew it on travel.

After years of austere living, it's no surprise that I eventually felt the urge to splurge. Instead of making myself wrong for that, I internalized the lesson: self-deprivation is a form of debt that eventually comes due. Now I focus less on restricting my spending, and a lot more on increasing how much money I have to play with.

I also upgraded my real estate strategy so that having a certain amount of savings was no longer a prerequisite. Now, my online course *Real Estate Empress* offers women practical tools for buying homes without down payments or banks — strategies they can also use to make a living as international property agents, funding their travels with real estate deals along the way.

Whatever your circumstances, I want to assure you that you're a lot more capable of attracting material resources and building a freedom-based lifestyle than you may have been taught — even if you think you've screwed up beyond redemption. Trust me, the Fertile Universe is way more powerful than that.

Wild Womanhood

When I lived outside, I would wash my clothes in the river, securing them under a few stones and leaving them there to be cleaned by the cold rushing water. I was initially surprised at how effective this was. I also swam in the rivers and in every natural body of water I could find, loving how invigorating and grounding it was. Other times, I would shower in the rain. One time, I knocked on someone's door and asked if I could hose off in their side yard (they said *yes*).

Usually, I slept in the forest and when in the city, behind bushes. Once I was hitchhiking and couldn't get a ride before it started raining at night, so I knocked on someone's door and asked to sleep on their front porch. The woman who answered made me a massive meal and I ate it all while watching the night sky and listening to the rain.

I knocked on someone's door one evening with an entire family and their friend and a dog and asked if we could all sleep in their backyard. I was prepared to knock on every door in the neighborhood until someone said *yes* — but luckily, the very first one agreed.

A few times, I thought it might be good for me to sleep indoors, but I found that I hated it. I missed watching the stars at night, feeling the cool air on my face and hearing the birds sing and the wind rustle through the trees.

By comparison, living indoors seemed like an exercise in sensory deprivation. I did feel safer indoors sometimes, but it didn't feel worth it for what I had lost. I just didn't feel like I belonged to that world anymore.

I felt so connected spending most of my day outside, like I was part of something much bigger than myself. I felt much more present as well, like I didn't need distractions or entertainment to pass the time. My instincts were sharper, I was speaking my mind freely, and doing exactly as I pleased each day. For the first time in my life, I was actually living like a human being instead of like a machine.

Living without money, or little of it, was the most freeing thing of all. I could see how humans had been tricked into spending most of our waking lives earning money, when life in the natural world had no price tag on it.

It's not that I never missed having a more comfortable bed or more delicious meals, it's that I was no longer willing to suffer for them. I would rather be free than enjoy the comforts of civilization at the cost of my happiness.

I'm not sure most people have actually done this cost-benefit analysis. If you haven't, I recommend it. For everything you have in life that costs money, calculate how many hours of your life you spent (or continue to spend) doing work you didn't love in order to buy it. Was it worth it?

Repeat this process for everything in your home, in addition to your home, your car, if you have one, and anything else you can think of. If you're already doing work you enjoy, then are the things you spend money on an accurate reflection of your values and what brings you joy?

I'm definitely not saying you should stop working or give away all your things, unless of course that feels right for you.

This exercise is about evaluating our relationship with work and money and stuff and feeling out where we are in alignment, or not, with ourselves. It's about taking ownership of our lives and claiming our power to create lives that we love, instead of the ones we were told we should want.

Doing this for myself didn't mean that I never used money again or never worked again or spent the rest of my days living out of a backpack. It meant that I had subtracted everything from my life that had cost me my time, energy or attention, so that I could find out what I actually missed and wanted to add back into my life, versus what I'd only thought I needed, but didn't actually care enough about to work for.

This is what owning our power as consumers and as creators looks like. This is what it looks like to be living on our own terms and using our resources consciously.

An "abundance mindset" doesn't mean always making the most expensive choice. It's about investing in what *you* want and what makes *you* feel best. Very often, these are not the same!

Don't make yourself wrong for doing something that feels right, just because it costs less. It doesn't mean you're "in scarcity" — it means you're *in control*. Being intentional with money and spending it on what *you* want instead of on what you *think* you should want, is the very foundation of wealth.

Once you know what really matters to you and what you couldn't care less about, you have the power to relate to the working world and the material world in ways that work for you.

You're no longer in the rat race, keeping up with the Joneses or chasing money just because that's what everyone else is doing. You're doing *just enough* to get what you need and want, and then you're getting back out.

Advertising has no effect on you because you know that buying into the images you see on the screen means paying with your life force energy. The media puts distance between you and your direct experience of the world, and you see through it every time.

You might want the house, the car, the clothes, or the gadgets, but you won't be a slave to them. You might decide to buy them, but you know they might just as easily come to you another way.

Since you know that you can be happy with very little or very much, and that things come and go, no one and nothing can have power over you. You're a sovereign woman, loyal only to your own desires and values, holding boundaries with civilization itself.

In choosing this path, you remember: you're not losing your mind, and you're not losing "everything" — you're only losing what's standing between you and the wild and free woman you were born to be.

A Woman's Place Is Wherever She Wants to Be

People sometimes ask me things like, "So should every woman leave her husband right this second and take her children to live in a community in the forest?"

I mean, sure… if she wants to? But liberating ourselves from patriarchal society is not about making big drastic changes in our lives based on what someone else tells us is the right thing to do. It's also not about making ourselves wrong for the ways we depend on men, or even about trying to change the fact.

A woman's liberation must come from her own desire, otherwise it can only be a symptom of disconnection from her own power. Reactionary and shallow changes are why social movements throughout history have failed. Why intentional communities fail, even having the best of intentions. Why one despot is replaced after a bloody revolution by yet another despot. Why the grandchildren of holocaust survivors grow up to support genocide. Why the United States of America was supposedly founded on the principle of freedom, and well, look at it now.

The common thread is that there needs to be sufficient inner growth to support transformation in the outside world. When trauma, grief, or external authorities are running the show, change will not be sustainable. The motivation for change has to come from a place of power within, or it won't stick. When change is forced from the outside, the uncomfortable truth is that no real change has occurred.

This concept can of course be wildly misinterpreted if approached from an individualist lens, which is common in Western culture. This gives us the New Age belief that one person's positive thinking alone can prevent a war — unless this person is the one initiating the genocide, that's not how this works.

My experience living without money shed light on this tension between individual choices and systemic limitations. I learned that there are many kind and generous people in the world. But the only reason I could have the experience I did, of hitchhiking and being fed and housed in strangers' homes, was because those people were still working regular jobs and paying their bills so that they had a car and a home and food to share. It seemed I was more of a mooch than a revolutionary.

The generosity I discovered still pointed toward the innate human trait of compassion, but it wouldn't be practical for everyone to do what I did all at once. For each one of those people I met to be able to quit their jobs, there would need to be massive structural change to enable freer collective access to resources, so that we could all be meeting our needs without the intermediary of an employer. If everyone had direct access to food, water, shelter and other necessities, and used means of production that could be sustained without depleting the land base, then this might work on a larger scale. In order for everyone to be free, we would need to reclaim a lot more than just our minds.

This is why large-scale social change cannot be brought about by individual action alone, and why positive thinking without aligned action is impotent. This is why it's best for us to wait until we are clear on what we want, and not what others think we should want, before making major life changes.

If we act based on what we think we *should* do, rather than what we really want and feel ready for, we will be disappointed by the results. We either won't get the results that we expected, we won't be happy with them, or we will achieve them and then lose them as quickly as they came.

Whenever possible, we can replace "should" with "can" — the first traps us in a matrix of guilt and obligation, while the second opens us to a world of possibility and personal power. When we want to let go of a self-destructive habit, instead of telling ourselves we "can't" do the thing anymore, we can tell ourselves that we "don't have to" — framing change as liberation rather than constriction. As women, we don't need more rules to follow —we need to figure out what we want.

The language of sovereignty and responsibility empowers us to break free from the world of permission and punishment. Shame traps us in subservience, but desire awakens our leadership.

So, how do you know what you really want? Desire lives in the body, not the mind. Our bodies are vessels for creativity and truth. Our bodies bring new life into the world — the most profound act of manifestation possible. Our voices are a manifestation of our inner reality, expressing the frequency we are on independently of the words we speak. When we speak, we can feel whether or not our words resonate with truth, as can others with heightened auditory sensitivity, or clairsentience. This is why we might say that a particular statement "rings true." Words and emotions vibrate like the ringing of a bell.

Often, it's women with a male partner being dragged into the homesteading lifestyle, which may be easy to romanticize until she finds that she is the one tasked with compensating for the inconvenience of living outside the system with endless unpaid labor. If a woman really wants to abscond to the forest with her babies, awesome! But if she feels even sort of icky about being far out in nature away from society and would rather raise her kids near their favorite waterpark so that they have social contact and lots of fun stuff to do without putting her in the position of singlehandedly growing all of her family's food, then that could be a better choice for her.

I bought land when my daughter was a baby, and lasted all of about half an hour out there before I decided it wasn't for me. I wanted friends. I wanted groceries. I wanted cozy coffee shops and talking to strangers and not having to drive for thirty minutes to get to a restaurant when I didn't feel like cooking. I was finally living the dream, but once I had it, I realized it wasn't really *mine*.

The same goes for starting a business. If it feels better to keep a job, or to try to get a better job rather than start a business, then that's the move for you. No one has the right to judge you for choosing a path that feels safer or more stable, even if it doesn't match society's idea of what "radical" living should look like. We can learn to tell the difference between holding back because of limiting beliefs, and holding back because we are waiting for something more aligned. We can do this by getting in touch with our body's wisdom — where fear and desire conflict, can we trust desire? Fear isn't to be demonized, though — after all, it can keep us alive. It's our job to decide whether our fears are rational or based on an expectation of danger that no longer exists.

There is a time for making big, shocking moves in our lives, and a time for baby steps and for balance. We don't have to move from guilt, fear or shame. We can trust that our desires and our intuition are leading us in the right direction. We may want something else down the road, and we may eventually become ready for something more "alternative," but for now, we can trust that what we secretly want most is just perfect. Rome wasn't built in a day, and it didn't fall in a day, either.

It's also important to recognize that there are challenges we face collectively that are not possible for us to overcome strictly as individuals. We can trust that there will come a time when things fall into place that we have been trying force without success. Our job is to prepare in any way we can now for when larger forces in the universe become supportive of our vision.

Hold onto the frequency of what you want, even — and especially — when it's not reflected in your surroundings. The absence of instant gratification does not reflect the worthiness of your desires.

Forget everything that you think you *should* do, want, be or have — and instead consider the many things you *can* do, starting from exactly where you are right now. More clarity will come as you go, so trust the process and your inner knowing. Your place in the world is wherever you want to be, you have all the wisdom you need to get there, and your power is always now, in the present moment.

Traveling the World for (Almost) Free

The cheapest way to see the world? Hitchhike to a new city, commit a nonviolent crime, and enjoy a weekend at the local JailBnB. It's like an all-inclusive resort where you're guaranteed three meals a day, interesting people and unforgettable stories!

Oh, you have kids? Then the best way to travel on a budget is by pet sitting.

If your kids are mature and self-aware enough to be safe around animals, pet sitting is a great way to raise empathetic, responsible, confident and knowledgeable children. Animals provide comfort and a lot of fun and opportunities for connection. It's a great way to keep kids grounded and active in an increasingly digital world, especially for kids who are homebodies or "indoorsy" and prefer nature to come to them.

Often, kids also have as much or more energy than we do for various pet care tasks like feeding, grooming, and playing hours of fetch. It's fun for them to learn new skills, meet new animals, and have the experience of caring for other living beings. I would never force a child to do animal care or expect them to shoulder any real responsibility, but the opportunity is there.

If you're willing to go where the wind blows, you'll have no shortage of wonderful surprises awaiting you in the form of fascinating new cities, cultures, and animal experiences. You can charge money for sitting to fund your travels, or sit for free if you can afford it. While many women imagine that having kids is a disadvantage to finding pet-sitting gigs, I didn't find this to be true at all. For every time I've been passed over for having a child, I've been sought out twice by hosts whose pets prefer women or who just don't want strange men lumbering around their homes. A lot of them were single women themselves, lesbians, or otherwise female-only households.

I've been a pet sitter on and off for over ten years, starting from when I was pregnant with my daughter. I had been sleeping in a friend's van, and one day got a burst of inspiration to advertise myself as a pet sitter on Craigslist. The next day, I had an email from a woman down the street offering my first paid gig. The rest is history!

Well, almost. After my daughter was born, I tried living a normal life again with a lease and all the stability that comes with it. But I missed the freedom of travel, the variety of animals I'd had for company as a pet sitter, and there were just so many places I wanted to go. Once again, a burst of inspiration led me to put up a profile on an online pet-sitting platform. We got our first assignment right away, packed up our car and headed two states away to begin a new adventure.

My daughter and I traveled as pet sitters for a full year when she was a toddler, never paying a cent for accommodation. We drove around from gig to gig in a beat up 1990 Volkswagen Fox that someone had given us when our van broke down one freezing Montana winter. The car had a lot of character — the windows could only be raised by pushing up on the glass with your hands — but we had wheels and we were free and we were happy. I found cheap flights to Europe (under $100) and we did a few pet-sitting gigs there, too. We got amazing reviews from hosts from the start and easily built a great reputation and demand for our services that allowed us to travel full-time as pet sitters.

Our adventures took us from the Pacific Northwest U.S.A to Edinburgh, Scotland, where I was thrilled to be able to explore my ancestral heritage and lands. I got to see my distinctly Scottish facial features and sense of humor in a new light — one of belonging. It was a real homecoming experience. We also got to visit Peppa Pig World in Southampton, England, which my daughter still cherishes as her earliest memory!

One of my favorite memories of that trip is watching my daughter engage three Irish ladies on the bus one afternoon, asking each of them in turn whether they preferred snow or rain. The women were amazed at her conversational skills at only three years old, and I felt proud of having created a life where we could spend so much quality time together and where I could raise her on real-life experiences.

Even without pet sitting, our family has almost always had animals in our care, fostering many dogs in the U.S. and Mexico until we could find them forever homes with enough acreage for them to live happy lives. In Puerto Vallarta, we took in two kittens who we instantly knew were family, and decided it was a sign for us to settle down for good. But it wasn't meant to be — the road called again and we set off for a new adventure, now traveling with pets of our own.

I was very happy to have the company of our sweet kitties and at the same time, sad not to be pet sitting anymore. About a year after we adopted them, we began putting out ads for pet sitting once again, this time with cats in tow! I was amazed at how many people were okay with us bringing our cats along for sits, even paid ones. It probably didn't hurt that I had over a decade of experience by then, and had built up a long list of five-star reviews from past clients.

I eventually turned all of this into a course called *The Pet Sitters' Passport*, but it all started with a beat-up VW Fox, a curious toddler, and a Craigslist ad.

Women Need a Whole Fuck Off Life

I made an interesting observation about my mind in the early stages of building my first online business. Whenever my work seemed overwhelming or I was facing something deeply uncomfortable — for example, anxiety about being more visible in the public sphere — I would often find myself drifting into romantic daydreaming.

My nervous system was grappling with the terrifying prospect of becoming a financially independent woman. Even though I'd never been married or ever relied on a partner for material support, it felt like my brain carried an ancestral blueprint: that survival meant attaching myself to a man.

My daydreaming wasn't about attraction or love, it was an intrusive thought that wanted to convince me it was safer to do things according to patriarchal tradition.

As I progressed in building wealth, I found that these thoughts eventually quieted down (accepting defeat, I assumed), and also that the more money I had, the less I cared about what men thought of me in real life, or what they might want from me. I specifically noticed feeling less self-conscious about my body and about whether anyone found me sexually attractive. Like a fish in water, I hadn't realized how much my preoccupation with being physically desirable was tied to my economic vulnerability. Becoming financially secure in my business rewired my brain on a subconscious level and shifted my attitude toward men and toward myself in ways I never could have imagined. I found this both fascinating and liberating.

I can't help but wonder: What would happen to the multi-billion-dollar beauty industry if dating and marriage were simply options for women, rather than survival strategies? If women had no material security whatsoever to gain from sexual relationships with men, imagine what would happen to the dating "market," the sex industry, and the institution of marriage. Women rarely admit to marrying for money, but in a patriarchal society where marriage usually does increase our access to material resources, either directly or indirectly, and in which we have been epigenetically programmed over thousands of years to associate heterosexual marriage with increased prospects for survival, it's almost impossible to know for sure.

I wouldn't be surprised if our drive for material security informs many other decisions, ways of being in the world, and thinking patterns that we aren't aware of on a conscious level. One thing I know for sure: Women's desires for sovereignty and self-respect are revolutionary, and there has never been a better time to claim them.

The Wonderful World of Online Business

The internet is a pretty amazing tool. It has completely redefined how we can earn a living, make an impact, and build lives that align with our values. You can literally sit on your couch and make money from your phone, doing what you love most.

My mind was blown when I first learned digital marketing — not because of the patient attraction strategies I supported clients with, but because it had never occurred to me that I could just post on social media to advertise a service, and then have people *actually buy it*. I had done this to an extent when I started pet sitting, and later with my jewelry and raw chocolate businesses, but that seemed like small time stuff compared to charging high-ticket retainer fees for ad management services to people I'd never even met in person, enabling my family to travel the world on passive income.

I decided to start my first online business after a year of full-time pet sitting. I still loved pet sitting, but didn't want to *have* to do it anymore to get by. We were ready for a higher quality of life that allowed us to pick and choose which gigs we wanted to do — especially after having landed in the English countryside for a last-minute sit and being told that our job required touching a live electric fence!

I rented an apartment back in the U.S. and gave myself two years to set up a reliable remote income stream and get moving again. By the time two years came around, I had achieved my goals and we were ready to go. It felt wonderful, but strange, to feel supported by the universe in this new level of wealth and freedom. When all we had wanted was a free place to stay in exchange for pet sitting, we had found it, dozens of times over. Having set my sights higher, the universe continued to respond, as if it had just been waiting for me to claim more.

I ran my digital marketing agency for a few years before I felt ready for something new. The beauty of online business is that with low overhead, pivoting can feel less like starting over and more like a natural evolution. Online businesses, in contrast to brick-and-mortar store fronts with physical inventory, allow a lot of flexibility. I started working with holistic healthcare clients more closely to refine their messaging and improve the effectiveness of their organic marketing, and then I began working with coaches and spiritual entrepreneurs on the inner transformation that would help them tell more powerful stories and attract the people they most desired to their programs. This later evolved into supporting unschooling parents in finding balance in the juggling act of online business, raising kids and self-parenting. This often involved sharing my marketing expertise and facilitating the deep inner work that I focused on in previous iterations of my business. Now, supporting women in living their own Second Childhood brings all of this together — with an added focus on whole-life creative sovereignty, playfulness, joy, manifestation and cosmic justice.

While I'm at a very different place in my entrepreneurial journey than where I began, each stage has helped me get clearer on what I want to experience in my professional life, and how to get there. Everything I do today is built on the foundation of everything I have ever done. Each mentor I've worked with has taught me invaluable lessons, and each mistake I've made has gotten me closer to where I am today.

Entrepreneurship has absolutely been a natural extension of my healing journey and supported my reclamation of sovereignty in all areas of life — creativity, relationships, finances, emotions, intellect, spirituality, sexuality, and beyond — as it also has for my clients. There's no shortcut to the growth required of us as entrepreneurs, but I hope that by sharing my journey I can save you time, energy and maybe even some heartache.

20 Ways to Ignite Your Business

Just starting out in online business? Here are 20 nuggets of wisdom to fast-track your success:

1. Don't be intimidated by "the competition" — it means there is a market for your services! No one out there is exactly like you, so be yourself and trust that the right people will come your way.

2. You can make money starting exactly where you are now. You don't have to be an expert, or the best in your field — you only need to be able to solve someone else's problem, which you can often do if you know a little more than they do, or are a few steps ahead of them.

3. Talk about what you do, how and why you do it more than it seems appropriate. No one who is meant to play a role in your life's purpose will think you're annoying when you do, and who cares what anyone else thinks?

4. Always ask for testimonials — social proof is your most powerful marketing tool. Video is best, written is second best. Share all of your client reviews, testimonials and successful case studies publicly. Craft them into compelling narratives — stories sell.

5. The best marketing comes naturally from being head-over-heels in love with what you're offering and truly wanting to share it. If you're not obsessed with what you're selling, go do something else.

6. When something's gotta give, don't let it be your vision. Find somewhere else to cut corners (hint: look at what you're investing time and energy in that you don't really enjoy or secretly resent).

7. If you're just starting out, you can work for free or set your prices low enough to get a few good case studies or testimonials, but don't undercharge after that. Never charge a price that leaves you feeling resentful of your clients — charge whatever makes you feel *excited* to serve them!

8. Never offer something for free or low cost if it will reduce the quality of your service — this will tarnish your brand and damage your relationships with clients and potential clients. Charge however much brings out the best in you, and allows you to take exquisite care of yourself.

9. Never make business decisions out of fear. It's not worth the cost — and fear always comes with a cost. Adopt the attitude that you can't afford to make moves from anything less than a full-bodied "YES!" Consent matters in our relationship with our business — not just in our personal life.

10. *You* are your most important investment. Eat well, get plenty of sleep, relax and enjoy life — more than seems reasonable. Most of your best ideas will come when you're not "working."

11. There are no "business problems" — only personal problems manifesting in your business. When you don't know what's wrong, come back to your body, your truth, and your pleasure.

12. If you do it right, your business will trigger the living shit out of you — and then it will heal you. Approach your business to be the biggest personal growth journey of your life, and you'll succeed.

13. Understand your failures as nervous system successes — embrace pain and fear in your business and hold a safe place in your heart for blocks and limiting beliefs so that they can integrate and shift.

14. Befriend your inner child instead of making her your enemy, and she will help you build a business that feels playful, joyful, delightful and fun.

15. You will always make exactly as much money as you subconsciously believe is safe for you — and the same goes for building wealth. Learn how to calibrate your nervous system to surpass your limits.

16. The main thing standing in the way of most people building a business is their own brain. Learn how to have this thing working for you rather than against you, and you'll be unstoppable.

17. Focus first on the type of lifestyle you want, and then build your business around that — do this, and you'll never feel like a prisoner to your business.

18. No one starts with all the answers — just begin, and trust that the path will become clear as you go. You have

to make the first move *before* you have evidence that it's working. So go first!

19. Instead of modeling your business to look like other ones you see, create something that reflects your own unique gifts, needs, and desires. Innovation and authenticity will set you apart.

20. Learn about your Human Design — it will become your personalized roadmap from feeling lost and burned out to building the life and business of your dreams!

The Worst Boss Ever

Despite making money and progressing toward my goals in my first year of online business, I was always stressed, anxious and too tired to enjoy the freedom I was creating for my family. Somehow, I'd started a business to free myself from workplace toxicity, and proceeded to become the worst boss I'd ever had. No breaks, no food, no emotions, no sunlight, no sleep…

I was finally in charge of my own time and energy, so what in the illegal sweatshop was going on here?

While I had removed myself from the toxicity of the 9-5 world, I hadn't yet removed that toxicity from myself. Despite my intention to create more joy in my life, decades of school and work had programmed my nervous system to find comfort in self-denial. As much as I had hated the unhealthy dynamics of the school/work day, I subconsciously still believed I needed to neglect my own needs to find success.

Without external boundaries and cues to limit my workday, entrepreneurship felt even worse than working for other people... You know, because employers have to follow these things called "labor laws."

I'd actually spent the previous decade focusing on self-care, but fell off course with the triggers that came with starting a business. And the bro-marketing culture my mentors modeled didn't help any.

When things got so bad that I caught myself fantasizing about veering into oncoming traffic one day, I knew I needed to completely overhaul my approach to business.

I took a massive leap of faith and slowed down — way, way, down, to the pace of a joyful life. Here's what that looked like:

I made time for my feelings — not when my workday was finished, but as soon as they arose.

I scheduled mealtimes and food prep into my calendar, sat down to eat, and ate slowly.

I made playing with my child a top priority and made sure to do it every day.

I took daily trips to the beach or hikes in the forest — rain or shine.

I set boundaries with my work and clients that allowed me plenty of sleep and downtime.

I made time for creativity, being silly and doing things just for fun.

I started meditating each morning, to connect with myself and nurture my inner child — no matter what was going on in my business or in the world.

I stopped rushing to get anything done and instead took cues from my body about what I truly desired and had energy for — my conscience became my new to-do list.

Instead of trying to force things to move forward on an arbitrary schedule, I waited for ideas, timing and opportunities that felt aligned.

I learned about my Human Design and applied this new self-knowledge to every aspect of my business, so that I was working *with* my energetic imprint and not against it.

Despite all the extra time I was spending giving myself love and attention and rest, and hanging out with my kid, I soon realized that I was actually getting *more* done this way, in less time…

First of all, I was actually getting my best ideas when I was not even working! Clarity on important business decisions would just randomly drop in while I was enjoying a hike or watching a show.

The quality of my work was also much higher when I was well-rested, fed, in a good mood and working with my body instead of against it. So, I was more efficient and didn't need to spend as many hours in front of my laptop.

New business actually came in more easily when I stopped hustling — in fact, my biggest client ever showed up one day out of nowhere, asked to work with me, and stayed for years!

Most rewarding of all, my relationship with my child improved, because we were connecting more and having more fun together… And she started saying "I love you" again.

As I grew in trust of myself and of the universe, I came to believe that respecting my needs, inner guidance, desires and natural rhythms was not a distraction from my goals, but the most sustainable path towards them.

Let me be clear: this was hard. *Really* hard. Working humanely triggered the crap out of me because I truly was afraid I would fail if I didn't keep up... And slowing down to make time for all the feelings meant that I was crying, like, all the time.

My business triggered the shit out of me, time and time again — but each challenge I faced became an opportunity to heal, allowing my business to grow into something that now deeply nurtures me.

I started out in business as the worst boss ever, but over time, I became the best boss I could imagine — and this is how I've built the business of my dreams.

We all have conditioning from family, work, school and society that no longer serves us, as well as childhood and ancestral traumas that can hold us back from creating the lives and businesses we want, in a way that feels good to us. This is another area of life, in addition to parenting, where being in touch with our embodied power as women is so important — if we don't know what feels good to us, and what it is that we desire, we won't be able to create it.

The most common refrain I share when working with other entrepreneurs recovering from workaholism is this: the more stressed you are, the more rest you need. Do the opposite of what you think you should do. When your brain insists you'll be unsafe unless you go against your body's needs, take a deep breath, go for a walk, have a nap, schedule a massage or book a vacation.

Show your inner child that it is okay to have these thoughts, but that you aren't going to let them run the show.

Let go of your fear around doing business in a way that feels good in your body, and you'll be amazed by how much more time you have to rest, play and spend time with your kids.

Bring Your Inner Child to Work Day

Throughout my journey as an entrepreneur, my daughter — who was home with me almost 24/7 — complained frequently about all of the calls I was taking. When I was running a marketing agency, it was sales calls. When I pivoted to coaching, it was coaching calls. Even if I only had a few sessions scheduled the entire week, she noticed and she hated it.

Sure, she was lucky to have as much time with me as she did, compared to other families who worked 9-5 and only saw their kids for a couple of hours from dinner to bedtime. But to her, it was torture. And I got it — I also wanted to be able to hang out with her or take a spontaneous day trip without having to end either our fun or a client appointment abruptly. Fortunately, I had the audacity to insist on more, for both of us.

After careful consideration of what my clients *really* needed from me in our work together, and untangling that from what I'd been taught about how a coaching business should run, I made a drastic change. Within a matter of days, I had restructured my entire business to offer *only* voice message and text coaching instead of scheduled video calls. This setup accommodates my need for flexibility as a parent, which means being available to my child throughout the day.

I have found that this also works better for my clients, who can now reach out and respond when it's convenient, instead of being bound to a specific appointment time. Asynchronous voice and text message coaching means I can run a business and still put my family first, and my clients can also get the support they need while putting *their* families first. There are no rescheduled appointments, last-minute cancellations, or no-shows, because there is no appointment to miss.

Now, I know for sure that taking time in the middle of the day to play video games or go for a swim with my daughter won't limit my productivity — in fact, play has become the most important part of my work! The more I play and nurture my inner child, the better I am at finding unconventional solutions to help myself and others live more authentically. Being willing to play with "the way things are" has led to innumerable improvements in my family life, in my work and in the lives of the women I work with.

I recommend that anyone who believes that they don't have time to run a business while parenting unschooling kids reconsider whether the business model or structure they currently have could be tweaked to better meet everyone's needs. In my experience, this can lead to unexpected win-wins as we often find that what works for us also works better for our clients, too.

Play isn't a distraction from work, it's the magic our work needs most! Sometimes, all it takes is one person willing to question the way things are — even when we've been told it's *the only* way — and take the leap to try something new.

When we center play, everyone wins. Make every day "Bring your Inner Child to Work Day" — I double dare you!

Building a Business from the Inside Out

One of my favorite things to do with entrepreneurs is to help them choose an area of focus that artfully plants their passion and their experience in the fertile ground where the business can grow robustly enough to support their desired lifestyle.

This is an important formula, because a successful business is based on not only offering something of value, but also being able to provide value *sustainably*. Doing what you love and doing it *on your own terms* is the best insurance against burnout. So, I always recommend that clients consider their desired lifestyle before moving forward with a new business. What is planted with joy, will be harvested joyfully as well. If your business becomes a real pain at any point, it's a good time to ensure that you're heading down the right path by working with your natural energy.

Here, "fertile ground" refers to a viable market where there is a demand for your service. A business needs revenue, and people pay for things that they want and need. Honing in on a specific group of people to serve in your business can make it easier for them to find you, but this can be a tricky piece to figure out. When it clicks, it's like magic.

One of my clients wanted to travel the world with his family. He had just left the military to pursue his true passion — finance — and was thinking about starting a consulting firm, but didn't know where to start. I could tell his time in the military had meant a lot to him. When I suggested that he offer financial services to military officers, his eyes lit up. He started talking about how many people he knew in the military who could benefit from his knowledge, because so many of them had not been well-paid before their enlistment and were unfamiliar with a long-term approach to financial planning.

It turned out that military peeps could see the value in hiring a professional to help manage their finances, and they loved that his guy understood them because of his military service. This father was able to start a business that provided abundantly for his family and which also had a great deal of personal meaning for him, because he was able to do work that he loved and was really good at, for people he really cared about and who wanted his help. And because he was able to work remotely as a consultant, he was free to make his own hours and travel the world with his kids.

Of course, there are also plenty of successful financial advisors who work with anyone and everyone, or who have different ways of setting themselves apart from other financial advisors. Choosing a specific group of people to serve in your business isn't always necessary or even practical. But sometimes other people can see what we have to offer more clearly than we can, such as when a potential niche might be staring you in the face. It's wonderful when you find that a group of people you're already connected to is perfectly suited to receive your expertise.

When you're heading in a new direction, believe that none of your life experiences will have been wasted. Sometimes it's just a matter of time and perspective before you see how all the pieces fit together in a way that feels exciting and purposeful. This can be so important for those of us determined to derive meaning from our work. If you know that you can't be satisfied in your profession without finding a way to alchemize the challenges you've faced into pearls of wisdom for others, don't let go of that. No amount of money can substitute for work that deeply fulfills you.

Keep in mind also that there's no need to "niche down" in a way that feels sad or constricting to you. I've sold everything from a real estate course to Human Design readings to a sugar addiction recovery program to the same group of people, because these things are all connected through my brand. Reality check: no one gets confused about "what Target does" as a result of the store selling so many different things. People don't need niches, because *we* are not products. Products need niches — people need brands.

Your business is an extension of who you are. When you build one from the inside out, you end up with a business that loves you back, and a life that feels like home.

The Surprising Look of Success

Once, a business coach predicted my future with chilling resonance, down to the existence of this book, and the color of the curtain on the stage I'd be speaking on within five years — but said she didn't think she was clairvoyant. Similarly, an astrologer laid out the last year of my life for me in detail (it's all become true!), but shied away from calling herself "psychic."

Why are so many women with obvious spiritual gifts so reluctant to claim them?

Maybe it's witch-burning trauma. Maybe it's that so many highly gifted and sensitive women have been labeled "less than" and convinced they aren't capable of making a living. Or maybe we have this image of the mysterious seer in a silk head wrap with a crystal ball who is the "real" deal, and let that stereotype undermine our abilities.

The same way a lot of people don't see themselves as "real" business owners for lack of the "right" connections, upbringing, wardrobe, branding, face — whatever we project is holding us back.

But comparing your insides to other people's outsides is a trap. You might be surprised to know who you look up to that struggles with impostor syndrome, or what other massive inner and outer obstacles they had to overcome to get where they are now.

Success doesn't have a singular "look." Just as you get a "beach body" by bringing your body to the beach, you "dress for success" by wearing clothes that feel good to you and being fully yourself in them while building your badass business.

Pave the way for others like you by claiming your spot, and when people start projecting that you had it made from the start, tell them what it used to be like so that they know success looks like them, too.

Shaking Off the Prey Instinct

Is it any wonder that we are afraid to be seen, when for millennia women's survival has been tied to our worth in the eyes of men? Is it any wonder that we struggle to assert ourselves in business, when we've historically been locked up — or worse — for speaking up?

In patriarchy, women's access to resources has depended on us appearing and acting a certain way, regardless of how we felt on the inside or what we really wanted in life.

In addition to ancestral trauma and our adult circumstances, if getting our needs met in childhood depended on us pleasing our parents, teachers or other authority figures, we have probably displayed lifelong patterns of concealing our true selves in order to stay, and feel, safe, and to rely on others' perceptions of us for validation, approval and our sense of self-worth.

Anyone living in captivity could learn self-abandonment to survive, but we are especially vulnerable to this conditioning when our brains are still developing and we are deeply impressionable.

Breaking free from this cycle involves both creating lives where our survival doesn't depend on unfair judgments of us by others, and undoing the psychological patterns shaped by life in captivity.

Navigating this journey means accepting that we will be deeply uncomfortable in healing from the trauma of being unseen and unloved and in making moves toward taking up space in the world unapologetically.

Building and maintaining a relationship with ourselves as our own loving parent is essential to reclaiming our sovereignty on the journey of entrepreneurship, lest we become prey to others who attempt to control or influence us by triggering our childhood emotional wounds.

Along with the many other tasks of building a business, we can take time to release ourselves from the shame, fear, and guilt we have incurred from harmful attachments to overbearing authority figures. We don't need to become predators, but we can look out for ourselves and let our anger guide us.

This inner work will give us the resilience we need to take risks, make mistakes, stand out, stand up for ourselves and be seen for who we really are, so that we can build businesses that reflect our true needs and desires instead of unsatisfying, vacant imitations of someone else's dream.

Staying true to ourselves and our inner authority is hard work, but who said trailblazing would be easy? We are not only reclaiming our nervous systems from crumbling patriarchal institutions, we are also paving the way for the girls and women who will come after us.

Your Five-Year Plan Sounds Like a Prison Sentence

I have never been one to sacrifice happiness in the moment for a future hypothetical reward — a tendency which has been validated by decades of experience. Things haven't always been easy following the call of joy, but I've always had enough, and I've always had my freedom, and wouldn't have it any other way.

I often see people pursuing expensive and time-consuming degrees and careers that drain them, all in the name of financial security and the promise of enjoying life during retirement. But money and freedom don't have to come at such a high price!

When I was a new single parent, I set the goal of making $60/hr with my jewelry business. It seemed like an outrageous goal, but I trusted my desire and in a very short time, I did it.

When I wanted to live on mostly passive income so I could homeschool my child and travel the world, I invested my last $1000 in a digital marketing course. I made my investment back many times over with my agency and achieved the lifestyle I'd dreamed of.

When I wanted to break into the IT field to revolutionize alternative healthcare cybersecurity, with no certification or degree in that area, I told myself I belonged in those spaces, kept an attitude of service, and just went for it. I built a server, worked up the nerve to charge $99/mo for web hosting, and my customers were thrilled with the service.

I don't want to make anyone feel bad for not trying harder; I want you to consider that maybe you're already working harder than you have to. What if there were more direct, enjoyable and profitable ways to get where you're going?

This comes to mind when I come across someone in the throes of self-deprivation as part of the F.I.R.E. (Financial Independence Retire Early) movement. It's great that you know your needs from your wants (most people don't!) and that you're willing to eat nothing but rice and beans for a decade to achieve the freedom you desire. After all, I saved up enough money to buy land with a cabin on it by living on the cheap for a few years and spending under $50/month.

But are you *also* willing to change your ideas of how money can come to you, and how much of it? Are you willing to reconsider who you can be in society, challenge the gates and ceilings that appear before you, and let go of what you've been told you need to achieve before getting what you want?

I'm just saying, I would never have gone to college if I'd known then what I know now about what was possible. Formal education can be a wonderful thing, but if you're not truly enjoying it, I hope you will consider alternatives. School puts so much pressure on children and young adults to decide what they want to do for the rest of their lives, without giving them the chance to experience the world and see what's out there. They are expected to follow a rigid schedule of back-to-back education programs, and go deep into debt for it, without even having the guarantee of any specific outcome for a degree, such as a stable income or even a viable career.

The truth is that I never really used my university degree, except for the classroom teaching jobs that required a bachelor's degree, but which nearly killed me. The businesses I've had that provided me with a joyful livelihood could have been started without any formal education at all.

Certifications definitely have their place, but confidence and courage can open a hell of a lot of doors.

School is clearly not the only pathway to financial success, and it's often not the fastest or most pleasant one, either. The number of college graduates having existential crises, panicking over student loan debt and complaining about low earnings and poor working conditions — and that is only if they are able to find work in their field at all, or any work — should make all of society question whether formal education is such a smart move.

It's never too late to go back to school, and it can be an empowering choice if an education program presents a clear pathway to a specific career goal or personal fulfillment. But the value of formal education should be considered on an individual basis, and not just taken for granted. When the norm is for kids to go through sixteen or more years of formal education with no clear benefit to anyone besides the companies and governments selling degrees, it's time to wise up.

Having taken the path of pursuing my interests without pressuring myself to plan how things would turn out later on — and living to tell the tale — has given me the confidence to support my child in doing the same. I know that she will have the creativity to face challenges that come her way, because I did, and she's at least as smart as me!

If your game plan looks like a list of ways to make your life harder and more miserable, you're doing it wrong. Joy isn't a frivolous indulgence — it's a compass that leads to creative solutions and opportunities that you might have otherwise overlooked. So go directly to joy, pass *GO*, and collect $200.

When we let go of our fears of the future, we are free to enjoy the present. In the here and now, we have access to an internal power and sense of direction that no amount of professional qualifications could replace.

It can be scary to take that first step, but the incredible feeling we get when things start falling into place lets us know that we are on the right path and helps us gain even more trust in ourselves and in the Fertile Universe.

More Holes Than a Golf Course – and Way More Fun

I had major impostor syndrome when an organization asked me for my résumé in advance of my first online course launch. While I am proud of my many accomplishments, listing them in chronological order — or any order — doesn't really explain how I got where I am today, or who I am as a person.

A résumé is meant to impress people who value doing things the conventional way. I most certainly have not.

First of all, I have never had a permanent full-time job. Ever.

I've gone from waitress to classroom teacher to commissioned artist to hurricane relief manager to backpacker to charity fundraiser to summer camp counselor to inner space explorer to copywriter to dumpster-diving activist to mother to van-dwelling jewelry designer to raw dessert chef to owner of a digital marketing agency and web hosting company, and now a women's empowerment coach — all without much thought given to "my future."

The thing is, every new direction I've taken in life has felt quite natural. I've chosen jobs based on what I wanted to learn, experience or share with others at each particular time in my life.

And yet, when I was asked for my résumé, a wave of shame and fear hit me. *Shouldn't I have a clearer story? A more respectable narrative arc?*

This, right here, is impostor syndrome at work: that creeping feeling that our unconventional paths disqualify us from success — as though the value we bring must be measured by neat bullet points on a corporate-style document.

But my work has never defined me. It's always only been what I *do*, not who I *am*.

If my résumé shows a clear progression of commitment and responsibility to anything at all, it's to my own joy, values and peace of mind. I've always rejected the idea that life is meant to be dutifully suffered through, or that we have to choose between money and happiness.

Ironically, my obsession with finding win-win solutions is exactly how I found myself in the position of creating a course to help holistic health professionals claim more joy, abundance and freedom in their lives, while embracing their many ethical and financial obligations. Those gaps and bumps in my résumé are the very reason I was able to support practitioners in creating businesses that felt like a Second Childhood — making grown-up money with childlike joy.

The same supposed "flaws" that I've felt self-conscious about have also fueled an abundant lifestyle — one that has allowed me to work online, unschool my child and have the time of our lives traveling the world instead of stressing about homework, exams, bosses and deadlines.

Impostor syndrome told me my story was too messy. But the mess is where the magic happened.

So, you wanna know my qualifications? I'm a professional happiness consultant — just see my résumé.

Someone Always Goes First – Why Not You?

Some of the most brilliant people I know believe that they can't be successful without an advanced degree in their field.

My response? Of course you think that!

Degrees, certifications and other standardized measures of knowledge have been weaponized to stifle creativity, control influence, and discredit anyone operating outside the system.

These are the questions you're not supposed to ask in school:

If you're doing something that no one has ever done before, how could you possibly have formal training in it?

If you could have learned everything you know from a university, how would you have anything new to offer the world?

How could we evolve as a species or grow as human beings if we only ever did things the way they had always been done?

If conformity was such a successful strategy, why do we mostly celebrate people whose ideas have *changed* the way we think and live?

Why can't many of the richest and most successful people in the world spell to save their own lives? And why haven't we needed to write in cursive since the 5th grade?

More than facilitating the free exchange of ideas, encouraging originality or supporting innovation, formal education is a system of power and a propaganda machine that reinforces the status quo and discourages other paths to knowledge, creativity, and wealth.

Impostor syndrome is more than a "mindset issue" — it's *psychological and economic warfare.*

The truth is that you can't bring something new to the table if you've been sitting at it the whole time.

So if you feel like a fraud, great! You're probably really onto something worthwhile. Keep flipping over those tables you never had a seat at, until the whole world is upside-down. Or just be yourself unapologetically, and see who shows up to sit at *your* table.

Now, you're probably thinking: *that's a great motivational speech, but what if my clients are specifically looking to hire someone with formal training?*

Okay, do you know *for sure* that they won't hire someone without a degree in your field, or is that just what they *say* they want? Or is it entirely an *assumption* on your part?

Because if I had let that kind of thing intimidate me, I wouldn't have been able to:

Start a healthcare web hosting company with zero professional experience or formal training, launch a paid, accredited course in the acupuncture industry on the topic of HIPAA compliance without any formal education in healthcare, law or cybersecurity, or live on nearly passive income for years on end after taking a single online digital marketing course.

I didn't need years of formal training or degrees — I only needed to provide solutions to other people's problems, and to believe that being awesome at doing that was enough.

Formal training really only matters as much as it gives you the ability to support people in reaching a specific, desired outcome. But most degree programs don't even teach you how to do this!

Of course, many people value formal training as a form of social proof, which is why it's useful to share case studies and testimonials from clients you've worked with successfully. When you can explain exactly *how* you do what you do, and prove that it works, your authority becomes self-evident.

In articulating their process, my clients are *creating* the training that others will follow and *writing* the manuals that will raise industry standards.

They are overcoming shame, impostor syndrome, visibility fears and limiting beliefs, inciting rebellion in their bodies and minds and the outside world.

They are liberating themselves to say the things that no one else is saying, but that resonate with millions, becoming the leaders our planet so desperately needs.

They are making meaning of difficult life experiences, redefining themselves as heroine and heretic with an important message and way forward for humanity.

And they are getting *paid* to make a real difference in people's lives, with or without any qualifications other than being really amazing at what they do, and loving the hell out of it.

There is always someone who goes first. So why not you?

You Don't Need Permission – You Need Audacity

No one starts in business already having *all* the answers, so just get moving and trust that the answers will be revealed as you go. The idea that you have to know exactly what you're doing before you get started is bullshit. It's meant to keep you stuck where you are now. The only thing you need to get started is the desire to start.

Before you buy another business course or program — or even your first — ask yourself: *Will this investment benefit me as much as the person selling it?* Do you genuinely need it in order to move forward, or are you giving your power away by assigning someone else the job of giving you permission to begin your journey?

Gatekeeping exists in almost every field, particularly with regard to professional degrees. While I'd only want to go under the knife with a board-certified surgeon, it's not necessary to graduate from fashion school in order to be a professional designer. It's not necessary to have an MBA to run a successful business. In California and a handful of other states, you can even sit for the bar without going to law school — you would just need an apprenticeship, which is actually how things were done before academia stepped in. Doesn't it make sense to focus *at least* as much on real-world experience, as on books and theoretical knowledge?

In my entrepreneurial adventures, I have learned what I needed to learn when I needed to learn it. When I lacked the time, interest or foundation to learn something myself, I hired people who could fill those gaps.

I didn't need to know *everything* about the field or be an expert in order to start a business — I needed the audacity to begin, and the humility to ask for help when I was out of my depth.

The most successful people don't just sit around waiting for permission, or for someone else to validate their desires — they're the ones who have the courage to claim their space and make bold moves. Having the courage to put yourself in the spaces where you belong instead of waiting for someone else to recognize your brilliance can put you light years ahead of the game.

I have a natural tendency to ignore social hierarchies, which has worked out pretty well for me. When I felt ready to write a book, I didn't apply to MFA creative writing programs, write a proposal to an editor, get an agent, or send a manuscript to a publishing house — although these can also be effective ways to get published. I skipped right to claiming the identity of a published author, putting it in my social media bios and letting myself really internalize it. It was technically not yet true, but it's not like I was putting it on my résumé — although the thought of telling a prospective employer, "Erm, no, I haven't actually ever led a research team before. That was an *affirmation*," still makes me laugh.

Within weeks of claiming that identity, it was obvious that things were shifting. A friend told me about an essay contest that offered a book deal with a publishing house that she thought would be a great fit for my work. I entered and won. My essay was published in a collaborative book, and now here I am, writing this one.

All of my major life accomplishments have begun with a *decision* — that I would be a published author, that I would have a successful online business and travel the world with my daughter, that I would make a living doing what I love — that set things into motion in ways I could *never* have predicted or orchestrated on my own.

If your heart is set on something, *make the decision* that it will happen. Go all in, and watch the magic unfold.

If You Daydream About Being Hit by a Truck

It's normal for anyone who has spent their entire lives pleasing other people to struggle with knowing what they want. When we live for others instead of ourselves, we often deny ourselves not only fulfillment in life but also the pleasure of knowing and loving ourselves.

One trick I've used to get clarity on my desires is to imagine offloading my responsibility for taking action on them onto someone or something else.

Many of us who have been conditioned to fear our own power or associate initiative with guilt already do this unconsciously. We wish we'd get fired so that we'd have an excuse to travel. We pray an abusive relative would hurry up and die so that we wouldn't have to see them anymore. We secretly hope for an earthquake to close down schools in time for the big exam. We daydream about getting hit by a truck to escape the crushing weight of our financial responsibilities as single parents.

If that was too morbid for you, thank your lucky stars you've never been in such a dark place! For others, these types of thoughts can become repetitive and even obsessive when we are divorced from our power and waiting to be "saved."

Part of the work I do with clients is uncovering the desires and power hidden behind "if only."

If you wish you'd get fired, then maybe it's time to quit.

If you dread seeing a relative so much that you'd wish death on them, then either stop going to family gatherings or start telling your family why you don't want them there, and give them a chance to do the right thing.

If school feels worse than a natural disaster, then maybe it's time to consider a break, mental health support or an alternative path to your goals.

If providing for your family feels so overwhelming that you've lost your will to keep going, then let's talk about how you can start making some real money doing what you love, in a way that supports — not sabotages — your relationship with your child.

Another trick for getting in touch with our desires is to keep an eye out for jealousy. When we envy others, we usually want something that they have, but are denying ourselves.

Instead of letting jealousy fester, we can approach it with curiosity. When I have envied other women who were wealthier than me, there's a lot more going on under the surface. I've wanted what they had, but at the same time, judged and resented them for having it. My own self-judgment and guilt were holding me back from receiving the wealth I wanted, but which I would not allow myself to have.

When I worked through the fear of having more money, I started receiving more. I found that *I* had been the one holding myself back the whole time. I love when I notice myself feeling jealous now — it's a flashing neon sign pointing me towards my deep desires.

Getting clear on what we want often means lifting the veil of fear, guilt and shame to uncover the jewel of our desire. Once we know what we want, we can begin to work through the feelings that stop us from fully owning our desire and taking action toward it.

As adults, no one else is responsible for giving us permission to go after what we want in life — not our parents, not God, not strangers in the street. But we can find courage in others' examples to give ourselves the permission we crave. When we attune to the longings of our heart, we reclaim the power to make the deeper wishes behind our secret longings come true.

Do You Need More Money, or More You?

In a sense, money is a material manifestation of fear. If we knew for sure that we could trust the world to willingly provide us with what we needed, we wouldn't need to hoard money in order to guarantee it. Abundance isn't marked by the presence of money, but by the absence of fear.

Humanity is entering an era where relationships will trump money when it comes to getting what we want. Meaning that if you don't know how to get your needs met without exerting power over others, if people wouldn't help you unless you paid them because you're kind of a dick, prepare for a bumpy road ahead.

The good news? It's never too late to learn how to cooperate with people, and the persistent fear of financial insecurity will be lifted as you do. Besides, so much of our success in life depends on our *inner resources*, rather than the amount of money in our bank accounts. Once you truly feel you *are* enough, you may find that you also *have* enough!

Besides, I don't believe the New Age hype that *everyone* on Earth could be a multi-millionaire. Or if it *were* possible, I don't think it would actually be that great.

Here's why:

Let's say I have $100. Now, $100 is just some paper (or these days, computer code) and the only reason it has any value is because we have collectively agreed that it does. More specifically, the only reason my $100 gives me any economic power is because some people *don't* have it.

Think about it: Who is going to work as a line cook, store clerk or lithium miner if everyone wakes up tomorrow as a multi-millionaire? Where would I even *spend* my $100 if everyone already had everything they ever wanted, and no one needed to work? If everyone had $10 million, pizzas might cost $300 each because that's how much you might have to pay someone to get off their skidoo to make one.

If everyone had $10 million, then having $10 million simply wouldn't go as far anymore. See? It's the same concept as inflation — the more money that is printed and entering circulation, the less value any of it holds.

I'm not trying to rain on anyone's parade. I believe in and deeply cherish the concept of abundance. And I absolutely think *you* could have more money, if that's what you want! What I'm trying to show is that if abundance is truly available to everyone on Earth and not just for a privileged few, then abundance can't *only* be about money.

Money is just a *tool* — a way to help us get the things that we want and need. What if *more than enough* of what we want and need was available to us — *with or without money?*

Of course, at this point in human history, it's neither revolutionary nor practical for women to be moneyless. It's only recently that we have even been allowed to earn and use money, and this has made a massive impact on our quality of life. But even in the pursuit of cold hard cash, there are other ways to get it besides grinding for it to the point of exhaustion.

This distinction matters, because a lot of women who ask for my help getting a business off the ground, when we dig deeper, don't even really *want* a business. They want more money. They want more time. They want location-independent income. They want to make their own schedules.

Okay, awesome. But *why*?

Well, they want more time with their kids. They want a nicer place to live. They want to be able to buy healthier food. They want to take their family on adventures around the world. They want childcare so that they can have an uninterrupted bath for once, or even (gasp!) pursue a hobby.

All of these are completely valid desires. But what if there are *far more direct paths* to fulfilling them besides pouring time, energy and money into building a business?

If the whole point is to spend more time with the kids, a business might actually be the *worst* way to get there. As we've discussed, there are ways to build a business that don't require staring at a computer screen all day, and that work just fine with children running around screaming at the top of their lungs. But the first step is making sure that what you really want *is*, in fact, a business, rather than just the revenue or other outcomes that you imagine a business would bring.

So, before you start a business, ask yourself: *Why?* Is it to quit your job and homeschool your kids? To experience the satisfaction of sharing your gifts with the world? A little or a lot of both?

Businesses often fail when people underestimate the energetic alignment and ongoing investment required to make them thrive. You might like the *idea* of having a business, but when the day-to-day reality hits, you might find that your heart isn't in it enough to make it work. The most successful, long-lasting businesses are the ones run by people who really love what they do. If that's you, great!

Getting clear on what exactly you want from a business — time, income, location freedom, impact — will help you determine both whether a particular business is for you, and also *how* you do business. This clarity will keep your business boundaries on point so that your business doesn't end up running *you*. If it's important to you that you're available to your family at any time of day and can make your own hours, don't start a web hosting company — or if you do, be ready to hire customer service reps from the get-go. If you'd rather step on a Lego porcupine in the middle of the night than manage inventory, then don't do dropshipping.

Choosing a business model is something that deserves careful consideration rather than being an afterthought. It's incredibly helpful to talk to others about this — both those who are already living it and can share insights into the day-to-day reality, and someone with broad knowledge of the online business world who can help you clarify your needs and suggest what kinds of businesses might be a good fit.

But if you don't really want a business? Also fantastic!

What *do* you want?

To sit on a beach writing poetry while your kids splash in the gentle waves, the smell of grilled seafood wafting toward you from a nearby restaurant?

To take your kids to a theme park in a foreign country and make memories with their favorite cartoon characters while you sip a gourmet cappuccino?

To experience the beauty and peace of rural living in a gorgeous home with no neighbors for miles?

You could book a hotel and buy flights the traditional way.

Or…

You could travel as pet sitters, getting paid to stay in someone's home *in the very town* where that theme park is located.

You could win a poetry contest, the prize for which is an all-expenses paid trip to the Caribbean.

You could serendipitously meet a patron of the arts who loves your artwork, and who *just happens* to have an island retreat in need of a caretaker for the off-season.

You might be invited to speak at a conference in a location you've always wanted to visit, and have your whole family's trip expenses covered.

Or you might spontaneously reconnect with a distant relative who decides to leave you a huge pile of cash.

The possibilities are endless.

Abundance is about opening ourselves to the multitude of ways our desires can be fulfilled when we're living in our fullest expression. Adopt the attitude that anything can happen, with or without money, and let life surprise you.

When Trying Hard Makes Things Harder

The weird paradox about manifestation is that if you're *trying* to manifest, you're actually working against yourself by giving the universe the message that you don't really deserve what you want.

So what is it that makes you think you need to try so hard? What part of you insists that it *should* be hard? Often, it's feelings of unworthiness, fear or self-doubt. When we resolve these feelings, we dissolve our internal barriers to receiving that which we desire.

It can feel so messy and confusing...

You might wake up with a feeling of urgency, a vague sense that there is something you *should* be doing to create the life you want — but you have no idea what! So you figure you might as well start the day.

Regardless of whether today is the day you finally tackle those life-changing projects, the kids need to be fed, plants need to be watered, laundry needs to be done. As you move around your home doing the morning chores, the long list of things that you feel you should have accomplished by now but haven't, slowly dawns on your conscious awareness:

Oh! That was it. I'm a single mother whose only child has been begging me for a sibling... Oh! And I want to start an online business so that we can travel, but I have no qualifications... Oh! And I've been feeling so tired and sad lately, I need to figure out why so I can stop wasting away my life!

And on and on.

One by one, these undone tasks and unmet goals shock us into a state of horror at what's missing from our lives, and a sense of overwhelm because they are all so big and we don't know where to begin. So we start randomly taking steps towards them. Looking at coaching certifications. Downloading a dating app. Contacting a functional medicine practitioner. All the while feeling anxious that it's not enough and that nothing ever will be and so *what's even the point??*

In the rush to "fix" ourselves and our problems, we stray from the most powerful path available to us in resolving them: the path of self-acceptance.

Tending to the feelings underlying our drive to get shit done — the anxiety, the overwhelm, the sadness, the self-doubt — this is where the magic lies. Once we have processed these emotions, we may find that manifesting what we want is a matter of course. We no longer feel unworthy, and are no longer repelling that which we claim we desire with the incongruence of our internal state.

Sometimes we don't need another coach, certification or consultation — we just need to believe we are already enough.

The VIA Manifestation Method

The VIA Method is a three-step process to manifesting our desires: Visualize, Internalize, Actualize. I'll first break down what each of these mean, and then share an example of putting it all together:

Visualize

Getting a clear idea of what you want is the first step. This doesn't have to be a literal image, as in something that you can see in your mind's eye. For me, it's often an emotion. For others it could be a physical sensation or a sound. Some people benefit from crafting each detail — the exact color of their future house, the scent of a newborn baby's head. For others, these details seem distracting and unimportant. What matters is getting clear in a way that feels vivid and powerful to *you*.

Internalize

Allow that vision, feeling or other representation of what you want to settle into your body, as if it is already your reality right now in this moment. It might feel like lying to yourself, but what you're actually doing is preparing your nervous system for the fulfillment of your desire. This is where the deep inner transformation work happens: validating our desires, shedding old stories of scarcity and unworthiness, and confronting our investment in *not* changing our lives.

Actualize

This is the part where now, having grounded our desire in our bodies, we are moved to take inspired action. If we've done the previous steps thoroughly, this won't feel forced or awkward — it will feel natural, even inevitable. We've transformed ourselves into a person for whom having this particular wish granted is perfectly normal. So now, we do whatever *this* person would do. We can trust that our next moves will become clear, along with the right timing, if we are paying attention.

It's normal to need to revisit earlier steps during this process — whenever new blocks surface, this is actually evidence that it's working! If nothing were changing, nothing new would be coming up to be witnessed and alchemized.

The second step is by far the hardest for most of us, and often accompanied by plenty of tears and snot. As we allow ourselves to feel safe wanting and having something that we have been taught is "bad" or "wrong," we may uncover lifetimes of trauma stored in our bodies. This is also the place where we sometimes find that something we thought we wanted very badly, actually doesn't feel like that great of a fit for us when we "try it on." Passing an idea through the filter of our physical form gives us the opportunity to refine our wishes and orient our consciousness toward what will *actually* bring us the happiness or fulfillment we seek.

The important thing is not to try to control or figure out in advance *how* things will fall into place, and to stay connected to how you will *feel* when you get what you want — and to let this new reality sink in bone-deep. From there, trust that you'll be moved where you need to be. Whether that means signing up for the songwriting contest or a pet-sitting platform, reaching out to connect with someone or mend a relationship, or even just going outside for a walk, you'll know what to do as long as you stay connected to the feeling of already having what you want.

Straying into strategy at the expense of your feelings won't get you far. While an attitude of "this, at any cost" might get you the thing you wanted, you probably won't feel the way you thought you'd feel when you do. Staying true to our values, honoring our feelings, and maintaining our integrity means believing that we are *enough*. It's a tall order, especially for those of us who have been taught that we have to pretend to be someone we're not in order to get what we want and need in life (I'm guessing, that's most of us!). So trust the process, and stay true to yourself. Manifest — don't manipulate.

Here's a story about how the VIA Method has worked in my life:

A couple of years ago, I was sick of running my business and wanted nothing more than to take a year off to reinvent myself, spoil my inner child, and rediscover my creativity without the pressure of needing to monetize it.

There was no logical way this was going to happen — I had no savings, no potential patrons. But I didn't let that stop me from fully acknowledging to myself and to the universe what I really wanted. I validated this desire in myself, and really and truly felt in my body that it would be good and right for this to happen for me.

This opened the door to magic.

Once I let go of the self-judgment around receiving a ridiculous amount of money in exchange for absolutely nothing, it soon arrived — and from the last place I ever thought it would.

I spent a glorious year doing exactly what I wanted, and it was everything I'd dreamed it would be.

The only thing I did to make this happen was to share my feelings in a phone conversation — an action inspired by having allowed myself to believe in my inherent deservingness. If I had fixated on *how* things were going to turn out the way I wanted, I might have inadvertently sabotaged the way they were already coming together. The takeaway is this: I didn't strategize or scheme to achieve an end result — I simply owned my desire with every fiber of my being, and let the universe take care of the rest.

We are not operating in a vacuum — we are co-creating with the universe, our ancestors and forces beyond our comprehension! The VIA Method is an invitation to let go of how you *think* money, resources, opportunities and gifts of all kinds should, or could, come to you, and be open to the infinite possibilities of the Fertile Universe.

I created my own Second Childhood by imagining what it would *feel* like, and letting that feeling shape my reality. What's your idea of a Second Childhood? Use the VIA Method to bring it to life.

A Life You Don't Want to Escape From

Unlike many business growth gurus, I would never tell an aspiring entrepreneur that they have to give up Netflix to be successful.

Instead, I tell them that once they connect to their soul's purpose, distractions just lose their appeal.

Once you're living your own story, starring in your own movie, you don't want to dissociate because numbing feels boring compared to what you're creating.

You don't need to be relieved from connection with yourself anymore, because your body and soul are no longer filled with pain.

Your body feels good

Your life feels good

Your work feels good

Your relationships feel good

And when they don't, you have the tools to handle it, and the commitment to do so

Movies and tv become art appreciation rather than addictions

Imagine a life you don't want to escape from

Imagine living your Second Childhood

Imagine Netflix telling *your* life story, because believe me, it's worth paying attention to!

Poof! You're Queen of the World

You can do or have anything you want.

You can have $10 million dollars. You can run naked across the freeway. You can swim with sharks.

It's when we start putting conditions on things — like survival and avoiding prison — that things get complicated.

These are ridiculous examples given to illustrate a point: We are often so attached to the way we *think* things will come together, or what the end result will look like, that we block it from happening.

So, consider: what are the *conditions* you've put on your dreams? What do you think you'd have to do or be to be worthy of them? Feeling unworthy is exactly what could be blocking you from receiving what you want *now*.

Remember that story I told about buying a cabin on land when I was homeless?

There's a lot of other ways this story could have gone. I could have said, well I'm only getting $500/month, might as well spend it. If I had just looked at the facts — that I didn't have what seemed like enough money to buy a house — I wouldn't have even tried to save up. But because I could save up the money, I did. Holding onto the hope that I'd find a house I could afford called to me more than spending cash on stuff I didn't really need or want. In taking steps towards a dream that I had no evidence could become reality, I took responsibility for my future and opened my mind to the possibility that there was a way — even if I had no idea yet what that was.

What are your values and priorities? These are different for everyone. Which conditions can you be flexible on? If something seems impossible, try revisiting your priorities to find a way. When you *believe* there is always a way, and you don't give up until you find it, you will. I am great at finding a way to make things work, because when I want something, I am like, *obsessed*. I don't let anything get in my way, except my conscience. This helps me brainstorm out-of-the-box solutions that defy the "rules" I've been told I needed to follow.

Poof! You're Queen of the World — what's your next move? What would you dare to want if you had absolute freedom and power? How could you accomplish this if you placed no conditions on achieving it? What are you *not* willing to give up in order to make them come true? What if the limitations you imagined were just a matter of adjusting your priorities? What if there is a way to achieve what you want that *doesn't* require you to compromise in the way you've been taught?

It's time to put on your crown, believe unconditionally in your wildest dreams, and live audaciously enough to make them come true.

Lucid Living for Liberation

I had a lot of lucid dreaming experiences as a child. I loved the freedom of being able to play in a make-believe world that felt so real, but in which there were zero consequences. It gave me a lot of insight into what I really wanted in life, provided me with the opportunity to do things I would never do in waking life, and also allowed me to practice things before trying them out in real life — such as talking to someone I felt too nervous to approach. I've found lucid dreaming much harder as an adult, but I've tried to distill the most important lessons and tools from the experience and use them whenever possible today.

Imagining that life is a dream can be a powerful pathway to the subconscious, even when we are wide awake. Pretend for a moment that none of your life is real, that it's all a dream. What would you do right now? What would you want to experience? Who would you seek out, and what might you say to them? If you could make someone or something magically appear, who or what would it be? Does imagining life without consequences help you get clarity on what you would go after in life if you didn't have to fear something bad happening as a result?

It can also be helpful to imagine life as a movie. It can be fun to ask, what would you want for your character currently? What happens next in the story? The empowering perspective that lucid dreaming or pretending to be a character in a movie gives us is that reality is just a story, and we are the authors. If you often felt trapped, helpless or powerless in your first childhood, this is a fun way to gain your power back for round two!

Try freewriting, where you fill blank pages of a notebook without stopping. What comes out may not seem to make any sense, but the point is to get past your conscious mind, so disregard whatever self-judgment it comes up with. Also keep in mind that just because an idea pops into your head, that doesn't mean you need to go do that thing, or that you even really want to. Look at it as useful information for getting to know yourself on a deeper level — the more, the better. Get curious about your impulses and how they reflect your programming, or what they reveal about any repressed feelings, unmet needs or disowned desires.

For example, maybe you'll get an idea to rob a bank! Now, this is real life so there are consequences — are they ones you're willing to live with? If not, implore yourself to examine the impulse and what it means for you. Do you crave the experience of receiving something for free? Do you wish you had unlimited wealth? Do you feel owed by life? Do you feel drawn to fun, adventure, risk? You can play with your ideas and desires as much as you play with the process of inviting them. There are no limits! It's your story to live, and you are holding the pen. Or, maybe it's just a story you want to write and explore in the hypothetical — this is what fiction is for.

Interpreting our actual dreams can be another useful way to get to know more about ourselves. I don't give much credence to the dream interpretation books that say having a dream about losing your teeth always symbolizes a lost job or relationship. You may find those interpretations useful but they have never resonated with me. When I look for meaning in a dream, I simply connect with the *feeling* it left me with upon awakening. Fear? Guilt? Hope? These are messages to me, from me, about what's going on in my emotional life, often related to events many years past that I haven't fully processed, current life experiences or those yet to come. Whether or not I can connect the events in the dream to real-life experiences, I treat the feelings in the dream as real, and integrate them.

Our bodies store unprocessed emotions as tension in our tissues. When we sleep, our bodies relax and emotions can be released, so it makes sense that they sometimes come through in our dreams. I make a point of checking in with my body and my emotional state upon awakening to see what information I may have been given from the night's rest. Dream journaling can be a really useful tool for uncovering our subconscious fears and desires, and helping us understand what our inner child needs from us, and what would make us feel happier and more fulfilled in life. Sometimes our emotions seem more "real" in the dream world than they do in waking life, and tapping into our subconscious through sleep or creativity can be ways of unlocking them.

When we liberate and nurture our desires, life becomes a waking dream.

My Standards Are My Responsibility

People say that when you raise your standards, the universe rises to meet them. To an extent, this is true. But it's important to recognize that our standards are still our responsibility. When we raise our standards and still don't get what we want, it's often because we have not done our part.

Here's an example from my pet-sitting days. My daughter and I were doing a lot of one-week and two-week sits, because those are the most common lengths of time for people to go on vacation. But the constant moving around was stressful; it took us a while to settle into a new place and we didn't want to have to pack everything up again right when we were getting comfortable.

So, I decided that I didn't want to do one- or two-week sits anymore — I only wanted ones that lasted a month or more, and ideally three months. I changed my search settings on the house-sitting platforms, changed the messaging on my profiles to attract long-term invitations, and did the mindset work so that I really *identified* as someone who did only long-term house sits.

As a result of all of this, I did get a few longer house sits, which was great, but I still wasn't finding as many as I wanted. My ideal was for us to *never* have to sit for less than one month at a time, but we still had gaps of a week or two to fill.

I could have felt like a failure because of this. I could have wondered what I was doing wrong to not be manifesting the thing I wanted. But I knew that the *real* reason I wasn't finding what I wanted is simply because not many people go away for a month or longer. It does happen, it's just much rarer.

The key thing to understand here is that we're not manifesting in a vacuum — as complicated and unfortunate as it may seem, other people's needs and desires are always going to be part of the equation. In the Fertile Universe, we don't have to see this as a problem. We can accept it, and adapt our approach.

What I came to realize was that I didn't just need to become the kind of person who could attract one-month or longer house sits; I also needed to become the kind of person who was willing to supplement house sitting with other types of accommodation if that was necessary to provide my family with the kind of travel experience that we wanted. I had to take *responsibility* for my standards by finding ways to meet them when one strategy I tried didn't work. After all, it wasn't so much that I was obsessed with pet sitting itself — we definitely loved animals, and they were often the highlight of our travels, but pet sitting was primarily a way for us to see the world.

My standard was that I wanted to stay no less than a full month in any one house; the reality of the pet-sitting industry made that unrealistic. Instead of lowering my standards, blaming myself for being lousy at manifesting, or becoming resentful at the industry, I took responsibility for creating the lifestyle that met my standards. I found ways to increase my income, so that we could afford to stay in vacation rentals instead of relying strictly on pet sitting for accommodation. The decision to start an online business ended up giving me so much more than better travel options — I grew personally in ways that I never would have if we had continued to pet sit exclusively. It's truly been the journey of a lifetime.

This is the thing about manifestation: if we are too attached to one specific strategy for getting what we want, we not only risk missing out on it but also block countless other gifts that we can't yet even imagine. When we let go of the way our minds tell us things are supposed to happen, we create space for them to happen in ways even better than what we could have planned.

Making Our Own Damn Luck

Having total autonomy for the first time in your life can be surprisingly hard to get used to. Once I had built an online business and had the freedom to travel anywhere in the world at any moment, I actually missed having an assignment.

Previously, I'd used work, volunteer and education opportunities to justify my desire to travel — I'd gone to Mississippi to support the Red Cross with disaster recovery, moved from Los Angeles to Baltimore after college for a teaching job, and studied abroad for a year in Australia through my university.

I enjoyed the challenge of adjusting to a new place and making a meaningful life in situations where not everything was within my control.

Having the power to decide where I lived at all times — and no longer needing to rely on "opportunities" for travel (essentially, external authority) — threw me in a bit of an existential crisis.

Sometimes, this led me to hold back on taking trips I really did want to take, at times where I couldn't think of a good reason to go — "a good reason" meaning that my going somewhere served *someone else's* agenda. I eventually realized that I had sort of a kink about being told where to be, and for how long.

I attribute this to the "father wound" created by a capitalist economy in which powerful men create opportunities for survival, and incidentally, travel.

I'd never been supported in pursuing my own desires to travel the world, outside of choosing from a list of limited options. I'd only ever known how to make meaning out of fulfilling *others'* desires, calling it *luck*. Because depending on others to call the shots had once been necessary, I had unknowingly fetishized a lack of control in my own life.

Taking on the role of loving parent for myself. I gave myself permission to create my *own* assignments based on pleasure, play, connection, joy, and whatever else motivated me to travel. I had to communicate to my inner child that it was now *safe* and *good* to move around the world without waiting for permission, and assured her that I could have an *even more* meaningful life by following my own desires than relying on good fortune.

I could still be proud of how adaptable and resourceful I had been before, and now I could apply those skills to a new set of priorities — like handling the inevitable hiccups of international travel.

By reclaiming my power to redefine what gives life meaning, I have been able to travel for all kinds of fun reasons that would previously have seemed frivolous to me — taking my daughter to meet her online best friend, visiting theme parks around the world, going to Ireland to connect with my ancestral cultures and lands.

I stopped waiting for opportunities, and started *creating* them.

In doing so, I've taught my daughter that she doesn't need anyone's permission to heed the call of freedom or to follow her heart's desire, and that she can make her own damn luck.

Grounding on the Fly

As a full-time traveling family, our lives are admittedly less grounded than most, simply because we don't have a deep relationship with anywhere we live. Driving and taking trains and airplanes that move us around the world faster than the speed of life can be disorienting and make it challenging to maintain a connection to our felt sense, as well as disrupting the routines we rely on to stay grounded.

I've learned that we need intentional grounding practices to counteract all of this. One of the most powerful tools I've found is play.

Both my daughter and I are highly sensitive individuals who can be easily overwhelmed and overstimulated by the unfamiliar sensory input of new surroundings. Play is a great way to "unfreeze" ourselves and begin to engage with a new place in a way that feels gentle, safe and lighthearted. Play connects us, lowers stress, and reduces hypervigilance so that we can feel at home in a new house or town.

We love a game of hide-and-seek when we first get to a new place. Not only does this help us figure out where everything is in the house, the physical movement also helps us manage sensory overload and integrate new experiences. After a few rounds, it's no longer a big new scary house with weird colored walls and a creaky floor and scratched-up Teflon (I swear to god, how much do you have to pay for an AirBnb to get decent cookware?!) — it's a playground with surprises around every corner. A board game or video games can have a similar effect. Doing anything creative can also help process the transition and take ownership of our presence in a new place. There is something powerful about tuning into a beloved television show, cooking a favorite meal, putting on good music, and engaging in other sensory and physiological comforts that can help to make a house into a home.

I also travel with a string of colorful fairy lights, scented travel candles, a palo santo room spray, and other self-care goodies that provide familiar sensory experiences to help us adapt to a new sensory environment. And sometimes that also includes thick, heavy silverware with smooth edges — because a lot of people who furnish temporary rentals don't seem to appreciate the difference between an eating utensil and a homemade prison weapon.

For those who travel frequently, there are ways we can structure our adventures to make us feel more grounded and stable. By making travel plans in advance (rather than at the last-minute), deciding in advance how long we will spend in one place, staying a little longer in each place at a time, going back to the same places repeatedly or seasonally rather than always exploring new places, can provide a sense of predictability and connection to place.

If you're like me, planning far ahead doesn't appeal much to you. I prefer to spend a minimum of one month in any given location to make orienting to a new place feel worth the effort, but I also tire of big cities after a week or two. Staying just outside of a big city can make it more tolerable. Three to six months is perfect for a place that I really like but where I don't see myself being able to stay long-term. Barring visa restrictions, I usually wait for a clear sign from my inner authority that it's time to go, and sometimes that means booking flights only a few days in advance or leaving a new place much sooner than expected when the vibe is just off.

Beneath this globetrotting lifestyle has always been our deep desire to find a place to call "home" — a place where both my daughter's needs and mine are met, a place that feels equally nourishing to us both. For now, we play it by heart. We visit all the places she loves, even if they don't fully meet my needs, and move on when I've reached my limit. And when a place fills my cup but drains hers, we adjust accordingly. Staying somewhere long-term that only works for one of us is unsustainable.

For as long as a more permanent home eludes us, we'll keep traversing the globe, making ourselves feel right at home — one game of hide-and-seek at a time.

Soul-to-Soil Longing and Belonging

Portugal — a country that I was advised to consider for relocation — is incredibly gorgeous and very "liveable" in every measurable category. But when I went there, it just didn't feel like home. It's easy to idealize a place based on appearances and objective measurements, only to find that something deeper is missing.

Americans have historically been really good at reducing beauty, meaning and life itself to aesthetics: dressing ourselves to fit the images we see in magazines, romanticizing soul-sucking careers because of how good they make us look, and fantasizing about making enough money to travel to the places on our desktop screensaver and nature photography calendars.

Those of us who break free to live nomadically can still fall into the same trap — objectifying places, people, and even our experiences.

We take the trip and gush over how beautiful the postcard picture is in real life, and nevertheless, there persists a quiet emptiness inside. We realize we've traveled all this way just to meet our own projection. We don't have a relationship to these places — we have only bought access with our points and miles credit cards. We are lacking a soul-to-soil bond with the land, and we have largely forgotten what that feels like or even means.

We often experience places through our senses, rather than by truly being in them, or of them. There is a painful degree of separateness inherent to ongoing migration. What we jokingly refer to as "travel addiction" is a trauma symptom from our loss of connection with the Earth, with place.

The craving for this connection never leaves us. Time and time again, the wind whistles through our exposed roots as we pack up our things and catch another transatlantic flight.

Traveling to Ireland to visit my ancestral homelands was an incredible experience, but the person I'd become since my family's initial emigration didn't fully fit in there. There's an art to holding the past, present and future all at once — juggling your identity, needs, and vision is like living inside a snow globe that never fully settles. Eventually, you start to feel most at home when you're shaking it.

I stopped planting gardens years ago, when I reached a point where I couldn't bear to abandon one more sunflower or tomato crop. Now, I share photos of the beautiful places I travel to because they delight me, and because I will always find pleasure in a flower, even if I don't truly belong to the place where it grows.

But as glad as I am to be able to travel the world, this isn't my idea of peak fulfillment.

I crave a place that feels like home to my soul, where my body can root deeply in devotion to the soil, where my work is enriched by relationships steeped with time, and where the children who seek out my presence in wild spaces can know for sure that we'll meet again.

Maybe the time and place haven't been right yet. Maybe this is an impossible dream. Even so, I refuse to pretend it doesn't matter. The courage to hold hope, grief and gratitude all at once — this is the art of being human. And I bring them with me, everywhere I go.

Bloom Where You Belong

From a land-based spiritual perspective, every search for God is ultimately a search for home — a deep sense of belonging to the Earth, to place, and to ourselves. Many of us have intergenerational trauma as a result of forced migration from the land, culture and people who felt like home to our ancestors, and often to us as well. Attachment trauma is not only caused by a failure of the parent/child relationship — it's also a result of our loss of connection with the land and our ancestral cultures. We can reparent ourselves expertly and it still won't be enough to fully heal us unless we are in right relationship with *place*.

After I got sober, I started feeling drawn to Ireland, and even had flashes of memories of being there, even though I had never been there personally. I realized that the alcoholism that ran in my father's family could be partially due to the relatively recent loss of connection to place incurred by moving to the United States. It's possible that I was the first person in our ancestral line to process the grief around this, thanks to the ability I gained to feel my emotions in sobriety. I never bonded with the land in the United States or the area where I grew up and always felt a deep longing for somewhere else — a place I had never been personally, but where I nevertheless felt a deep sense of belonging.

One of the New Age phrases I despise most is "bloom where you're planted," because it insinuates that the desire to travel is misguided and that all the fulfillment you could possibly seek in life is available to you wherever you currently reside, if only you do enough "inner work."

What about displaced persons, the global diaspora? What about colonial settlers? Shouldn't they go home instead, if and when home calls them? Who benefits when people bond to a landbase that they and their ancestors have no relationship with, or when a bond is severed with a landbase that is everything a people have ever known?

Wisdom must be rooted in the land as well, in order to be practical. That phrase, "bloom where you're planted," like any other saying, was born from a specific place in a specific time. Wherever that place is, that's where it's relevant, and that's where it's meant to be shared. The Fertile Universe has boundaries. Being present in our bodies, and nurturing a connection with our own landbase, can help us discern which advice is for us, and which isn't.

It's possible that the saying had an entirely different meaning when it originated, that has been lost due to misinterpretation from being uprooted from its original context. Maybe it was even intended to *discourage* colonialism. Much New Age thought is created by uprooting indigenous wisdom from its landbase, and then universalizing it — invariably, with the result of being really fucking obnoxious. So maybe the saying "bloom where you're planted" should take its own advice, and go back to wherever it came from.

Arriving on Irish soil for the first time in my life was a revelation. I had never felt so at home before in a place. While there are practical considerations that would prevent me from making Ireland my permanent home, traveling here has been an important part of reclaiming my identity and integrating the experiences of my family.

Sometimes the place you'll bloom most fully isn't the place where you were born, or the place where you live now. Don't let anyone keep you from finding your roots, or from going somewhere you feel a sense of belonging. Home is your birthright. When and wherever home is calling you, go.

Rewilding – But Make It Make Sense

When I first began my healing journey, I put an unhealthy emphasis on nature immersion. I fantasized that my problems would magically disappear if only I had a perfect little cabin in the woods all to myself. The prescription that "nature heals" is true in a sense, but in my case, I was projecting onto wilderness an idealized mother figure that I hadn't yet been able to source from within. I was still looking "out there" for something that would fill the gaping hole inside of me, using nature as a way to avoid facing the immense losses of my childhood. In truth, I was not yet fully willing to grieve the mothering I had needed and deserved as a child, and which I would ultimately never receive from another human being.

Since recognizing this pattern in myself, I've seen this unacknowledged mother wound fester in many nature-oriented individuals, groups and settings such as ecovillages, van-dwelling communities, and outdoor education programs. The common thread is an attempt to go "back to nature" without restoring women's sovereignty, wisdom, and collective leadership, which are what made land-based matriarchal and matrilineal societies successful and sustainable. Retaining patriarchal models of governance, thinking and relationship leads to reproducing patterns of emotional immaturity, interpersonal conflict, oppression and leadership failure that characterize our modern world — just with prettier scenery.

Attachment trauma is hidden from collective awareness just as the work of mothers and the value of mothering is underrecognized and underappreciated. This is no coincidence — when women lack an understanding of their value and power, they are more likely to leave mothering and leadership to men and patriarchal institutions, and in turn, children's unmet attachment needs make them a lot easier to control and exploit.

Mothers are nature, too. We can't fully rewild ourselves without acknowledging the losses caused by missing or complicated relationships with our mothers and ourselves, and taking steps to address those unmet needs. We can't expect to buy land with a bunch of traumatized adults and magically create anything resembling utopia, nor can we just send children into the forest every day and assume they will mature into emotionally stable adults. The attachment bond is vital for human development and essential for the survival of any species in the wild.

Idealizing nature as the ultimate "safe place" is a projection that reflects our desperation to escape from the violence and discomfort of the human world more than it reflects the reality of life in the wilderness. Modern society shields humans against our ignorance of how nature really works. Learning how to survive outside of civilization can't be achieved just by reading a book. More than knowledge, it requires developing relationships with the land, and with one another, which takes time.

Many, if not most, land-based societies have been violently displaced, and much of indigenous knowledge has been lost. Learning about the indigenous culture(s) where you live or where your ancestors are from is a great way to build an understanding of the immense complexity of social and environmental relationships in sustainable, land-based societies. Rewilding can mean cultivating a sense of belonging within the larger web of life beyond human relationships and deepening our appreciation for the sacred within and around us.

Ultimately, when nature experiences offer healing, it's because they help us find our *own* nature. While my imagination wildly exaggerated the benefits of beaches, waterfalls and forests as cures for childhood trauma, it's still helpful to live somewhere relatively peaceful, because nervous system healing requires safety. This is definitely easier to do away from the noise and chaos of civilization, especially at first. Getting away from the sources of our conditioning helps us externalize them and come to an understanding of who we are on the most essential level. Once you get the hang of it, it becomes easier to do in less favorable environments.

So I'm not saying that anyone should suck it up and live in the middle of a city even if it hurts — I'm super sensitive to my environment, too, and definitely prefer smaller towns and quieter, more rural areas — just that the fantasy of living outside of society can be a lot more pleasant than the reality.

It's also good to consider before investing in a big move that could potentially destabilize you, whether your physical or emotional wellbeing depends on resources or routines that tend to be more accessible in cities. If you're feeling called, definitely go — just don't forget the practicalities of self-care along the way. There's no magical location on the planet that will relieve us of responsibility for the day-to-day stuff that keeps us alive, and it's important not to rewild ourselves in ways that cause us harm.

Sometimes the most practical approach to healing and growth is to spend time in places where comfort and nature co-exist.

I've felt profound connection during long walks in ancient forests and immediate relief of tension from spontaneous swims in wild rivers. It can be incredibly restorative to co-regulate with the Earth, and to bring our body's rhythms in sync with the natural pace of life. As a sort of hedge witch who bridges worlds, I love offering private family retreats on the edge of civilization, inviting mothers and children to recalibrate in environments that support expansion and leadership-building through connection and playfulness.

Since you *are* nature, you can be wild in ways that don't require you to uproot yourself physically — such as by nurturing your emotional needs, being more playful in your daily life, raising children outside the system, following an ancestral diet, exploring the wonders of plant medicine, sharing your gifts with the world or liberating yourself from social norms to follow your dreams.

Nature excursions and immersions can bring us clarity about what's missing from our lives, but we don't necessarily need to stay long-term to find true happiness. The goal of our Second Childhood isn't to escape the world, but to find harmony within ourselves, with one another and with the Earth. This journey can unfold anywhere, and wherever we go, it requires deep exploration within ourselves.

For years, I dreamed of buying land, living on it, building a sanctuary, and permanently leaving society. And I did try it — more than once — but something always kept bringing me back. It wasn't that I missed the comforts of civilization (although I'd be lying if I said that wasn't a factor), it was that my soul's purpose could not be fulfilled in isolation. Part of rewilding is reconnecting to other humans in ways that nourish us and allow us the freedom to be our authentic selves, fully expressed. When we rewild together, we have a chance to transform the society we live in rather than just escaping it.

While I loved the peace and quiet of living on the land, and often didn't want to leave, it still never felt like home. It didn't feel right to settle in a place where I had no ancestral ties — the feeling that I was in someone else's home never left me. Land ownership is not necessary for rewilding, and can actually feel quite unnatural if we don't have a personal connection to the place we live, or if we feel weighed down by the commitment. Living a nomadic lifestyle has also been a part of my rewilding — a way to reclaim my personal freedom while connecting with more relaxed and instinctive ways of life, as well as my own ancestral lands and culture.

Rewilding isn't necessarily about running away from civilization — it's about awakening to the wild woman in ourselves, wherever we are, and wherever she may lead us. Nature has so much to offer, but let's remember: we are nature, too. We can start rewilding right where we are, with consideration for our needs, compassion for ourselves and a willingness to reconnect with our bodies, to each other and to the Earth. Nature is all about balance, and so naturally, rewilding ourselves also requires a balanced approach. With respect for the gradual unfolding of who we are at a pace our nervous systems can handle, we also rewild ourselves by learning to trust the process.

Pledging Allegiance to the Earth

In nature, *belonging* exists in the form of interdependence among differentiated and sovereign beings, not the forced grouping together and homogenization of captive beings.

School teaches kids the exact opposite.

Rather than belonging to our bioregion and to the diverse community of species that live around us, students are told that they belong to Miss Moore's Fourth Grade Class, and are encouraged to identify and socialize (but not too much!) exclusively with the kids in their class, who are all of a similar age and developmental level. Beyond that, they are expected to identify with their families, their school, their town, their country — all patriarchal social constructs that alienate humans from our true nature.

The pledge of allegiance is the soul contract anchoring workaholism, materialism, and money worship into the cultural psyche. If you've never released yourself from it, I recommend trying. It should lose power naturally when you see it for what it is — when I internally renounced allegiance to the flag as a "lower power," I felt an immediate and profound sense of wholeness. Speaking truth out loud can also help ground it more deeply into your body.

What if adults and children alike woke up tomorrow and pledged allegiance to the land they live on, instead of to their flag and the fake god of corporate control it represents? When we recognize ourselves as an integral part of nature and members of a larger web of life, the artificial hierarchies imposed by humans lose their hold on us. Challenging these hierarchies may land us at odds with much of society, but the upside is feeling freer and more deeply connected to ourselves and the life around us.

We can only truly belong when we stand in sovereignty, and we can only experience true sovereignty when we honor our belonging to the Earth and to one another.

In Solidarity with the River

A letter I wrote to the United States Army Corps of Engineers in response to their proposed plan to bulldoze hundreds of trees from a beloved stretch of the American River:

I was walking a 2.5 mile stretch along the river the other day, like I do every day. A couple of miles in, I saw three tough-looking older teenage boys walking toward me on the trail. My body tensed up.

But when we met, I smiled.

And then they proceeded to talk to me, very excitedly, as if they were little boys, about their adventure down at the river.

One of them told me how the water had risen up and soaked their shoes and pant legs ("accidentally on purpose," I guessed). Another told me that a bird had flown so close to his face that it had almost touched him!

They were so thrilled with their nature excursion, their faces awash with pure joy and grinning ear-to-ear. After we parted ways, I was also grinning ear to ear, filled with joy. In fact, I have not been the same since.

Their delight was contagious!

I was amazed at how these street-savvy-looking young men had been transformed into playful little children by their encounter with the river and the life and habitat it supports.

My appreciation for this little strip of land grew after that encounter, and I have come to value nature access on a new level.

What if every boy or man had spaces like these where they could experience this same sense of wonder and awe?

Towards the natural world?

Towards life itself?

Towards women and girls?

Towards their own capacity for delight?

This area is not just a wildlife habitat, a running path, a dog walking trail or a scenic spot for families. It's a place where transformation happens — where hardened exteriors soften, where connection blooms, and where we remember what it feels like to belong.

This place is not only valuable to those of us who come here, but to our larger community — each one of us who is touched by the magic of this place passes on the magic to others as well.

The value of this space for residents, human and otherwise, is immeasurable. It cannot be replaced. There is no substitute. We must protect it and other wild places as much as possible. So, let's play with potential solutions until we find a path forward that works for everyone.

Because while flood protection is important, what our souls long for most is the return to innocence I witnessed in those three young men that day — and which I also experienced through our encounter.

The tragedies we have collectively faced in this area and in the world make it clear that humanity is desperate for a Second Childhood.

We can't miss this opportunity.

Stop Feeding the Bloodsucking Parasites

I've recently had the opportunity to see how my approach to environmental activism has changed since experimenting with Human Design, and committing to more deeply embodied living.

Years ago, I felt compelled to participate in a variety of political activities that I can now see were not a good fit for me, including things that put me in physical danger and made me especially vulnerable as a woman, costing me my mental, emotional and physical health.

Due to my conditioning, I felt emotionally compelled to meet others' expectations of me, and to contribute as much as I could, regardless of the cost to myself personally. The high instance of alcohol and drug abuse in the environmental movement was definitely a red flag for me as a sober person, but it was easy to rationalize that saving the Earth was more important than individual wellbeing.

Over time, I noticed a pattern: women's voices as leaders and wisdom-bearers weren't valued as much as our physical and emotional labor. Men still floated effortlessly into positions of power, spoke over women, and perceived themselves as vanguards of the revolution. We were trying to change the world, while at the same time reproducing the same patriarchal dynamics that had gotten humanity into this mess to begin with.

As a result of the stress and overwork in my activist career, I burned out hard. I stayed as far away as possible from anything remotely connected to environmental activism for years afterward. While I felt resentful of how much pressure I'd been under to neglect my own needs for a greater cause, it took becoming a mother for me to fully accept that my own survival and wellbeing were worthy causes in their own right.

It was obvious to me that my child deserved to live, and live well. I reasoned that if I deserved to live enough to raise her, I also deserved to be happy and healthy. No one else was as well-positioned to prioritize our needs as I was, and as much as I truly did care about the planet and its inhabitants, the do-gooder industry had proven to be a bottomless pit of toil and misery.

However, this inner transformation went way beyond logic — the mama bear in me had been activated, and a fierceness arose in me that gave me the courage truly not to give a fuck what anyone else thought. I became willing to put myself and my child first, unapologetically, which eviscerated any remaining guilt I had around making money and being compensated fairly for my work.

In the years following, especially through the process of becoming an entrepreneur, I've uncovered so much about what specifically *I* have to offer the world. I know now that sharing my perspective in the form of speaking and writing is the most powerful way for me to make a difference in the world. My favorite part of activism was always writing and speaking at rallies, which was a clue that these were a good fit for me energetically. I know now that I can trust what feels good and easy.

Focusing on making an impact with my natural gifts and energy type, instead of trying to fit myself into others' expectations and assessment of my value, has given me the ability to overcome feelings of obligation. Now, if something isn't aligned for me, I can just say "no," without needing to explain or defend myself. It's not costing me my health or my sanity anymore to make a contribution, and I have plenty of energy to do it because I'm saving my energy for the things I do best.

Women are often expected to sacrifice themselves to clean up the wreckage left by men's wars against each other and the Earth, on top of all our other responsibilities and the personal traumas and injustices we are already navigating. We definitely need to prioritize our landbase as a society, but when our approach to this involves going to war with ourselves, it's a recipe for burnout and repeating cycles of abuse and exploitation.

In deciding that we will give only where and when we can give joyfully and enthusiastically, we ensure that we are well-nourished enough for our gifts to be used well. It's important to remember that we are nature, too — and also worth saving!

At first, I found it really hard to write this book. I felt that it wasn't worth all the paper it would require to print, thinking of all the trees cut down for the purpose of human expression and entertainment and the devastating impact of clearcutting I'd personally witnessed.

Finally, I'd had enough of my thoughts — something more powerful was coming through. I stood up from my laptop and shouted, "I deserve to write this book!" With these words, and the burst of trapped energy behind them, I claimed my right to write this book with my entire body and soul. In doing so, I also claimed my right to occupy the space within myself, in my life, and in the world that had been colonized and taken by and for others.

In retrospect, I can see how I used environmentalism as an excuse to avoid speaking up for myself as a woman. Although I had no problem speaking up for the Earth, and I still do this, I was terrified to be seen and heard advocating for myself and for other women.

The dozens of journals I had filled with my thoughts, feelings and raw process in early recovery, and then threw into a dumpster, I secretly wished would be found and turned into a book. That turned out not to be the most direct way to become a published author — while other people have been indispensable in making this a reality, I had to decide I was worthy of it, and take responsibility for making it happen.

I know now that I'm responsible for doing my part in the world, but nothing more. The rest is for others to do in alignment with their own soul gifts, according to how they want to offer them. Scientists have discovered mushrooms that eat plastic and plants that dissolve toxic compounds — we are not doing this alone! Instead of wringing our hands over environmental degradation or losing ourselves in despair, we can do our part by refusing to work in a way that is unsustainable for *us*. Our current exploitative economic system would collapse immediately if everyone woke up tomorrow and acted as though their creative sovereignty *mattered*.

If women around the world were free, there's no way environmental degradation could continue at the current rate — we would simply not be feeding, fucking and fueling the bloodsucking parasites who are destroying the planet.

So, you want to save the planet? Dump him. Quit your soul-sucking job. Do what lights you up. Rest when you're tired. Stop to smell the roses.

Trust that what you *really* feel like doing is more than enough, because a world built on guilt and obligation has a built-in expiration date. Respecting yourself is one of the most powerful ways to change the world. When you honor your gifts and share them on your own terms, you not only liberate yourself from the old system, you stop being complicit in the harm it perpetuates.

My journey of differentiation according to Human Design has been about reclaiming spiritual sovereignty and claiming my place in the world by listening to my inner authority. I've found that my genius zone is the part of me that comes from beyond me, a strength that I channel in service to myself and others.

I'm not depleting myself when using my gifts; I'm actually making myself stronger, more inspired, and more energized. Giving 100% no longer means giving everything I have until I'm completely depleted and can't even take care of myself — it means giving only as much as I can give joyfully.

When my enthusiasm fades, that's my cue to look at where I've slipped out of alignment and begun leaking energy. The pull of homogenization is insidious and requires ongoing awareness. Activism can be a dangerous trap for women who don't love ourselves enough.

As a sovereign woman, I'm in charge of *all* of my resources — my time, energy, attention, money, and talents. I decide what moves to make, and when. It's only natural!

A Vision for the Future

I envision a world in which all women have financial, emotional, physical, sexual, intellectual and spiritual freedom:

To choose where we live, and with whom, and the freedom to change either at a moment's notice.

To raise our children — if we choose to have any — from a place of deep inner wisdom, free from government interference, psychological manipulation, and economic coercion.

To pursue joyful and meaningful work that puts our natural gifts to good use, and still have all the time we need to rest, play and nurture our inner children.

To experience the material security, emotional availability, and flexibility in our daily lives to respond spontaneously to our children's needs and desires, and to do so with pleasure.

We are creating this world for ourselves, in every moment of every day — both as individuals and collectively, as we follow our authentic desires to propel the evolution of humanity as a whole.

We are nurturing our talents and our inner children and overcoming the traumas stopping us from showing up as our most radiant, powerful, joyful selves.

We are creatively reimagining inherited ideas, structures and systems around work and parenting in order to make them work for *us* and for our families.

We are thriving outside patriarchal institutions of education, finance, law, health, and relationships that limit our expression and expansion.

We are supporting our children's natural drive for exploration and expression, and modeling for them what believing in ourselves, living authentically and honoring our dreams looks like.

We are reclaiming a childlike sense of wonder about the world and our place in the cosmos, daring to find meaning in places we have been told not to look.

We are valuing our vision for our lives, our families, our work and our world — even if it's simply to enjoy these — and continuously leading ourselves toward it, again and again.

This world isn't a distant dream, it's a reality we're already creating, one playful invitation, one joyful moment, and one courageous step at a time.

Tag, You're It!

I wrote this book over the course of our travels in eight different countries. Although I thought at times that it might make more sense to stay in one place to focus on it, my soul knew that I could only write this book by continuing to *live* it.

Each place we visited added a richness to our lives — the clawfoot tub in Paris overlooking a rose garden, connecting with online friends face-to-face, the rugged and wild beauty of Donegal — experiences of freedom, joy, pleasure, belonging and play that helped me breathe life into these pages.

Two weeks before my first draft was due, a new friend I'd met while living in the Irish countryside invited me to lunch. My daughter was sound asleep — it was prime book writing hours. Still, I chose joy.

As I walked along the water's edge toward the cafe, the final words of this manuscript flowed effortlessly into my mind — proof, once again, that prioritizing play *works*.

Writing this book throughout our travels, I found a sense of home — rooted not in a specific place, but in my life's purpose.

So…. *Tag, you're it!*

This is your invitation to reclaim, live and create your own story, as author, muse and star of your Second Childhood. It's never too late, you're never too broken, and you're never too broke. It doesn't matter how you got here or what you've lost along the way. All that matters now is *this moment*.

Whether you want to spoil your inner child, engage in spirited homewrecking, manifest a house like you stole it, make money with your magic, or raise your outer child in a way that would make your great-grandparents roll over in their graves, the Fertile Universe is ready to play with you.

All you need is your imagination, the courage to own your desires, and the willingness to take the first step in the direction of your dreams.

Go ahead — write your own damn happy ending.

THE EVIDENCE

[1] Centers for Disease Control and Prevention (CDC). *About Child Sexual Abuse.* U.S. Department of Health & Human Services [Online].

[2] Michael & Russell. (n.d.). History of Women and Divorce in the United States. [Online].

[3] History.com Editors. (2019). Magdalene Laundry Abuse in Ireland. [Online].

[4] Daeva, E. (n.d.). Before War.

[5] ScienceDaily. (2009). Early Trauma Linked to Adult Health Problems. [Online].

[6] Bureau of Justice Statistics. (2021). Female Murder Victims and Victim-Offender Relationship. [Online].

[7] National Coalition Against Domestic Violence. (1989). Domestic Violence Statistics.

[8] YaleGlobal Online. (n.d.). Should Women Stay Single? [Online].

[9] Miller, Anna. "Husbands Create 7 Hours of Extra Housework for Their Wives." *HuffPost*, 19 Feb. 2016. [Online].

[10] Killewald, Alexandra, and Ian Lundberg. "New Evidence Against a Causal Link Between Premarital Cohabitation and

Marital Instability." *Demography*, vol. 55, no. 2, 2018, pp. 587–606.

[11] Johns Hopkins Medicine. (2021). Anti-Parasitic Drug Slows Pancreatic Cancer in Mice. [Online].

[12] Britton, W., & Lindahl, J. (2019). Meditation Research at Brown University. [Online].

[13] Global Initiative to End All Corporal Punishment of Children. (n.d.). Reports on Every State and Territory: USA. [Online].

[14] The Atlantic. (2015). Corporal Punishment in Schools. [Online].

[15] Anda, R. F., et al. (2006). The Enduring Effects of Abuse and Related Adverse Experiences in Childhood. The Permanente Journal, 10(4), 44–52.

[16] Chesney-Lind, M., & Pasko, L. (2013). The Female Offender: Girls, Women, and Crime (3rd ed.). SAGE Publications.

[17] Geller, Jeffrey L., and Maxine Harris, editors. *Women of the Asylum: Voices from Behind the Walls, 1840–1945*. Anchor Books, 1994.

[18] Marnie Rothschild Shiels, Esq. "Spousal Rape Laws: 20 Years Later." *National Center on Domestic and Sexual Violence*. Volume 5, Number 6, August/September 2000, pp.85–86.

[19] Showalter, Elaine. *The Female Malady: Women, Madness, and English Culture, 1830–1980*. Pantheon Books, 1985.

ABOUT THE AUTHOR

Kelly Moss is a comedian, speaker, and trauma-informed coach who helps women and girls reclaim sovereignty, joy and meaning through practical tools and no-B.S. wisdom — fueling the rise of a modern matriarchy.

To learn more, visit **thesecondchildhood.net**

www.ingramcontent.com/pod-product-compliance
Lightning Source LLC
Chambersburg PA
CBHW071144070526
44584CB00019B/2651